25/12/99

CW00347005

THE POISON

THE
POISONED BOWL

Sex and the public school

ALISDARE HICKSON

Duckworth

First published in paperback in 1996 by
Gerald Duckworth & Co. Ltd.
The Old Piano Factory
48 Hoxton Square, London N1 6PB
Tel: 0171 729 5986
Fax: 0171 729 0015

First published in Great Britain in 1995 by
Constable & Company Limited

Copyright © 1995 by Alisdare Hickson
The right of Alisdare Hickson to be identified
as the author of this work
has been asserted by him in accordance with the
Copyright, Designs and Patents Act 1988

ISBN 0 7156 2709 0

A catalogue record for this book is available
from the British Library.

Printed in Great Britain by
St Edmundsbury Press Ltd
Bury St Edmunds, Suffolk

CONTENTS

ACKNOWLEDGEMENTS

I had the good fortune to find many willing contributors – well over one hundred Old Boys, schoolmasters and headmasters – without whose good will, enthusiasm and generosity this book would have been impossible. They include: The Marquess of Aberdeen and Temair, Rupert Allason MP, Lindsay Anderson, Dr Edgar Anstey, John Arden, John Arkell, the Revd Canon Reginald Askew, Alan Ayckbourn CBE, Hugh Barclay CB, Timothy Barnes QC, General Sir Hugh Beach GBE KCB MC, Sir Martin Berthoud KCVO CMG, Professor Edwin Besterman FRCP, the Rt. Revd John Bickersteth KCVO, Professor John Blandy FRCS, Lord Campbell of Eskan, John Campbell CVO CBE MC, Oliver Clauson, Dr Euan Clarkson, Nicholas Colchester, the Revd Frederick Copleston SJ, the Rt. Hon. Sir Frederick Corfield PC QC, the Revd John Coventry SJ, Dr Raymond Crawfurd, Donald Crichton-Miller TD MA, Quentin Crisp, Julian Critchley MP, the Revd Philip Crowe, John da Silva CMG, Dr Nigel Davies, David Dean, Conrad Dehn QC, Dr Alec Dickson CBE LLD, the Hon. Peter Dickinson, Professor Freeman Dyson FRS, Dr Duncan Egdell, Major-General David Egerton CB OBE MC, Alan Elliot-Smith CBE, Dr Peter Elmes, Colonel Sir Geoffrey Errington, Gavin Ewart FRSL, the Rt. Hon. Viscount Falkland, Dr Hugh Faulkner FRCGP, Sir Ewen Fergusson, Sir Maurice Fiennes, Desmond Flower MC, Lord Gainford, Peter Gardiner, John Gleave, Viscount Glenapp, Lord Glendevon, Rear-Admiral John Hervey CB OBE, Sir Henry Holder, the Rt. Hon. Lord Holderness PC DL, Michael Holroyd CBE, Geoffrey Holroyde, Sir Benedict Hoskyns, Sir Havelock Hudson, Major-General Richard Jerram CB, Professor Humphrey Kay FRCP, the Hon. Christopher Layton, Air Commodore James Leathart CB DSO, the Marquess of Londonderry, Major Colin Mackenzie MC, Roger Martyn, Bill Mason, Michael Mason, the Ven. Richard Mason, Michael Meyer, Professor Donald Michie DSc, Lieutenant-Commander John Miller GC, Captain John Moore RN, David Moreau, Michael Morgan CMG, Rear-Admiral John Myres CB, Professor Colin Pennycuick FRS,

Dr John Rae, Surgeon Vice-Admiral Sir John Rawlins KBE, John Rowley, Adam Ruck, Richard Shepley, Professor Charles Shute MD, Ian Small FRSA, Harold Snoad, the Most Revd Robert Taylor CBE OGS, Robert Walker QC, Professor John Waterlow CMG MD FRCP FRS FRGS, Sir Rowland Whitehead, Rear-Admiral David Williams CB DSC and the Viscount Woodstock.

And I am of course equally appreciative of George Melly's incisive humour evinced in the foreword, of Peter Tatchell's kindness in writing a recollection of his talk to the Shelley Society at Eton and of the generosity of all those other contributors who are not listed above, such as that of the Old Marlburian who bravely lent me the only copy of his extremely amusing but unpublished remembrances of school and allowed me to use them as the basis for his anonymous contribution.

I must also thank the staff of the British Museum Library, the London Institute of Education, the Archives at King's College Cambridge and of all the many libraries in Wandsworth for their patient help, enabling me to track down even the most obscure references.

During the three years of research for this book I have relied on, and quoted extracts from, a huge number of books and I am deeply indebted to all the authors and their publishers. I hope the sources of all quotations are sufficiently acknowledged in the notes, but I should like to acknowledge specifically the *London Magazine* for permission to quote a large portion of a poem by T.C. Worsley. I should also like to thank Robin Baird-Smith, Professor John Honey and my best friend K.K. for reading my typescript and offering helpful advice about both the content and presentation, and Jon Haynes for his editorial help with the book. But the greatest credit of all is owed to my mother, whose reservoir of strength, inspiration and saint-like patience helped ensure that this project was finally published.

ILLUSTRATIONS

FOREWORD

When two middle-aged, middle-class Englishmen meet it is not long before they reveal or are somehow obliged to reveal, as part of that dog-like sniffing to establish their exact social status, what public schools they went to. The upper classes are less obsessive. They take it for granted that they were at Eton, Harrow or perhaps Winchester (or, if elsewhere, because they were too stupid or idle to pass what in my youth was called 'the common entrance' – perfectly acceptable excuses).

For the middle classes however, despite Major's classless Britain, it still seems to matter, although the defence mechanism is to compete ironically as to how frightful the experience was: who had the worst food, the least baths, the more eccentric masters and, above all, the most savage system of corporal punishment. It is unlikely however, unless the competitors are both gay or intellectuals, that the subject of the relative prevalence of homosexuality will come up; still less their personal experience of it, whether voluntary or imposed. This omission Alisdare Hickson has set out to correct.

The book is in two parts. The first and shorter is historical: a demonstration as to how homosexuality, tolerated or at any rate ignored in earlier times, became by the middle of the nineteenth century the dragon whose defeat was the most important task of the proliferating public schools. To render it impotent, social intercourse between houses was forbidden and so was friendship between boys of different ages. Architecture was co-opted to frustrate it. Like a prison, everywhere could be overlooked. In some cases even the choir-stalls were rearranged or abolished so that the older members of the congregation couldn't feed their lust by staring at the prettier choristers. Cold baths, inadequate blankets, ever-open dormitory windows, public flogging followed by expulsion, were all weapons thought to discourage any resort to mutual masturbation, sodomy, oral sex and, worse, any love or affection which such acts might express. Even 'self-abuse' was proscribed: its practice – or so the boys were told – leading to blindness or the penis 'dropping off'. And yet homosexuality itself was seldom or never named or described. One of the more comic aspects of the book is the evasive and impenetrable attempts by head-masters and their staff to dissuade their charges without making it clear what they were warning them against. I especially like the apocryphal Eton story of 1900 where the headmaster announced in chapel that 'a most undesirable element has reared its head amongst us', and the boys thought he said 'ele-phant'.

Yet Eton, being among the oldest, was also the most relaxed. So much so that when due to social pressure things began to tighten up, the wife of a master proclaimed disdainfully, 'It's the traditional ancient aristocratic vice of Eton' — a wonderful blend of snobbery and tolerance.

Dr Hickson examines the various reasons for the growth of homophobia: the many new schools founded to accommodate the burgeoning middle classes, needed to administer the growing Empire, had no previous history of tolerance to draw on; their heads created instant traditions, mostly savage and puritanical; they tried to encourage prigs and sneaks, dividing in order to rule. They also tended to employ bachelors, many of whom were inevitably pede-rasts, sublimating their desires through sadism or, if losing control, suffering immediately by dismissal on the grounds of a 'nervous breakdown'. All in all a wicked and potentially damaging form of institution which has indeed turned out many thousands of inhibited, reactionary, pathetic alumni during the last hundred and fifty years or so.

What prevented total disaster was the boys' natural instinct to revolt. Sex, like smoking and drinking, was anathema to authority and therefore an excel-lent form of protest. Often it was much more. To be surrounded only by one's sex at the height of puberty is to ensure homosexual activity. For many boys it was almost a duty. It created its own traditions of courtship — of calf-eyes and *billets-doux*.

This is clearly demonstrated in the second half of the book: an alphabetical description of over thirty fee-paying boarding schools, amplified by accounts from Old Boys of their homosexual memories Forty Years On. These are both revealing, fascinating and at times pathetic or monstrous.

The recollections were solicited through a questionnaire or less often by a personal interview. Being unacquainted with the author I can't say how he decided whom to approach. There are for example a surprising number of the aristocracy and politicians, but there is also a wide spectrum of retired service officers.

There are several anonymous contributions including several from gays who seem to be out of the closet. Others remain incognito so as not to upset their wives; some are prepared to give their names and admit their 'crushes', 'crashes', 'pashes' or 'patches' for a 'bijou', 'bum boy', 'doud' or 'lustknabe' (all slang terms particular to different schools), but usually neutralize such confessions by insisting firmly that they are now happily married and with several children. They remind me, these qualifiers, of the character in *The Jew of Malta*:

'Thou hast committed –'
'Fornication? But that was in another country, and besides the wench is dead.'

The respondents swing between the hysterical – 'I owe it to my old school, and to my contemporaries there, to tell you that this [homosexuality at Eton] is, and always was, a lie' – and the humorous, with a certain amount of fudging in between. Only one adult homosexual wonders if his school was perhaps responsible for his orientation. Another, aware that he was gay, tended to avoid group sex for fear of detection. Several commentators come across as very naive in expressing surprise that a contemporary, notorious for his active seduction of boys, should in later life have proved himself equally obsessed with girls. Many of the professional authors quoted or referred to in the text blow the gaff on their school's version of the 'dirty little secret'. Both Evelyn Waugh and his brother Alec had books banned at their respective schools: Alec Waugh for his novel *The Loom of Youth*, Evelyn for his autobiography.

My general impression on finishing this book is a reinforced loathing for the cruelty and hypocrisy of the public schools in general and admiration for those boys who defied the status quo. I feel that while caning and whipping may well have worked for the benefit of certain severe ladies given to leaving their cards in telephone boxes, few or none of those boys who turned out to be homosexual did so because of their sexual quarantine at school.

Of course today things have in the main much changed: austerity has given way to comparative luxury in many cases and there are girl sixth-formers, but the author is possibly even more unhappy in that while many of the staff have accepted the concept of Gay Lib, in theory at any rate, most of the pupils have become surprisingly homophobic and give anyone suspected of deviance a hard time. In consequence, while sometimes affecting to be gay to scandalize their peers or the public, it is the boys themselves, according to the author, who perform the suppression of homosexual activity, replacing, more efficiently, the creeping housemaster and pyjama-examining matrons.

Of course no public school is ever going to include open sex as a part of the curriculum. To suppress sex, whether hetero or homo, will always be on the agenda. Hickson quotes Roxburgh, the first headmaster of Stowe, as pro-posing in his cynical drawl that the only solution for controlling sex in a public

school would be to install a brothel on the premises. That proving unacceptable it will always be a cat-and-mouse game. This illuminating book, among
its many other virtues, shows how in this field too everything changes but
everything stays the same.

To finish on a personal note may I assure the reader (for I know very well
one of the reasons I have been asked to contribute a preface) that to the best of
my belief – and as much as I would have liked to – I never seduced Sir
Peregrine Worsthorne on the art school couch.

GEORGE MELLY

INTRODUCTION

For a hundred years, coinciding with the heyday of its history, from the mid-nineteenth to the mid-twentieth centuries, the boys' boarding school became the battleground between two systems of values. On the one side, ashen-faced headmasters issued cryptic warnings and zealous housemasters prowled dormitory corridors. On the other, the schoolboys remained stubbornly indifferent to the staffs' obsession with homosexuality as a moral issue.

In the outside world, or at least in the more literate sections of it, homosexuality was gradually being defined by science as a condition and a terrible sickness, the roots of which could be traced back to childhood. But such abstract theories, restricted as they were to the jargon-camouflaged text of scientific journals or to discreet conversations between knowing individuals, were slow to permeate the monastic pupil culture of the boarding school. Here reality ensured that in a single-sex environment, all physical sexuality was naturally homosexual.

Unaware that they were playing on the edge of a supposed psychoanalytic abyss, boarding school boys looked on homosexuality as a form of release, like drinking, fighting or smoking, which was in no way incompatible with boyish machismo or having interests in girls. Despite the inventiveness of pupil lingo and the numerous school-specific terms for older and younger partners in relationships, boys rarely had a word for 'homosexual' and they had no fear of being labelled or stigmatized for expressing a sexual or romantic interest in other pupils. Consequently pupil discourse was often blatantly and unashamedly homoerotic.

This situation was a great threat to the school authorities and not just because the wider culture of which they were a part was virulently homophobic. An additional fear was that homosexual romance between seniors and juniors would undermine the divide and rule system upon which schools depended to keep their ever increasing pupil populations under control.

Headmasters and school governors alike felt that something had to be done. So the boarding school became the testing ground for a series of ever more desperate attempts to manage boys' sexuality. So much so that for the last 150 years it has been the fear of homosexuality, more than any concerns about children's education or health, which has shaped the experience of boarding school life. It initiated the move towards smaller, single-aged dormitories and changed the layout of beds, it brought about the introduction of phased going-to-bed times, it enhanced the importance of the housemaster in regulating leisure time activities, it gave rise to the night-time torch rounds, it affected the layout of pews in the school chapel, it was reflected in the regulations and taboos that grew up around friendships between boys of disparate ages, it swayed decisions concerning the content of the curriculum and the Sunday sermon, it spawned modifications to existing school uniforms, it was the *raison d'être* of the cold shower and it dictated the acceptable bounds of art classes and dramatics societies. In fact, every aspect of boarding life from school sports to school architecture was decisively influenced by homophobia.

But if homophobia was pervasive, it failed to restrict homosexuality. Instead it enhanced the schoolboy code of collective secrecy in the face of determined inquisitions and often gave the young homosexual practitioner the popularity of the outlaw. Boys often embraced homosexuality either with a passionate but quiet sincerity or as an amusement shared between friends, a distraction from the rigours of school life. It seems to have had little or no effect on actual sexual orientation either then or later. Indeed those who were worried about their sexuality sometimes remained aloof from the homosexual games and machinations plotted by their colleagues. As for the more boisterous boys, it was only to the teachers and later as adults that they developed a reluctance to talk frankly about their sexual activities. Of course there were a few exceptions, individuals who were genuinely unaware of or uninvolved in any homosexuality throughout their school lives. Perhaps some chose to define homosexuality as overt physical homosexuality. Certainly, in most single-sex schools, with little or no opportunity for heterosexual contact, few boys can have been untouched by homosexual feelings.

This study focuses on boys' public schools in Britain and mainly on those schools where the majority of boys boarded, which excludes several famous schools including Merchant Taylors', Haberdashers' Aske's and Whitgift.

For anyone unfamiliar with the British educational system I should point out that it is divided between the state and private sectors. The private sector has always provided most of the boarding places, and within this category there is a group of about two hundred schools which are affiliated to the Headmasters' Conference. They are often described as 'public schools'. Originally these were endowed grammar schools which were under some form of public management, as contrasted to schools whose sole purpose was profit.

Later, however, the term came to be applied to those endowed grammar schools which had evolved into large fee-paying schools and to new private schools set up on the same basis.

Besides public schools, I have also paid occasional attention to other types of boarding school, including orphanages and naval training ships, because they have historically shared many common features with the more prestigious public schools including a limitation on the possibility of heterosexual contact and a marked concern among the staff about homosexuality.

I have not addressed the issue of homosexuality at girls' schools. This is partly because my own experience as a pupil has been restricted to ten years at single-sex boys' schools. It is also partly because I felt women would not be willing to disclose intimate details of their personal life to a man; but the decisive factor was that homosexuality in girls' schools was not a mere mirror image of homosexuality at boys' schools, and I wanted in particular to address the machismo and homophobia of all-male institutions.

The book is split into two sections. The first is based on autobiographies, biographies and school histories. It deals largely with the period up to the 1930s. The second part is a collection of contributions by letter and interview which demonstrate both the continuity and changes in school life from the earlier period. These cover the six decades from the First World War to the 1970s and collectively form a fascinating mosaic of memory.

PART I

HISTORICAL BACKGROUND

None can pass through a large school without being pretty intimately acquainted with vice; and few, alas! very few, without tasting too largely of that poisoned bowl.

Dr Thomas Arnold, headmaster of Rugby 1828–1842

DEVILISH DESIRES:

THE DEMONIZATION OF HOMOSEXUALITY

'The authorities in their desire to deprive us of all occasion for
illicit intercourse deprived us of all occasion for any
intercourse at all.'
Harold Nicholson

When Kenneth Pexroth once labelled the public school 'a seminary for sodomy', he felt there was no need to substantiate his allegation.[1] Headmasters and housemasters had long been characterized as being paranoid about the possibility of out of bounds heterosexual liaisons and indifferent to dormitory homosexual escapades. Ironically, the truth was very different. Far from turning a Nelsonian blind eye, public and other boarding schools had long since introduced wide-ranging *modus operandi* to control homosexual passions.[2]

School life outside class had changed radically from the almost anarchical freedom of Byron's age. Worried that the devil might find work for idle minds, Victorian headmasters had been anxious to implement all necessary measures to prevent any boyish tendency towards homosexuality, so that by the early twentieth century the public school made even the rigorous regimentation of a giant penitentiary appear relatively congenial. 'Anyone who has been to an English public school,' commented Evelyn Waugh, 'will always feel comparatively at home in prison.'[3]

There were at least seven types of control that operated in the early twentieth-century boarding school:

1) *Demarcation:* The old ruse of divide and rule. Boys' loyalties and friendships were confined to one house, one dormitory and one year-group.

2) *Denunciation:* A boy faced a relentless barrage of propaganda on the evils of sexual experimentation.

3) *Diversions:* A boy's free time and 'surplus energy' were restricted through his participation in arduous sports.

4) *Defeminization:* A masochistic machismo, of the cold baths variety, was encouraged in order to fight moral weakness.

5) *Debarment:* Some schools deliberately excluded African and Asian pupils because they were considered to be dangerously promiscuous.

6) *Detection:* Housemasters prowled dormitory landings after lights out and in general kept a keen parental eye on their boys.

7) *Deterrence:* Any boy found guilty of homosexuality was savagely beaten and promptly expelled.

Let us now look in greater detail at how this worked in practice.

DEMARCATION

During the Victorian era the house system was established in most of the larger and many of the smaller public schools. Superficially the arrange/ment seemed quite innocuous. Each new boy was allocated to a specific house on arrival which remained his residence for the rest of his school/days. The highest authority in each house was a housemaster who was responsible for discipline and order. He was usually an elderly bachelor master with many years of school experience and exercised authority with the help of the prefects and senior house prefect, sometimes known as the head of house.[1]

The house prefects would be selected by either the housemaster or head/master from among the more eligible senior boys. Once appointed they were able to wield very considerable powers within their house, often having the right to beat boys who broke house rules, but unless they were also school pre/fects they had few formal means by which they could control or discipline boys in other houses.

Their powers might therefore appear to have been somewhat limited since technically a house was merely a residential part of the school where boys slept and spent much of their leisure time, but in reality its importance was far greater. Meals in many schools were always held 'in house' so that it inevitably became the focal point for communal table talk and gossip. School sports too, except for occasional games with other schools, were usually organized on a house basis. This served to ferment what loyalists termed *esprit de corps* or 'house spirit'; a doctrine which automatically cast a cloud of suspicion over any boy who was friendly towards the inmates of other houses.

'Which are you – A or B?' was frequently the most baffling question which greeted first-year boys,[2] who quickly learned that friendships with boys in other houses were contrary to either the rules or 'tradition'. The newspaper editor Ian Stephens recalled: 'Never, never, till you'd reached your third year, could you walk in public with a boy of another house . . . You'd be beaten or "tunded" by a prefect (flogged with ash-sticks on the buttocks) if you were seen doing so.'[3] In the year of Ian Stephens' arrival at Winchester, 1916, a former teacher published a memoir on his experiences at 'Winchborough' in which he described how, at one staff meeting, the head had insisted on a clampdown on inter-house mixing:

> And now, gentlemen, to pass to the next point, I propose to bring in a new rule about boys going from one house to another . . . I do not think any good is to be derived from too much communication of boys with one another outside their own houses . . . Masters will therefore see to it that in future no boy is entertained at their house unless he happens to be a member of that house. I have several adequate reasons for this . . .[4]

At Wellington boys had to wear a cap with the coloured ribbon of their house. This enabled a housemaster to know instantly if one of his boys was entering another house or if any boy of his was associating with others from a different house. So important did house tutors consider this system of instant recognition that it became a beatable offence to be found anywhere in or out of bounds without one's cap.[5] Consequently it became virtually impossible for boys from different houses to associate together, as the writer Brian Inglis recalled:

> In one respect it was the worse for me, through arriving in the summer term as the only new boy in the house . . . Beside the school hall . . . I encountered another new boy from Riggs Hall – Haydon's house; we fell into conversation, and it turned out he came from Dublin. Ball had an agreeably friendly way with him; how lucky, I thought, to fall in with a likely friend from the start. [But] during the time we shared at Shrewsbury I was never to speak to Ball again – except on the mail boat back to Ireland . . . There are few more rigorously enforced conventions than that the boys from different houses must not be seen together . . .[6]

The other great chasm which opened up during the nineteenth and early twentieth centuries was that between boys of different ages, who faced increasing proscriptions against socializing together. The writer and artist Osbert Lancaster felt that these restrictions at Charterhouse in the 1920s were so severe as to seriously handicap him for the rest of his life:

> To ask the way or the time was, at best, to be greeted by a stony silence and a shocked stare, at worst, to provoke a major ticking-off for gross impertinence. So permanently inhibiting did this tradition prove that even today I find it almost impossible to overcome my reluctance to address a word to anyone, from a fellow-passenger to a shop-walker, to whom I have not been formally introduced.[7]

A cold 'gentlemanly' formality was required of all new boys. In an American lecture the novelist John Galsworthy described how at Harrow almost any display of emotion was frowned on:

> In that queer life we had all sorts of unwritten rules of suppression . . . You must not walk two abreast till you reached a certain form; nor be enthusiastic about anything except such a supreme matter as a drive over the pavilion at cricket, or a run the whole length of the ground at [rugby] . . .[8]

No wonder that the famous Old Etonian Governor of the Bank of England, Montagu Norman, was renowned for his ability 'to hide his feelings under a bland exterior'. His biographer, Andrew Boyle, described how even as he became the scapegoat for the collapse of the economy following the Wall Street crash, he continued to behave with a 'magisterial restraint'.[9] A somewhat more morbid example is the case of Jeremy Bamber, an Old Greshamian, who murdered his entire family (mother, father, sister and two nephews) in 1985 and was able to conceal almost any hint of emotion both during the funerals and the subsequent police interviews. Bamber attributed such robot-like self-control to the rigours and formalities of a public school education.[10] One of those formalities required that boys learned to refer to each other by their surnames only. They often found that this took some getting used to. The future King Edward VIII, on his arrival at Osborne Naval College, told the other boys his name was Edward. 'Edward what?' was the somewhat impatient response, to which the future king replied, 'Just Edward'. The prince was duly punished, his head being thrust through an open window and the sash slammed down on his neck.[11]

Violations of the age taboo could prove equally hazardous. A new boy had to learn quickly the many unwritten laws of conduct, often as complex and uncompromising as the Hindu caste system. At Lancing College a glance exchanged between boys of disparate ages was deemed a virtually capital offence,[12] while at Oundle younger boys were not supposed to smile in the presence of a senior; such an informality was considered especially dangerous as it was 'a go-ahead to depravity'. For the broadcaster Arthur Marshall it was a difficult lesson to learn: 'I found it well nigh impossible not to smile, never having been previously required to desist, and for a time I was considered to be rather "fast"'.[13] In some institutions severe penalties were applied to prevent inter-age socializing. New boys at one religious seminary near Manchester were forbidden to talk to any of the senior boys on pain of expulsion.[14] This Iron Curtain mentality was also reflected in the architecture of schools. Out went the old system of a few huge dormitories comprising boys of all ages; in their place smaller dormitories accommodating just a few boys of similar age multiplied. At Eton the infamous Long Chamber, a dormitory 172 feet long and fifteen feet high which accommodated seventy collegers, was subdivided into separate cubicles and the number of boys quartered there was reduced to twenty-one. The remaining forty-nine were allocated new rooms.[15] Until this rearrangement in the 1840s, it was said that whenever 'Eton's name is heard the Long Chamber is a proverb and a reproach'.[16] Old Etonian Edward Thring, who later became headmaster of Uppingham, remembered how 'seventy boys were locked (into the chamber), utterly without supervision, from 8pm until the next morning' and recalled 'the wild revelry and fun and rollicking freedom of that land of misrule.'[17] It was exactly the sort of fun that Victorian headmasters were afraid of.

By the 1880s this philosophy of age-segregation was being copied in Japanese boarding schools with much the same motives:

'When younger students live in close proximity to older students,' explained the headmaster of Osaka Middle School, 'they become accustomed to improper language and activities. Younger students who have not yet developed their own independence will seldom imitate the best behaviour of older students; instead, they will fall victim to improper amusements.[18]

Another major cause of anxiety was the common procedure of sharing beds which had enabled the boys, often in freezing, window-vandalized dormitories, to keep warm. In the eighteenth century this practice had not attracted any notably adverse criticism. If, as in the case of some boarding houses, there were enough beds to enable some of the boys to sleep singly, the exact arrangements appear sometimes to have been left to the boys themselves. A letter written by a parent in 1758 detailed the particulars in one Eton boarding house:

. . . the present way of settling is that Stephen and William are to lie together. Ophaly a bed to himself in the same room, and Charles in a little one by them; for neither Ophaly nor Charles like to have bedfellows; besides, they kick off the clothes so that other boys don't like to lie with them, and I'm told Stephen and William agree mighty well . . .[19]

It seems that Stephen was probably at least two years older than his compan-ion as he had entered the College two years before William and was to leave some four years earlier than his friend. One can only assume that in the eight-eenth century the school authorities were either blind or indifferent to the pos-sible consequences. By the early nineteenth century such arrangements were certainly attracting voices of disapproval. The philosopher Jeremy Bentham was one of those who called for change: 'On the present plan [boys] are often forced together under circumstances still more favourable to it [homosexual-ity] by the custom of lying naked together in feather beds'.[20] Physical warmth had to be sacrificed in order to preserve moral innocence. In the case of the more financially hard-up institutions, such as Christ's Hospital School, this led to decisions by the school governors to cut numbers. At other schools extra beds were added, even when there was not sufficient space. When Thackeray (later to become famous as the author of *Vanity Fair*) arrived at Charterhouse in the 1820s he had his own bed, but it was jammed tight between other beds in one long room.[21] The space at Charterhouse between beds grew gradually larger as the century grew older and by 1902 the school architect Felix Clay outlined this plan of a model dormitory: 'The beds are 3ft 6in apart, with a passage down the centre of the room 11ft 6in wide in which are placed the basins. The room takes twelve beds, and measuring 46 by 23ft, allows 88 sq ft per head . . .'[22]

During the second half of the nineteenth century classrooms were reorga-nized so that boys of similar age were grouped together. Prior to the 1860s boys in most of the public schools had been assigned classes according to their success in the end of year exams. A difference of age of three years or more between boys in the same class was common and there were cases at Shrewsbury, Harrow and Rugby where the age gap between boys at adjacent desks was up to six years. T. W. Bamford in *The Rise of Public Schools* noted that size of class had nothing to do with such arrangements and it seems likely that it was fear of sexual relationships, rather than any organizational necessity, which motivated headmasters to 'reform' the class system.[23]

School authorities were also unhappy with the traditional classroom layout in which boys were able to pass notes and get up to all sorts of 'indecent' mis-chief, sheltered by the ranks of desks. Some schools tried new arrangements in a vain attempt to solve the problem. At Sherborne, in an excess of zeal, desks in one classroom were lined up facing the wall so that the boys had their backs to each other and the prefect. But, as with most such crude interventions, the resulting resentment undermined attempts of staff to win boys' trust and the unpopular experiment was soon dropped.[24] In many other areas however the pace of reorganization accelerated.

Many public schools decided to narrow the age range of the boys by raising the minimum age of entry. Gradually more and more new schools were established so that those aged eight to twelve could be educated away from the covetous gaze of older boys. Sometimes, as at Eton in the 1860s, this process occurred in two stages. The first being the accommodation of the juniors in separate boarding houses and a gradual reduction in their social and formal connections with the rest of the school which led inevitably to the second stage, the decision to remove the junior school to an entirely separate locality. These junior schools became known as preparatory or prep schools, the inference being that their purpose was to prepare younger boys for life at public school.[25]

Ironically, the public schools, though now accommodating a much narrower age range, were becoming ever more anxious to 'protect' junior boys. As a consequence of such fears even the chapels of some schools were rebuilt so that the pews no longer faced each other. Supposedly the old arrangement had allowed too tempting an opportunity for flirtatious glances during services.[26] At Tonbridge, Charles Long (headmaster 1907–1922) agonized over the dangers created by juniors in the choir, dressed in their pretty surplices. In his opinion they were a blatant distraction to godly thoughts. He decided that something had to be done, however unpopular it might prove to be with the traditionalists, and so he outlawed the wearing of surplices. For ten years they remained on their pegs in the vestry before finally disappearing altogether. The verdict of D.C. Somervell, author of *A History of Tonbridge School*, was that it was 'a hideous waste of ecclesiastical lingerie'.[27]

Schools also faced the common problem of thwarting older–younger boy liaisons in the evening. By the end of the nineteenth century the commonly accepted practice was for each age group to go to bed at a different time, summoned by a bell, often in enforced silence. Tom Hopkinson, the future editor of the *Picture Post*, would never forget the strict bedtime procedure at St Edward's:

At night we undressed in silence; the prefect lolling in the corner might appear to be reading, but would detect the slightest whisper. 'Prayers!' he would shout, and in a second we were all on our knees to our Creator and must remain there motionless until he shouted 'Time!' . . . A quarter of an hour exactly was allowed for getting into bed, and every head must be on the pillow as the chapel clock, which also sounded quarters, finished strik⁄ing 9.30.[28]

No boy was ever allowed to trespass into another dormitory. To prevent toilet visits being used as a pretext for night⁄time flirtations, chamber pots were fre⁄quently placed under each bed or at the very least one to a dormitory. At some schools every boy had to pee into his pot before 'lights out', that being the last permitted opportunity before the morning call, and so denying boys of the most obvious excuse for subsequently leaving their beds. At Abbotsholme, where the toilets were open air cabinets outside the building, any boy needing to visit them at night faced an intimidating procedure. According to the guide⁄lines:

> If after reaching his dormitory he be forced to go to cabinets, before going to bed or during the night or on getting up, he will use the one appointed, and report the matter at the earliest opportunity to his Captain, who will report it to the Medical Officer in the dispensary after dormitory parade.[29]

But boys were often ingeniously and frustratingly inventive. 'Oh, I must have been sleep⁄walking' was one of the favourite ways of explaining away a visit to a neighbouring dormitory and in at least one Sherborne house a standing order was posted demanding that the boys immediately report any 'sleep⁄walker' to the housemaster.[30]

Another tactic employed by older boys when soliciting their younger beloved was to summon the boy from his dormitory on some official pretext. In Roy Fuller's *The Ruined Boys* (1959), based partly on the author's own expe⁄rience of a Lancashire boarding school in the 1920s, one of the senior boys is particularly adept at such strategies:

> 'Thorp, you've left your towel on the floor in the bathroom and the lid of your dentifrice off,' Dyce said, in a voice of oleaginous reasonableness. 'Come and tidy them up.' 'All right, Dyce,' said Thorp, and jumped out of bed. When the light had been put out again and the two had departed, Gerald surprised himself by saying: 'Well we know what those two are going to do.'[31]

As an impediment to liaisons the architects of schools frequently sought to maximize the difficulty of getting from one dormitory to another. At Cheltenham College gates were placed on all staircases and were locked at 10.30 every evening.[32] At Radley all doors were locked and iron bars placed on ground-floor windows.[33] At Wellington College the dormitories radiated like spokes from a central hub which was constantly monitored so as to make inter-dormitory visits almost impossible[34] and at Quentin Crisp's school the authorities devised an 'H'-shaped block with dormitories on each of the furthest ends. Crisp described it as an inevitable Romeo and Juliet set-up and one night one boy chanced it. He was caught in flagrante delicto.[35]

In some schools each bed had its own partition, often lockable only from the outside, with a single key in the possession of the head boy or housemaster. In the 1860s E.W. Benson, the headmaster of Wellington, even considered nailing a wire lattice over the top of each cubicle as an extra security measure.[36] In the end he did not resort to such extreme measures. Others, however, continued to invent new and ever more ingenious anti-vice strategies. Edward Lyttelton, when an assistant master at Eton, related how a headmaster of another unnamed school had boasted of successfully preventing wickedness in dormitories by balancing a heavy wooden bar on the top of every cubicle partition so as to make it virtually impossible for boys to climb over without sending the bar crashing to the ground.[37] But Lyttelton was dubious about the effectiveness of such tactics: 'As soon as we openly defy boys' ingenuity, we challenge them to circumvent us, and this they seldom fail to do.'[38]

The introduction of cubicles was not welcomed by the boys themselves who from the first moment were suspicious of their purpose. 'On coming back to school,' related one troubled headmaster in the *Journal of Education*, 'they sniffed over the unaccustomed accommodation with as much suspicion as the Trojans showed at first of that fatal horse, contemptuously reviling the cubicles as "loose-boxes" and "dog-kennels" ... then it cost I know not how many scoldings and punishments to get the rule observed of keeping each to his own compartment.'[39] Nevertheless cubicles soon became an integral part of dormitory architecture in many schools and a large number remained in place up to and during the Second World War, despite the danger such wooden structures would have posed had the dormitories been hit by incendiary bombs.

In the case of open-plan dormitories every pupil had his own clearly defined space with his chair and belongings on one side only of his bed. Each boy was forbidden from entering another's space and in the case of my own prep school, one frightened lad went down to the matron to ask permission to pick up his teddy which had fallen on the 'wrong side'. If anybody persistently flouted such rules he was regarded with suspicion, and ultimately, as in the case of Rudyard Kipling, transferred to a room of his own: 'Dunsterville told me on Wednesday, in the plain ungarnished tongue of youth the why and wherefore of my removal according to [my housemaster], and by the light of later knowledge I see very clearly what that moral but absolutely tactless Malthusian must have suspected.'[40] If more than one or two boys were involved, then the whole dormitory might be forbidden to talk either to each other or to anyone in the rest of the school. One boy, whose dormitory had been forbidden from participating in any sporting activities after such an incident, later described the enforced silent walks as having the same atmosphere as a convict gang on the march.[41]

Even in normal circumstances the strict segregation system cast a shadow over every part of public school life. In the dining room boys messed with the same companions at breakfast, lunch and tea, week after week, term after term, year after year. On the sports field boys could only play in their house teams. Country walks were also closely supervised. A solitary stroll was permissible, three or more boys in a group was preferable, but two boys together, never![42] 'To guard against danger,' explained Robert Singleton (headmaster of Radley, 1847–51), 'no one is at liberty to go out by himself; in fact he may not stir from bounds unless he can form a company of three – all engaging on their word of honour that they will keep together.'[43] Even the short walk from a boy's house to his classroom was often closely regulated. At Winchester the fellow one walked up to books (class) with was called a 'socius' and had to be approved by one's housemaster.[44]

DENUNCIATION

By the Victorian period, sexual experimentation was viewed with horror. Not only was it seen as a manifestation of moral weakness, but it also supposedly formed part of the slippery slope down to the underworld of homosexuality. At every available opportunity public school housemasters and headmasters warned their sheep of the dangers of straying from the fold, alluding to unforgivable sins and unspeakable perils that awaited any boy whose vigilance momentarily lapsed.

In contrast stood a boy's experience at prep school. There the schoolmaster was too frightened to give any verbal definition to such fears, lest the early innocence of youth be corrupted at too young an age, for whereas the public school was seen as a nightmarish abode in which no evil went unpractised, prep school was considered to be a Garden of Eden where boys had not yet eaten from the Tree of Knowledge. Nevertheless, that crucial moment always came when the senior prep school boy, having completed his time, would have to be forewarned of the imminent dangers.

The moment chosen was usually either on the day of final departure or, at the very earliest, on the evening preceeding it. Every precaution had to be taken

to prevent the knowledge leaking from the leavers to 'contaminate' the lower
ranks of the school. At Summerfields the headmaster demanded that all boys
attending his 'highly classified' lecture should first promise not to divulge any
information disclosed to any other boy,[1] while at Durnfield Prep School each
boy, having been warned individually behind the closed door of the headmaster's study, had immediately on exit to take his place on the bus for Swanage
station.[2] The warnings themselves were nevertheless expressed in a generalized
and confusing way, the headmaster always afraid of being too explicit.
Normally the talk would take a tortuous and embarrassing route, starting with
some simple fact. The headmaster of Sandroyd began 'Some of you have
sisters'[3] and the headmaster of Horris Hill with the breeding methods of the
birds and bees.[4] From there a headmaster would usually broach the subject of
'normal sexual intercourse'. One lad remembered being told that 'if you want
to have a baby you put what you have dangling down into her hole and you
relieve yourself into it.'[5] As if all this was not confusing enough the head would
then warn vaguely of perversions of this sexual act and of the dangers of being
approached by an older boy. A typical, though fictional, account is given in
E.F. Benson's *David Blaize* (1916) in which the prep school headmaster warns
David:

> You don't understand me now . . . but you will. And when you do under-
> stand, try to remember for my sake, if that is anything to you, or for God's
> sake, which is best of all, that there are things worse than stealing. Things
> that damn the soul, David. And now, forget all I have said till the time
> comes for you to remember it. You will know when it comes. And don't
> listen to any arguments about it. There is no argument possible.[6]

The end result was that most boys, while usually unable to piece together all
the cryptic clues of the facts of life, were nevertheless made uncomfortably
aware of unspecified dangers that waited to entrap them. But the leaving lec-
tures could also prove counterproductive for they reinforced the impression of
boys that sex was an issue that could not be discussed easily with the school
authorities and they imbued both its theory and practice with the allure and
fascination of being daringly subversive. The Revd A.A. David, some years
after retiring from his post as headmaster of Rugby (1910–21), criticized the
leaving day sermonizing which had by then become a long established and
routine procedure:

> The perils indicated are very imperfectly understood by the average boy,
> and the general impression left upon his mind is that here is a dangerous

subject which his elders find distasteful. And yet he is drawn to it, not only by the fascination of the forbidden and the unknown, but also by new sensa/tions and impulses in himself which he does not understand and is there/fore the less able to control.[7]

However, a boys' leaving day jaw was often merely the first of several sermons on the subject of sex. While the prep school headmaster was now able to wash his hands of further responsibility, parents often considered the long summer holidays preceding public school as a time for further warnings. Even if they did not anticipate such a need their optimism was often shattered by a letter from the boy's prospective housemaster. 'I should be glad,' explained one Harrow housemaster to the parents of Walter Monkton (later a cabinet min/ister), 'if some time before he comes, you will take an opportunity of warning him of the moral dangers of a large public school. I shall speak to him myself but I like to know I have your support in the matter.'[8] Parents were often highly embarrassed in attempting to fulfill such obligations and sometimes even the basic facts of reproduction were forgotten in the trauma of spelling out the perils their boy was about to confront. Sixty years later the writer Edward James could still recount every painful detail:

> She [my mother] was looking very unattractive. Because it was late, she had taken the wig off and was wearing a lace cap. She had forgotten that one could see through the cap and that she was almost bald under it. She had a lot of grease on her face and she had been working herself up to break the horrible news that a bigger boy at Eton, some horrible boy, might try to assault me sexually or make sexual advances to me. I don't know who had told her about this, perhaps some other mother. She had entirely forgotten that she hadn't told me anything else, so the very first fact of life I learned was the danger of being assaulted by another boy, and to tell me this she had made herself so unattractive I might have been put off sex for ever[9]

Robin Maugham's mother warned her son that such an assault might come

> When you're out for a walk in the woods. And then this older boy may tempt you to commit with him an act which in the Bible is called 'fornica/tion', and is forbidden by God because it is very wrong and very evil. And if this happens, then you must tell the boy that you will never agree to the act and that you've been advised by your parents to tell the headmaster if the boy ever suggests doing such a thing again.[10]

So, by the time a boy arrived at public school his housemaster might hope that some sense of apprehension had already been hammered in. Nevertheless it was the housemaster's duty to ensure that all in his charge fully understood the dangers that surrounded them. An experienced housemaster would rarely give such warnings to boys collectively as that risked open ridicule. One Etonian housemaster thought himself above such risks and dared to give his house a public lecture on 'boys putting their penises up other boys bottoms'. As he stood in front of an open fire, in his Corps uniform with its thick leather leggings, he preached the importance of self-control. For some time he had sensed that the fire's heat had been gradually percolating through from the outside, but suddenly the previously satisfying sensation reached scorching point and in his panic he struggled as clumsily as a clown to tear down his trousers, while the onlooking boys laughed hysterically.[11] Housemasters had also to consider the possibility that talks might 'contaminate' innocent minds and provoke 'evil desires' where there had been none before. 'I was obliged,' explained the Revd A.A. David (who was both a headmaster and housemaster), '. . . to take the risk that however carefully and reverently I dealt with the subject, I might stimulate the wrong kind of interest and provide material for more bad talk.'[12]

A favourite time for a tête-à-tête came just prior to confirmation. The house-master would begin by attempting to discover whether his confirmands had had the usual pre-school parental pep talk, a question to which a boy sensed the desired answer was 'yes'. Another commonly employed method of avoid-ing mutual embarrassment was the leaflet which could be shoved into the hands of the seated boy who was then asked if he had any questions to which the only polite answer was 'no'.[13] However, housemasters were not always so reticent. Lord Drogheda recalled that his Eton tutor, just before confirmation, began his facts-of-life talk with 'I have been told that you have been seen playing with yourself as you walk along the High Street.' Since the allegation had no foundation in fact, Lord Drogheda long harboured a suspicion that this was the usual opening gambit employed, at least by this particular house-master.[14] One Winchester housemaster upheld a virtual tradition of three confirmation chats, at the last of which he would elaborate on the perils of sexual perversion:

'Now Chitty, in the house we have three sorts of trouble,' he begins. 'Self-abuse.' Here his voice falls into a trough of portentous seriousness. 'Mutual self-abuse,' rising to a squawk of dismay. 'And buggery,' deep in the trough again, a horror beyond adequate register.[15]

Concerns about the dangers of sex talks that followed a regular and rehearsed formula were raised in a privately printed pamphlet on the *Causes and Prevention of Immorality in Schools* circulated by the Social Purity Alliance. Its author was Edward Lyttelton, then an assistant master at Eton. He already wielded considerable influence both inside and outside the college and his dynamism was soon to propel him into the headmasterships of Haileybury (1890–1905) and ultimately Eton itself (1905–16). In the pamphlet he spelt out the dilemma facing the housemaster when warning boys about homosexuality:

> If you speak plainly to them, you will rudely tear the scales from their eyes, and rouse them to a sense of a world of impure horrors they never dreamt of before. If, on the other hand, you speak in veiled language, you will only stimulate their curiosity, the most fruitful source of moral evil in the young.[16]

Lyttelton argued that therefore there was great danger in such talks becoming merely a routine procedure. Boys should not all be subjected to the same lecture at the same age. Rather, each case should be judged according to the perceived character and knowledge-level of the boy concerned: 'When it is remembered how infinitely different boys are, and how unfathomable their natures, it is foolish to recommend any one treatment as suitable for all alike.'[17] Though the housemaster was obviously in the best position to know the 'character' of his boys, the headmaster would sometimes consider the task of deterring sexual experimentation (both solitary masturbation and homosexuality) so important that instruction could not be trusted to housemasters alone, and he would decide to speak to boys either privately or publicly on the sins of the cities of the plain.

Boys may well have nudged each other in anticipation as Edward Thring, the great Uppingham headmaster, mounted the pulpit steps in chapel to address the school in vague metaphors on the subject of masturbation and to warn of its terrible physical consequences:

> And so the poisonous breath of sin keeps tainting and corrupting all the freshness and purity of young life: and the corruption spreads, and gets into the very soul, destroying all its power to do true work, and win even earthly credit; and the face loses its frank and manly expression; and the poison begins to be seen outwardly; and after disappointing father and mother, and family, and himself most of all, the wretched victim either sinks down to a lower level [homosexuality?] . . . or often finds an early grave, killed by his own foul passions.[18]

Thring was thankful whenever he had the courage to give such talks and once confided in his diary, 'At nine I had all the communicants in the Upper School to speak to on the subject of lust . . . I do thank God unfeignedly for the opportunity of putting these great truths before the school, so that none shall fall into that pit of hell unwarned.'[19] In 1884 he explained to the Church Congress at Carlisle:

> Ignorance is deadly, because perfect ignorance in a boy is impossible. I consider the half-ignorance so deadly, that once a year, at the time of confirmation, I speak openly to the whole school, divided into three sets. First, I take the confirmees, then the communicants and older boys, then the younger boys, on three following nights after evening prayers. The two first sets I speak very plainly to; the last I only warn against indecency in thought, word or deed, whether alone or with companions. Thus no boy who has been at school a whole year can sin in ignorance. And a boy who despises this warning is justly turned out of the school on conviction.[20]

A quarter of a century later, Dr Herbert James (headmaster of Rugby 1895–1910), while lacking the same eloquence as Thring, appeared equally anxious to instill fear into his pupils. 'If you touch it, it will fall off', he warned boys who had been summoned to his study.[21]

Sometimes headmasters tried to deal with the issue more obliquely. G.W.S. Howson, headmaster of Gresham's, lectured the entire school on 4 April 1909 on the dangers inherent in certain school friendships:

> I would speak of the unwisdom of unequal friendships, and, believe me, that there is a greater gap between seventeen and fourteen, between the big boy and the little boy, than between other ages, a gap that cannot be bridged without loss of dignity and without courting disaster . . . In friendship we open the gates of our city, and he who enters, if he is not our ally, is a treacherous foe.[22]

The warning was also sounded in novels written by schoolmasters as evinced in this extract from F. W. Farrar's widely read *St Winifred's or the World of School* (1862):

> For during the last few years Kenrick has entirely lost his balance: he has deserted his best friends for the adulation of younger boys, who fed his vanity; and the society of elder boys, who perverted his thoughts, and vitiated his habits . . . Within these two years – and his countenance betrays the fact in its ruined beauty – he has lost the true joys of youth, and known

instead of them the troubles of the envious, the fears of the cowardly, the heaviness of the slothful, *the shame of the unclean*.[23]

The struggle between purity and lust also found its metaphorical representation in some Victorian school art. *L'Ange des Splendeurs* is the title of one such painting which young Abbotsholmians passed on their way to the dining hall. It depicted an angel attempting to save a youth from serpents of vice and evil and beckoning him upwards to a nobler existence.[24]

In history lessons too, the lives of kings and queens also often served as metaphors of good or evil, and of correct or incorrect sexual conduct, especially when any hint of homosexuality appeared in the circumspect language of school texts. The most popular target was King James I, who was invariably held up as an object of derision and contempt because of his friendships with younger male courtiers. Senior boys must have understood only too clearly the similarity between such historical circumstances and their own situation as prefects, capable as they were of bestowing or withholding considerable favours on junior boys. But Shrewsbury boys at least appear to have ridiculed the constant moral lecturing:

> So, side by side, we shall rehearse
> How England went from bad to worse,
> And why the South Sea Bubble burst
> And what was wrong with James the First.[25]

But while the denunciation of homosexuality often appeared to take on the form of a ritual, there were also many unplanned and explosive episodes when masters, driven near to despair by some boy's demeanour or behaviour, would launch into a vitriolic tirade against the evils of indecency. Perhaps a boy was being a little too boisterous in the bathroom, perhaps scatalogical scribblings had been discovered in the 'bogs' or perhaps it was just a lad laughing at some ambiguous turn of phrase. The novelist Antony Powell recounted such a confrontation at Eton, which was detonated by a boy chuckling during a verse of the carol *Good King Wenceslas*:

> In his master's steps he trod,
> where the snow lay dinted:
> Heat was in the very sod . . .

The teacher, incensed that any boy should have such a wicked knowledge of vulgar vocabulary, proceeded to reprimand the offender, reminding him of the dangers of that 'most loathsome form of dual vice'.[26] Despite the apparent triviality of the provocation, what appears to us now as almost comical overreaction would then have been considered an appropriate and timely response to the first conspicuous symptoms of moral corruption.

A teacher always had to be on the lookout for early indications of depravity. The writer Beverley Nichols recalled how at Marlborough his form master was enraged by a simple postcard pinned to his desk. It was of Cézanne's *Les Baigneurs*, but despite the fact that, even then, it hung respectably in the Louvre, to a public school master it was like a red rag to a bull. 'Do you like this stuff? Do you like looking at the bodies of naked young men?' he asked, and with that he ripped up the postcard and tossed the remnants into the fire.[27]

Neither were boys to take any sort of interest in each other's bodies. At Ackworth two seniors spotted comparing the size of their thigh muscles were promptly reprimanded by the headmaster, who with a remarkable display of biblical knowledge, instructed them to look up the tenth verse of the 147th psalm and write it down. It read:

> He delighteth not in the strength of a horse:
> He taketh not pleasure in the legs of a man.[28]

On other occasions boys were also reminded of the consequences of immorality both on this earth and after, and they knew such language to be a euphemism for expulsion. So, even those boys who disagreed with the sentiments of their elders and cared little for their own spiritual welfare were nevertheless left uncomfortably aware of the seriousness of the repercussions, should any of them be discovered with their trousers down.

DIVERSIONS AND DEFEMINIZATION

By the late Victorian period a consensus prevailed that the two easiest ways to keep a boy's mind free of temptation were to toughen him up physically and to keep him busy. A tough boy could fight off depraved emotional tendencies from a position of strength. If he learned to survive the unheated dormitories in winter and the bedlam of the rugby scrum, it would (in theory) be no greater hardship to learn to live without a bosom friend. And if his free time could be carefully limited and controlled, there would be little opportunity for vice to gain a foothold. 'In schools where games are not encouraged,' warned Rugby's Medical Officer, 'there can only arise an unmanly precocity in self-indulgence'.[1] He advised that an emphasis on games would 'always furnish a topic for innocent conversation, which is an inestimable boon'.[2] Similarly, the author of *Our Public Schools* (1901) observed, 'It is the opinion of competent judges that the more athletics flourish in our public schools, the less vice will be found in them.'[3] Headmasters were also eager to generate among their boys an obsessive interest in games which would cloud out other 'less wholesome' temptations. 'Did you ever think what a priceless boon is the innocence of school games as a subject of conversation?' the headmaster of Clifton asked parents. 'You are, perhaps bored by the incessant talk about matches and runs, and place kicks, and scrummages; you think games occupy a disproportion-ate share of the boy's mind. You may be thankful it is so.'[4]

Such views won easy approval by the turn of the century but they reflected radical 'reforms' in the organization of boarding school life. A hundred years earlier the situation had been very different. While boys suffered the strictest supervision in class, their leisure time was extensive and virtually unregulated. A typical early nineteenth-century boarding school timetable ran as follows:

> [After morning wash we] were let out to play till the bell rang for breakfast ... At ten we were all in school again [until lunch] ... We went into school again at three. At five school broke up, and at seven we had our suppers of bread and milk; afterwards we could study or go out within bounds as we pleased.[5]

In many schools the rules governing leisure time were even more generous and boys could often be seen wandering daily with their friends in the countryside some distance from the school. Nor is there much evidence that even the famous Rugby headmaster, Thomas Arnold, appointed in 1828, shared any of the views of later Victorians on the moral value of compulsory sports.[6] As Lytton Strachey commented, 'The modern reader of *Tom Brown's Schooldays* searches in vain for any reference to compulsory games, house colours or cricket averages. In those days, when boys played games they played them for pleasure.'[7] At Rugby, boys had long been used to doing what they wanted with their leisure time and the situation was the same at most other schools. One Marlborough boy noted in his diary, 'For the strictness with which they conducted their actual teaching, masters atoned by an almost total indifference to the way in which a boy employed his leisure.'[8] In 1840 an unpublished book on Winchester lamented that the masters had 'little to do with the boys per-sonally except to hear them their lessons'.[9] After these each sixth former was allowed to take one or two juniors with him on trips into the surrounding countryside. Thomas Arnold, when still a pupil at the College, wrote home excitedly about how he had been so chuffed to drink cherry brandy with

Lipscomb 'at a village called Compton' and another boy recalled that much of the summer term was 'passed amid these fresh glades and sparkling waters'.[10] At Ackworth it was a similar story with boys inventing their own games such as 'Greeks and Trojans' and 'Farmers and Robbers', which despite having nominal rules, were usually little more than free-for-all rough- and-tumbles, sometimes degenerating into angry fights.[11] An Old Boy of the King's School at Ely recalled: 'Our playground was extensive; we had the range of the whole College. In bad weather we sheltered in the cathedral; and incredible as it may seem, we span our tops and trundled our hoops without interruption.'[12] Perhaps some of the most bizarre pastimes took place at Loretto, Scotland's oldest independent boarding school, where in the after-noons masters wrestled with boys and every Saturday evening the whole school danced![13]

But gradually the amount of unregulated leisure time was reduced. Compulsory sports were introduced and inter-school and inter-house competitions were arranged, and as the spirit of patriotism and Empire height-ened, some schools also encouraged boys to join an Officer Training Corps that would organize field exercises at weekends. Little by little, the schoolboy found his 'free time' increasingly regimented until ultimately 'the boys' days were organized down to the last minute of every hour'.[14] The actor Christopher Lee recalled the burden of military training at Wellington College:

> Late at night, the polishing, polishing, polishing of boots, buttons, buckles, webbing, plus pressing one's trousers, ate into one's sleep, which seemed to be wiped out altogether when we got up at an ungodly hour to continue with the heartbreaking process of getting the exact amount of space between each layer of puttee . . .[15]

Even on Sundays boys were not to be allowed the luxury of too much leisure time. Here for instance is the timetable at Radley as in force by 1860:

> 7.00 a.m.: rise. 7.30: learn collect and gospel. 8.00: breakfast. 9.00–10.30: litany and morning prayer. 12 noon–1.00 p.m.: Holy Communion and sermon. 3.30–4.00: say catechism. 4.00–4.30: wash and change. 4.30: dinner. 6.00–7.00: evening prayer. 7.00–7.30: tea. 8.00: roll call. 8.00–8.30: if in Black Book, sit in schoolroom and read; if not, go to tutor's room. 8.30: bed.[16]

At the same time schools strived to make school life less comfortable as a first step in the toughening-up process. In 1867, the Governors at Oakham School passed a resolution that 'the water closets, servants' privies and boys' privies throughout the Master's house and premises at Oakham be converted into dry earth closets.' This was done, despite the fact that the flush toilets had been installed at great expense only nine years before.[17] Similarly, at Abbotsholme, a boarding school founded in 1889, the existing water-closets were ripped out and replaced by a spartan row of open air outside 'earth cabinets'. The school's most famous pupil, Lytton Strachey, was so weakened by the regime of cold baths and meagre rations that he had to be carried unconscious to the sick-room, his weight down to little over five stone despite his height of five feet two inches.[18]

One factor which aggravated this situation was the assumption made by school authorities that evening meals could be a sexual stimulant.[19] Consequently schools tended to hold suppers early and ration food strictly. Cecil Reddie, headmaster of Abbotsholme, explained to those who might have otherwise questioned the school's austere diet:

> If boys at school are fed upon inflammatory food they are apt to lose control of themselves and have fits of irritability, leading very often to moral vice. Whereas, those fed upon a cooler diet of cereals and vegetables run far less risk of these storms of super-abundant vitality.[20]

At Fettes boys regularly raided the stores in the basement and stole potatoes from the fields[21] and at Radley their situation appears to have been even more desperate. Radleian boys became so hungry they took to eating flower bulbs and cooking acorns. The headmaster's diary demonstrates a callous disregard for the boys' situation:

> Yesterday evening (8 February 1848) the younger Elliot got up during tea time and coolly went to the bell and rang it. On my enquiring into the meaning of this extraordinary movement, he as coolly replied that 'the boys wanted more butter'. We were perfectly astounded at this impudence. I told him never to dare to do such a thing again without leave, and when Thomas came to answer it I said in an unmistakable voice that 'nothing was wanted'.[22]

It became standard practice in schools for boys to be allowed only a bare minimum of clothes, whether summer or winter, and at Loretto the maverick Tory MP Sir Nicholas Fairbairn remembers that even underpants were banned as sissyish.[23]

Such was the insensitivity of the authorities that despite the suffering of boys under such conditions, schools continued to consider cold showers and baths an essential ingredient for a healthy, hardy life. At Osborne Naval College each dormitory had its own cold water plunge pool.[24] At Winchester each bathroom contained eight 'sit' baths filled with cold water in which boys had to totally immerse themselves.[25] At Clayesmore a dormitory prefect counted slowly from one to ten 'while each victim shivered and pleaded',[26] and at Sherborne one housemaster proudly observed how 'senior boys, in order to set an example to junior boys of supreme joyousness, spring gaily to their cold baths at 6.30 before the smaller boys come down'. A suggestion by the same housemaster that a gramophone playing lively music should be positioned outside the bathroom door was 'received with considerable loathing'.[27] Perhaps the most bizarre procedure was that implemented at the Watts Naval Training School in Norfolk. Here, boys were amassed seventy-four at a time and made to stand in a large shower room. The cold tap was then turned on and remained on until the last boy stopped yelping. Then and only then, when everyone was completely silent, would the supervising master allow warm water to flow.[28]

Schools introduced a multitude of strenuous activities to complement the part supposedly played by the cold shower in the construction of the manly character. One early innovation was the compulsory cross-country run. By the 1880s Aysgarth boys had to run up and down the Yorkshire Dales even in midwinter.[29] But the cold and exhaustion was sometimes only part of the ordeal. At Uppingham a prefect with a hunting crop always accompanied the juniors on runs so as to punish stragglers.[30] Sometimes boys could not manage the pace. Around 1890, one Rugby boy wrote back to his mother:

> Thank you very much for your letter. Yesterday a fellow tumbled down in a run and died; he was a small town-lout [day boarder] and was found in the road in what seemed like his last gasp by some fellows; these got him some brandy and put him in a cab and drove him off to the san. But he died before he got there . . .[31]

A later innovation was 'Outward Bound' which comprised organized expeditions, often involving rock climbing and canoeing in the wilder parts of Britain. One of the early pioneers, Adam Arnold-Brown, contended, 'There is little doubt that creative activity during and after adolescence can bypass that energy-sapping, distracting, all-powerful interest in sex which can fill the vacant mind.'[32] But one teacher at Gordonstoun, the Scottish school where the Outward Bound movement was born, had a more cynical view. 'It seemed,' he wrote, '. . . that an idea was gaining ground at Gordonstoun that improvement of character comes from suitable expeditions, even if compulsory, as inevitably as hydrogen comes if you drop sodium into water.'[33]

It is unlikely that spartan conditions and the encouragement of sporting activities did anything to lessen homosexual passions. On the contrary, the apparent indifference of the school authorities to the boys' discomforts and pains can have only served to enhance the degree of solidarity and comradeship among boys, while staff insensitivity probably promoted homoerotic attach-ments between boys searching for the elusive warmth of an emotional relation-ship. But added to this, the extreme stress on the importance of games in the staff room was inevitably mirrored by the hero worship of athletic boys by their juniors.

The eulogizing of athleticism by headmasters and staff elevated the status of the 'bloods' to virtual deities. At St Edward's even one of the chapel windows was dedicated in honour of a certain William Bates, a member of the cricketing XI.[34] Such actions only encouraged boys of ordinary rank to indulge in crushes on the more successful sporting types.

Inter-school matches offered boys the opportunity to exchange knowledge and ideas about sex with boys from other schools. Many headmasters were very nervous about such possibilities and Dr William Sewell (headmaster of Radley 1853–1861) was one of several headmasters who always insisted on vetting visiting teams before they were allowed on their school premises.[35]

There was also a more direct way in which the cult of athleticism proved counterproductive as it inevitably created many sexual opportunities, whether between stragglers on a cross-country run or lingerers in the communal showers. So, all things considered, it seems unlikely that the idea that somehow sport and sex are diametrically opposed was ever proved in British boarding schools.

DEBARMENT

Ethnic minorities were often indirectly victimized by the institutionalized homophobia of public schools. It was commonly believed that homosexuality was more prevalent in foreign countries and particularly in India and Islamic societies. This was sometimes attributed to the supposed superiority of Christianity and sometimes to climatic differences; the hot, humid conditions of Africa and southern Asia were thought to favour homosexuality. One Englishman, soon after arriving to take over the headmastership of an Indian public school, was not at all confident that he could turn his boys into gentle-men of moral stamina:

The character of the boys is another difficulty. Both in its good and bad aspects it is feminine and weak. They have none of the straightforwardness and stubborn pluck of English boys: they can only be ruled by a rare union of ever-vigilant firmness and loving sympathy. This moral weakness is founded upon the feeble precocity of physical development incidental to the climate.[1]

Credence to these prejudices appeared to be enhanced by the uninhibited way in which Asian and African pupils frequently touched their friends, often placing a hand on a knee or an arm across a shoulder, entirely unself-consciously. School authorities, which looked on all such demonstrations of affection with extreme suspicion, were quick to condemn. 'After several weeks,' one Nigerian Old Etonian recalled, 'I slowly started to discover that at Eton, any form of physical contact or touching another boy was apt to be misconstrued. Putting arms around each other's shoulders and necks was considered a friendly attitude in Africa. It had also been quite common at my prep school, and nobody minded my doing it to them at all. But at Eton it was considered perverted.'[2] Such students were often unwilling or unable to change overnight habits of communicating friendship which they had learned over years. This convinced many that foreigners, particularly non-Europeans, were undesirable influences.

Until 1911, Haileybury accommodated foreign pupils in specially segregated houses[3] and in 1928 J.F. Roxburgh, headmaster of Stowe (1923–49) refused to admit the sons of a Maharajah. When asked why, he replied that 'schools which have open dormitories . . . ought not in my opinion to receive coloured boys.'[4] Even when Africans and Asians were admitted, they always felt themselves to be under even closer scrutiny than their white counterparts:

That was one of the disadvantages of being black at Eton . . . It was embarrassing and extremely disturbing to think that it was genuinely believed I was a homosexual . . . There were, of course, a number of boys all over the school reputed to be homosexuals. But none of them, I knew, had made half the name I did.[5]

This type of racism was all the more implacable because, besides being based on a deep-rooted belief in white supremacy, it also formed part of a relentless crusade to eradicate homosexuality through the redefinition of the acceptable limits of friendship and affection.

DETECTION

Boys being boys, no amount of segregation and lecturing was going to stop some from satisfying their desires. In fact a few no doubt found the added challenge titillating, but in the same way that no prison, deserving of its name, goes without a comprehensive system of surveillance, similarly no public school felt it could afford to lack all necessary means for detecting vice.

Generally, the headmaster himself was above the sordid day-to-day, or to use a more appropriate adjective, night-to-night task of eavesdropping. His role was as a Commander-in-Chief keeping himself at a respectable distance from the quagmire of battle. Much of his energy was devoted to coordinating the activities of his various agents (housemasters, classteachers, matrons, prefects and informers) and in ensuring they put loyalty to 'the school' (a euphemism for himself) above any foolish notions of friendship or, worse still, comradeship: for nothing could frustrate the head's ambitions more than the impenetrable wall of silence which frequently met any inquisition as to the state of boys' morals. The famous psychoanalyst Wilfred Bion later recalled the pitiable attempts of his own headmaster to win the loyalty of the boys in a desperate plea at Sunday chapel:

> But . . . surely if you knew that one of you, however esteemed for his games or work, was putting poison in the food of another boy you would go to one of the masters and tell him. Yet when a boy is poisoning the mind of another you say nothing.[1]

Thomas Arnold (headmaster of Rugby 1828–42) attempted a different technique, striving to inspire rather than merely berate his sixth formers: 'You should feel like officers in the army or navy, where want of moral courage would, indeed, be thought cowardice.'[2]

The headmaster's ambition was invariably the establishment of a pyramid of surveillance in which every member of the school was to play a part. But as in all systems of power some had a larger part than others. Next down in importance from the head himself, and occupying a position similar to that of the aristocracy in feudal Britain, came the housemasters. It was the opinion of many headmasters that these posts were too frequently sinecures filled by men of overly independent means. Some of these bachelor barons were more interested in being popular with 'their' boys, than in winning the respect of the head whose real powers had, at least in some schools, sunk almost to the level of some figurative boy-king.

Many housemasters refused outright to participate in what they knew the boys would see as ungentlemanly espionage. Others dragged their feet, some-times quite literally. In the 1850s one Harrow housemaster always changed into hobnailed boots before making his nightly rounds.[3] At Eton, where each boy had his own room, a tradition had long prevailed that 'M'Tutor' (the Eton term for housemaster) had always to knock before opening a boy's door. The students often took these rights for granted.[4] One newly appointed house-master was reminded by a prefect that his supervisory powers ended abruptly at a green baize door which was the Harrow equivalent of Hadrian's Wall. 'Everything that happens on this side of the door is your responsibility,' the boy explained. 'Everything beyond it is mine. When you wish to enter my side of the house you will knock and wait to be invited.'[5]

It was the strongly held opinion of all headmasters and even many house-masters that all this had to change. 'It is often forgotten,' complained the Revd Alfred Barry (headmaster of Cheltenham 1862–1868), 'that a boarding-house master is not merely charged to see after the food, lodging, and health of his boys, but that his influence must be very great, for good or for evil, in forming the moral tone of the school . . .'[6]

Headmasters determined to rid themselves of their more negligent housemasters. They could achieve this only by ending the gravy train of posts for life and the process proved a slow one. At Eton, where the lodging system had evolved haphazardly over many years, it was not until 1933 that the head-master managed to attain any right over the selection of housemasters. Until then, classics tutors were automatically given the post of housemaster, whether or not they had the headmaster's favour.[7]

As soon as a headmaster had won the cooperation and compliance of all his housemasters, the system of surveillance took on a new vigour. Like all net-works of espionage it depended on both astute groundwork and the immedi-ate disclosure of relevant information to the appropriate authorities (i.e. a boy's housemaster and, if sufficiently serious, the headmaster). The first necessity of good groundwork was a knowledgeable watchfulness. Was one boy seen too frequently buying lemonade for another at the tuck shop? Why were the same two boys always walking back together from the squash courts late every evening? Headmasters were always reminding housemasters of the importance of keeping a keen eye on their boys and particularly on the company they kept. Dr Arnold would sometimes take his assistant masters to one side and alert them to the necessity for vigilance. 'Do you see those two boys walking together? I never saw them together before; you should make an especial point of observing the company they keep: – nothing so tells the changes in a boy's character.'[8] A housemaster could never afford to assume innocence. One Eton boy bitterly recalled that:

Whenever we could, Tom and I used to play records in the Music Schools, only to be faced by regular grilling from M'Tutor when he came to our rooms last thing at night. 'Now I want to know what you were doing at the Music Schools this evening.' 'We were playing the Rachmaninov concerto, Sir.' 'But I want to know what you were *doing*!!'[9]

Housemasters prided themselves on having a detailed knowledge of where any one of their boys should be at any given moment. One famous housemaster used to conclude his introductory talks to new boys with the warning, 'Remember that I shall be watching you every hour of the day.'[10] Neither would a housemaster or any other member of staff tolerate any excuse for being in the wrong place at the wrong time. Even trips from a class to the lavatory were usually restricted to a certain number of minutes (normally about three) and at some schools had to be entered into a log book.[11]

Surveillance was a twenty-four hour responsibility. It was not sufficient for a housemaster simply to respond to excessive levels of dormitory noise, for while pillow warfare might be heard at a distance, mutual masturbation and other such 'devilish' acts of homosexual experimentation were more difficult to detect. It required considerable stealth and an element of surprise. The key weapons in these ambushes were slippers and a torch. One of the earliest practitioners of such anti-vice techniques was the Marlborough housemaster C.B. Canning. His silent patrols in carpet slippers earned him the nickname 'Foxy Ferdie' from the boys, after Ferdinand, king of Bulgaria, an ungentle-manly ally of the odious German Kaiser.[12] A more unusual technique was practised by one Winchester housemaster who hid himself in a strategically placed suit of armour in order to find what his boys were up to.[13] Less bizarre methods of surveillance were rapidly taken up at other boarding schools. By the 1920s the matron of one London orphanage was making her nightly patrols in stockinged feet. Any boy caught with his hands under the bed-clothes was immediately caned. Such was the fear of discovery that even years later ex-inmates still found it difficult to relax at night:

My wife asked me why I always slept with my hands on the pillow. I didn't realize the habit still persisted. As I told my wife the story I realized for the first time that Miss Mason had been afraid of masturbation. We were little more than babies then but Miss Mason had credited us with knowledge beyond our years . . .[14]

Many dormitories were kept lit during the night. Radley in the 1850s had a typical arrangement with a candle on every alternate cubicle partition and with a row of night lights in perforated cylinders along the floor of the central passageway. '[They] threw great shadows and circles of light upon the ceiling, looking down like watchful eyes upon the sleepers.'[15]

The boys, however, developed their own techniques of counter-surveillance. Often one boy would keep cave just outside the dormitory and warn the others of a housemaster's or monitor's approach. This was done either on a rota system or by a boy keen to enhance his popularity, as keeping cave was in itself a dangerous activity:

> When a fight was in progress, one of us crept out on to the landing and peeped over the banisters to keep watch. I peeped over the banisters at the exact moment that Nurse looked up. Our eyes met. My frantic dash back to bed did not save me. She vented the full force of her temper on me.[16]

The term 'to keep cave' (pronounced kave or kav-ye), meaning to 'keep a lookout', is probably itself an invention of public school slang, being derived from *cave*, the imperative of the Latin *cavere* – 'to take care' or 'to beware'.[17] The expression dated from the sixteenth century and by the Victorian era its use was widespread in public schools. Dormitory corridors were at best dimly lit, and the boy chosen 'to keep cave' would watch out for the light of the housemaster's candle. The best tactical position was often:

> At the top of the staircase . . . He then commanded for a great distance the only avenue in which danger was expected. If any master's candle appeared in the hall, the boys had full three minutes warning, and a single loudly whispered 'cave' would cause someone in each dormitory instantly to 'douse the glim', and shut the door: so that by the time of the adversary's arrival they would all be (of course) fast asleep in bed.[18]

The other necessity of counter-surveillance was information on a housemaster's movements and boys were always attempting to discover on what evenings and at what times he might be safely preoccupied with other duties. Headmasters often preferred to appoint bachelor housemasters for this very reason, that they might have more time available in the evenings to monitor boys' behaviour.[19] At one point Stowe had only one married man in a staff of thirty.[20] Roxburgh like most other school heads, thought that single men would be able to devote themselves more wholeheartedly to the demanding tasks of supervising boys than would married men. But even the most dutiful housemaster had occasional commitments. The writer Robin Maugham recalled the casual confidence of one late night intruder to his Eton study:

'I want to talk to you,' he said quietly. 'Talk to me tomorrow,' I whispered back. 'There'll be a hell of a row if you're caught here.' 'I won't get caught,' Drew replied. 'M'Tutor's done his rounds, and he won't come back because he's got a dinner party tonight. I saw all the cars outside.'[21]

Such moments of safety were far from being the norm. Even prefects were only too aware that a housemaster could fling open a door at any moment. Once, when a senior accused a new boy of having a magazine stuffed down his trousers during a caning, the lad started to undo them to prove otherwise. Whether innocent or guilty, it proved a wise move. 'The prefect, alarmed that he would be found in the sixth-form library with a new boy with his trousers down, immediately protested, "No, no, no, I believe you."'[22]

Nevertheless, doors proved to be something of a hindrance to the grand strategy of surveillance. Even when they were not lockable, there was a limit to the frequency with which they could be flung open by a housemaster before he would become open to ridicule. Besides, there was the problem of knowing which door to open first, as by opening squeaky study or dormitory doors sequentially a housemaster would lose any advantage of surprise. A number of ways were found to circumvent this problem. At Eton boys returned one term to find three holes drilled in every study door.[23] At other schools dormitory doors were sometimes kept propped open[24] and many public schools, including Winchester,[25] Rugby[26] and Marlborough,[27] kept all toilet cubicles doorless well into the twentieth century. Even when doors were placed on toilet cubicles they were designed so that 'neither the doors nor the partitions are carried down to the floor'. Then all it took was a quick glance by a master or prefect to determine how many pairs of feet there were per compartment.[28] Even so some schools resorted to additional measures. At Harrow, where lavatories had doors, only seniors were allowed to close them. Lord Rothschild remembered how one boy avoided the resulting embarrassment:

It was a three-year privilege . . . to close the lavatory door. A boy called Usborne did not go to the lavatory for a whole term as a result. We were much mystified by this feat of endurance but I suspected he secretly relieved himself at the Music School which, because of its cellular construction, was also the headquarters for homosexual activities.[29]

Another even more unpopular aspect of the surveillance system was the encouragement of 'honourable espionage'. While normally housemasters considered it improper for boys 'to sneak', where homosexuality was concerned informers were encouraged. 'Discourage actively confidences about a boy's surroundings,' advised an Eton assistant master, 'except in regard to the one all important question of purity.'[30] Sometimes valuable tip-offs were obtained in this way to the mutual benefit of the authorities and the informer. When one Harrow boy tried to blackmail Lord Rothschild into having sex with him, the little Lord took the matter up with his housemaster and was rewarded by becoming a permanent favourite, even to the extent of being frequently let off early morning school.[31] It took a lot less provocation for the young Eric Blair (George Orwell) to decide on the same course of action:

> Once, towards the end of my time, I even sneaked to Brown [my house-master] about a suspected case of homosexuality. I did not know very well what homosexuality was, but I knew that it happened, and that this was one of the contexts in which it was proper to sneak. Brown told me I was a 'good fellow' which made me feel horribly ashamed.[32]

But frequently the cultivation of espionage could backfire when the school's sense of what was proper came into open conflict with the schoolboy princi-ple of collective loyalty. One Eton boy who exposed a scandal was jeered at by an angry schoolboy mob.[33] Similarly Revd Bertram Pollock (headmaster of Wellington College 1893–1916) was hissed at by boys, who suspected him of encouraging informers. He only managed to restore order by caning three of the culprits on the spot.[34]

A less controversial means of surveillance was the delegation of night time supervisory powers to prefects, a scheme pioneered by Radley headmaster Robert Singleton:

> It is well known how extremely particular we are upon this point, in accor-dance with the injunction of the statute, *sileatur in Dormitorio*. Unless we can secure peace and quiet there, all our efforts at education will be futile . . . In other places the dormitory is only a second playground: here it is to be a sort of second chapel; sacred to devotion and holy rest. The prefects therefore are not to allow a word to be spoken, or a needless sound to be heard, either by day or night.[35]

New boys often had a prefect allocated to their dormitory who was held responsible for any misbehaviour. In 1902 the school architect Felix Clay observed that

> In large dormitories it is usual to find at one or both ends a fair-sized cubicle, which is occupied by a monitor or prefect, who is placed there to keep order

in the room. This room should have a window or an opening giving a good view of the dormitory.[36]

At Abbotsholme his task included explaining the minutiae of dormitory rules and submitting a report at the end of term on each boy's co-operativeness, cleanliness and moral standards.[37] 'Above all,' emphasized the dormitory rules, 'he is to maintain a healthy tone in the whole dormitory and a manly bearing in each fellow. He should discourage both effeminacy and roughness, but foster a frank and hearty comradeship.'[38] While at Loretto the headmaster would always write to each prospective dormitory prefect 'telling him that by far his most important duty is to keep up a high standard of purity, and to stamp out all really bad or low talk'.[39] Outnumbered by mischievous youngsters, it was often a difficult task. At Eton the nocturnal activities of Collegers at night-time so alarmed the authorities that they empowered the Captain of Chamber (the old dormitory of the College) to use a rubber siphon to beat the more unruly boys,[40] while at Osborne Naval Academy the cadet captains (two were assigned to each dormitory) could use the reveille gong-rope for the same purpose.[41] At most other schools dormitory prefects rarely had such Draconian powers and frequently the post's only merit was that the feeble protests of the senior boy would inevitably be heard by some passing master.[42] A more effective method was to delegate trustworthy prefects as 'prowlers' along the corridors outside the dormitories. The prowlers would then, without needing to directly confront junior boys, simply report any disturbances to the housemaster. A variant of this system was that seniors or 'landing boys' would be stationed at fixed intervals as sentinels outside dormitory doors.[43] This pre-empted the possibility of cave-keepers reconnoitring landings to warn of a housemaster's approach.

Dormitory romps became an extremely hazardous sport. By the early twentieth century a highly sensitive surveillance system had been introduced into most boarding schools. Such was the environment that nurtured the future author of *1984*. But this Orwellian despotism did not go without resistance, both passive and violent. In one Eton house boys covered up spy holes in their study doors with pieces of black card that could be hidden away each morning.[44] The same decade also witnessed a near riot against one particularly priggish Eton housemaster. Several boys decided to ambush Mr Goodhart on his nightly anti-vice prowl. As he got to the middle of a long dark corridor trays were hurled at his back. Furious and unable to discover the identity of the culprit he rang the house fire alarm and instructed boys to come 'immediately just as you are': 'Thereupon half the house tore off their pyjamas and came down naked or wearing only a pair of spectacles, a sock or a shoe – all of which made a farce of Mr Goodhart's solemn interrogation.'[45]

Nevertheless, these mini-rebellions were but blips in the gradual but continuing trend towards an almost suffocating degree of supervision. Whether in the music school or the dormitory, homosexuality had become a dangerous game. Gone were the days when housemasters simply let dormitories run themselves. Gone too, in many cases, was the trust boys held that housemasters would not abuse information given in confidence. There was to be no more turning the blind eye. It was a war and if homosexuality was discovered there were to be no prisoners. For the nature of punishment was changing too. Expulsion was no longer just the ultimate deterrent; it became a mandatory sentence, often forming the least painful part of the punishment package.

DETERRENCE

Until the mid-nineteenth century boys were rarely expelled for homosexuality. In 1730 a certain Henry Simms was expelled from Eton for 'keeping undesirable company' with two aristocratic youths,[1] but this case appears to have been an isolated one in a period otherwise totally lacking in schoolboy expulsion scandals.

The long era of *laissez-faire* appears to have come to an abrupt end in 1859. In the next three years several anti-vice purges shook the public school establishment. The biggest of all took place that first year at one of Britain's oldest schools, Westminster, where five senior boys were expelled, another five rusticated and eleven others caned in the library.[2] One of Britain's newest public schools, Wellington College, witnessed a much smaller, if equally portentous scandal. The headmaster Edward Benson (1859-73) was informed that a general's son had struck another boy between the legs. Some years earlier this may have been at worst a stand-in-the-corner offence, but coming so soon after the Westminster incident, Benson decided an early example was required. The culprit was locked up in the bathroom, while the general himself was summoned and informed of his son's expulsion.[3]

Expulsion was always a traumatic experience but there was no parallel to the almost unbearable sense of shame engendered by expulsion for homosexuality. A vivid portrayal of such a predicament is given in Simon Gray's (1967) novel *Little Portia*, where the hero Grahame Thwaite imagines that his affair with another boy has been discovered:

He walked from the library to the classroom, from the classroom to the house, with his gaze lowered. He could meet no one's eyes, and answer no one's call. Aprilson gave him a look. The others stared and smirked and gossiped. The masters circled around him in the cloisters on the way to chapel, and put their hands behind their gowns and their heads together, and talked of his dirtiness, which rose from him to fill the Upper Common, the classrooms, the library.[4]

By the early twentieth century anyone with any worldly knowledge could understand the whisper, 'Oh, he was sacked for the usual reason.' Expulsion had become almost synonymous with homosexuality. If a man could not hide such a blemish he could not hope to make any progress in society. Writing of the period just prior to the First World War, an Old Wellingtonian put a new perspective on the biblical passage on the wages of sin:

> It must be remembered . . . that at the time of which I write, their wages (if found out) was social death. For expulsion from a public school was gener-ally attributed to sexual depravity and any boy so disgraced would find uni-versities and professions barred to him unless, like one of Conrad's anti-heroes, he was prepared to expiate his guilt by service in some remote fever-ridden outpost of Empire.[5]

Shame would also fall on the house to which the boy belonged and when at Eton the Captain of Williams's was found to have seduced younger boys, the entire house football team was obliged to pull out of the final of the inter-house cup.[6]

But however dark the cloud of a sordid school scandal, it always had, at least from the head's perspective, a silver lining. Here was a golden opportunity, not only to set a stern example, but also to lecture the boys and imbue them with a collective sense of guilt and repentance. Like the biblical floods or the Great Fire of London, the drama of an expulsion provided a one-off chance for a new beginning. From the very first moment of discovery a reign of terror would overshadow the school. 'Twice before,' wrote Uppingham's headmaster to a parent in 1880, 'I have had to battle with it ['the evil of impurity'], probing each time to the very end every bit of evidence I got, and following every clue.'[7] Frequently, numerous boys would be summoned to interviews in an attempt to discover how far the rot had spread. They knew that there was little safety in numbers, for a school would often be prepared to sack any number of boys in order to protect the remainder. Perhaps the most bizarre example of this ide-ology was the Eton housemaster who, having unexpectedly gate-crashed a soirée in the house library, was surprised to find himself surrounded by dancing naked prefects sipping gin and tonic. He immediately summoned taxis and, reluctant though he was to be head of a prefectless house, expelled them all on the spot.[8]

The instant removal of those guilty of such 'depravities' helped to prevent 'the cancer of moral corruption' spreading, but sometimes the school authorities preferred to wait until the following day. Then, in the cold sobriety of the morning after, the whole school could be assembled for a public beating in which the obvious pain and humiliation inflicted on the culprits would hopefully deter any other wouldbe offenders. Just moments prior to the execution, the head would use carefully chosen words to express the sordidness and seriousness of the crime. Sometimes the words were too carefully chosen, as one spectator later testified:

> There was, when we were all gathered, a great and puzzling speech . . . Mostly there was decency, most boys were content to be boys according to some accepted definition; they got on soberly with their studies and their healthy games. But there were patches of mould. There were unspecified vilenesses. Two boys in particular were creators of corruption, and might become carriers if dramatic punishment were not imposed. This was the moment for it. Alas. The two boys were named . . . These boys, we were told, had been caught fooling about in the lavatories. I remember attempting to focus the wickedness involved . . . The lavatories? Had they been tinkering with the plumbing? Then something happened that was straight out of my Victorian school stories. The caretaker was summoned, and each boy in turn was hoisted upon his back, there to be tremendously flogged. We dispersed – most of us, I now think, quite baffled.[9]

In another, if somewhat surreal, version of the public birching, George Orwell remembered being lectured on vice in one room, while a boy was being viciously beaten in a room above:

> A long desolate wail rang out . . . A very small boy named Ronalds . . . was being flogged, or was recovering from a flogging . . . Flip's eyes searched our faces and settled upon me. 'You see,' she said. I will not swear that she said, 'You see what you have done', but that was the sense of it. We were all bowed down with shame. It was our fault . . . Then Flip turned upon another boy named Heath . . . I cannot remember for certain whether she merely quoted a verse from the Bible, or whether she actually brought out the Bible and made Heath read it; but at any rate the text indicated was 'Whoso shall offend one of these little ones that believe in me, it was better for him that a millstone were hanged about his neck, and that he were drowned in the depth of the sea.' . . . Ronalds was one of these little ones, we had offended him . . . 'Have you thought about that, Heath – have you

thought what it means?' Flip said. And Heath broke down into snivelling tears.[10]

Humiliation was a vital element in the punishment process. Humiliation, both of the culprit and of the whole school. Ideally this was intended to arouse the anger and indignation of all the 'innocent' lads who sometimes mobbed the beaten boy as he struggled with his suitcases on his lonely way to the station. In one instance, 'the route was lined with boys hurling eggs, tomatoes and filth'.[11]

However the severity and theatrical nature of the punishment more often than not rebounded on the school authorities. Instead of a cowed humiliation, the boys would be overtaken by a sympathy for the underdog. A martyr was created. The feeling of shared revulsion at the excesses of a punishment would undermine the school's struggle to suppress sexual deviation. Quentin Crisp recollected how after one particularly barbaric beating 'no one seemed to regard what they had seen as right. Some of us enshrined the culprit in our hearts as one of the saints of Aphrodite.'[12] Like many others, Crisp was a witness both to the inflexibility and futility of a system blinded by its determination to suppress homosexuality at any cost.

School authorities were adamant that there could be no tolerance of homo-sexual behaviour. Homosexuality was, they argued, highly contagious and only the expulsion of offenders from the school could protect other boys. Cyril Norwood (headmaster of Harrow 1926–34) explained:

> In the case of . . . active immorality, expulsion is not only necessary but just. Medical men who usually advise parents about these cases, and study them from the purely individual point of view, frequently argue that expulsion is the wrong treatment: they forget the responsibility of the school to the parents of the other boys. They themselves would never leave a patient with smallpox in a dormitory of healthy people, and it has always been somewhat astonishing to me that they should think that a schoolmaster should think twice about permitting a detected corrupter to range free inside a school.[13]

H.H. Almond, the headmaster of Loretto (1862–1903) expressed a similar view when he sacked a boy for indecent talk in 1899:

> What I least like is the idea that any boy living among our boys could think that such talk could make him anything but wished away. I am glad there has been one case, *pour encourager les autres* . . . Society would be a very unpleasant place . . . if well-disposed people didn't do everything in their

power to clip the wings and break the force of the bad ones. Evil doesn't observe 'laws of war' in dealing with good, and I have no hesitation in saying that I think good is usually far too squeamish about its weapons and tactics.[14]

However there were rare occasions when even headmasters acknowledged that they had too hastily expelled a boy. One English head of an Indian boarding school admitted in his memoirs:

My action implanted fear in the school, which hid from my eyes and ears for a time all sexual misdemeanours, but the boil festered. A year later a boy attempted to commit suicide, because he was worried by sex. Teachers, if they knew of masturbation or of homosexual practices amongst the boys, had kept the information from me. Boys, if they knew of anything, would hear and see and speak no evil.[15]

In such schools homosexuality often became more fashionable precisely because it was forbidden. The only assured result was that as long as masters waged war on boys' morals, so boys would make an equal effort to hide, even quietly to eulogize, such dangerous liaisons.

GOODBYE MR CHIPS:

THE TWILIGHT OF THE CANDID TUTOR׳PUPIL FRIENDSHIP

Thus there was lost entirely, that cordial intimacy, a mingling
of friendship and respect, between master and pupils without
which the labour of the educator is the greatest of
martyrdoms.
Santiago Ramon y Cajal in *Recollections of My Life*.

When Evelyn Waugh commented on public school teachers that 'some liked
little boys too little and some too much', he was encapsulating in a phrase the
absurdity of early twentieth century wisdom.[1] This held that all boarding
school masters walked a tightrope in which any immoderate inclination
towards informality could plunge the unwary into the abyss of infatuation and
indecency. Extravagant familiarity between tutor and pupil was supposedly the
root cause of sexual evil.

FRIENDSHIPS BETWEEN MASTERS AND BOYS

Boarding schools were a frightening and alien world to the new boy. One boy's
first impressions of Fettes are typical: 'I recollect very well the cold clean look
and cheerless sanitary smell of the passages, the chill echo of footsteps on their
scoured stone floors.'[2]

In such bleak, barrack׳like institutions, it is unsurprising that many boys
spent much of their time mourning the loss of the comfortable family environ׳
ment. Usually they were unable to see their parents for more than two or three
days in an entire term, and other boys, whose parents lived far from school,
were lucky if their parents 'came down' even once in a term. It was therefore

entirely natural that boys often looked up to masters as substitute father-figures. This desire had a strong counterpart in the obligation incumbent upon house-masters and tutors, and to a lesser degree on other teachers, to function *in loco parentis*. After all, the ambition of many boarding schools was to be the 'perfect family', turning boisterous children into gentlemen of 'reputable character'. Such an undertaking necessitated a certain closeness between schoolmasters and their protégés.

However, there was debate as to the wisdom of such methods. What seemed to some common-sense practice was deemed by others to be dangerous folly. 'It is no use pretending,' warned Frank Fletcher soon after leaving his post as headmaster of Charterhouse (1911–35), 'that a difference of years doesn't exist or doesn't count; a master who forgets or pretends to forget that he is not a boy is as objectionable as the boy who pretends or persuades himself that he is a grown man. The friendship between boy and master . . . ought not to be, and indeed cannot be, the same as the friendship between boy and boy.'[3] The opponents of too much familiarity between teachers and taught claimed that at best it led to a moral spinelessness and that at worst such intimacy might provoke indecency between tutor and pupil.

The dispute came to a head in the mid-Victorian period. In the first half of the nineteenth century affectionate attachments between masters and boys had never been looked upon with any suspicion. The poet Shelley, when at Eton in the first decade of the century, had not turned any heads on his frequent visits to a master's Windsor house.[4] There, ignored by the world, they had discussed Plato and his philosophy of 'virtuous lovers' and 'beloved youths', over tea.[5] Several decades later the headmaster of Radley College still had no obvious embarrassment in writing to a boy's father that his son who had been 'plainly suffering from a decrease of religious views':

> came to me in an agony of repentance, confessed his sins and implored for-giveness. After holding out for some time, I took him to my arms, where he kissed me all over, crying most bitterly; and I need not say that I kissed him as tenderly.[6]

It was gradually, almost imperceptibly, that the kiss became taboo. In 1814 the Prussian general Blücher had raised only a few eyebrows when on a visit to Eton he insisted on kissing many of the boys in continental fashion.[7] By the second half of the century, however, even the modest English kiss was merited only on a few significant occasions, such as when Sewell kissed a boy who had won a scholarship, or in the wake of some misfortune as when Revd William Wood (headmaster of Radley 1866–70) gently embraced a boy who had fallen

down the stairs.[8] But soon even these infrequent rituals of demonstrative tenderness were tolerated only with considerable misgivings, while any hint of
more casual expressions of affection was met with grave suspicion.

The career of one Eton master, Tom Cattley, almost came off the rails when
it was rumoured that he routinely kissed all the boys in his house good-night.
Wilfrid Blunt, who joined the staff in 1938, thirty-nine years after Cattley had
first been made a master, was critical, describing his alleged behaviour as 'reckless'. He added that he considered the kiss 'a perilous . . . if not a criminal act'.[9]
Rupert Hart-Davis, another member of staff, writing to a friend in the year of
Cattley's death, penned a brusque epitaph: '[I] didn't much like what I heard
about him . . . I'm sure he was a suppressed pederast.'[10] However, Lord
Drogheda, one of the pupils who was a 'victim' of Cattley's good-night visits,
was more accepting of his housemaster's antiquated and affectionate nightly
adieu. 'One felt,' he wrote later, 'there was someone warm and loving aching
to break free from his constraints.'[11]

At American schools the taboo on masters kissing boys seems to have come
much later. Even as late as 1935 Jack Kennedy's housemaster was able to write
candidly to the boy's parents explaining how 'For a year and a half, I've tried
everything from kissing to kicking Jack into just a few commonly decent
points of view and habits of living in community life, and I'm afraid I must
admit my own failure as well as his.'[12]

English housemasters by then may well have still resorted to kicking, but
never, never (without incurring considerable risk) to kissing and in an increasingly puritanical climate, it was not just the kiss which was seen as an indication of lurking dangers. Many members of staff also began to object to the
conspicuous closeness and informality of some tutor-pupil associations. Where
there had once been enormous latitude in what was considered acceptable
tutoring practice, there was now escalating opposition to masters who were felt
to take too keen an interest in their charges. Nowhere was this clash of wills
more bitterly contested or more critical to the outcome of this ideological war
than at Eton.

The climax of the struggle came in the 1870s. Two highly charismatic
housemasters, William Johnson and Oscar Browning, attempted to defy the
new dogma as fearlessly and as foolishly as sixteenth-century religious martyrs.
Their downfall was similarly inevitable, if a little less theatrical.

William Johnson was by far the most experienced, by reason of his age and
seniority. He had been appointed in 1845 and was Oscar Browning's tutor.
Browning himself joined the Eton staff in 1860 and soon became Johnson's
comrade-in-arms. But until his overthrow in 1872, Johnson remained the pre-
eminent influence. The historian G. W. Prothero called him 'the most brilliant

Eton tutor of his day'[13] and one boy later testified that his poetry had 'created a spirit which stole into every nook and corner of Eton.'[14] The source of his influence was ultimately the cause of his undoing – the intimate and impassioned rapport he had with his pupils. He encouraged boys to visit his rooms after school hours and to borrow any books they fancied from his extensive library. Then when he had wished the final lingering boy good-night, he would set about writing poetry or letters late into the night to those he felt needed consoling or reassuring. He was indefatigable and his perseverance earned him a certain status among the boys. He bewitched them with delightful eccentricities, sometimes wearing three pairs of spectacles one on top of the other, charmed them with his generosity and inspired them with his teaching. But not content merely to attempt conversion through example, he had the temerity to spell out his gospel of tutorial obligations. First, a teacher should always respect his pupil. 'If a boy stammers,' he wrote in his *Hints for Eton Masters*, 'do not scold him, but civilly ask him to take a full breath.'[15] Second, a teacher should not limit his attention merely to his own pupils and wash his hands of all responsibility as soon as a student had moved to another form. Third, a teacher should not lock himself away outside school hours but rather should see it as his duty to welcome boys who dropped by, whether to discuss academic or personal problems, or just for a cosy chat over tea.

Most of the staff were convinced that such ideas were dangerous and were furious whenever Johnson felt it his duty to give advice or time to boys who were not his official responsibility. No doubt some were also jealous of the fondness and admiration which many pupils showed for him.

In 1872, Johnson's long-predicted downfall was accomplished and he left for good. The curtain of silence which descended on the circumstances of his departure had probably more to do with protecting his enemies and eradicating the last vestiges of his influence, than to any noble desire to conserve his reputation. Nevertheless, his textbooks were so indispensable that they remained in use for a further eighty years, even though the name of their author was struck from them.[16]

Legend has it that a father discovered an excessively passionate letter to his son, but in the many letters that survive there is no evidence that Johnson ever attempted to seduce any of his protégés. A more plausible explanation for his resignation was that someone discovered a letter in which perhaps he had been too frank in his criticism of another tutor. In any event somehow his position was compromised and lacking allies in the staff room he was compelled to leave.

It was Browning who now became the focus of the moralist crusade. Realizing his predicament, he attempted to blunt his critics' invective by arguing that only through getting to know a pupil intimately could a master gain a boy's confidence and correct any tendency to indecency. But Browning set about this strategy in a highly extravagant manner. His hospitality to his young male guests exceeded even Johnson's. Students who called by were invariably invited to join him for a feast fit for princes, being attended to by a line of servants and sometimes also savouring the company of such eminent guests as John Ruskin and George Eliot.[17] His young guests were bedazzled and those boys who had been invited from other houses returned to their lodgings late, inspired by their host's iconoclasm.

Soon Browning's subversions became even bolder. He began to teach history right up to the beginning of the nineteenth century and, as if this was not itself a sufficient outrage, he posted Liberal election broadsheets on his windows. The final bombshell came when he wrote to Her Majesty's Commission on Public Schools complaining of the philistine emphasis on macho sports.[18]

The headmaster, Dr James Hornby (1868–1884), and most of the staff were now determined to be rid of Eton's turbulent priest. The first opportunity came when a housemaster, the Reverend Wolley-Dod, protested to Hornby that Browning had taken an improper interest in a good-looking pupil – George [later Lord] Curzon. Browning was duly summoned to account. His reaction was one of indignant fury. 'Do you mean to say . . . I took notice of a boy because he was good-looking?' to which the headmaster replied, 'I don't know, I'm sure.'[19] This opening skirmish was followed up by a relentless assault on Browning's reputation by Wolley Dod and his fellow conspirators; a crusade which received the back door blessing of Hornby. Few dared to support Browning, except the father of the boy who had provided the initial *causus belli*. He wrote a letter of appreciation and sympathy to his son's tutor:

> I exceedingly regret this very unpleasant complaint of Mr Wolley Dod's, with reference to your conduct towards my son George. I am fully aware of your warm feelings and keen desire that he should grow up a manly, true, pure-minded lad and though it is possible that your notice of him may have tended to annoy his tutor – I give you full credit for acting from the purest motives and I do not wish the kindly relations between you and my boy to fall through. I quite believe that you were instrumental in rescuing George from companions of more than doubtful repute, and that your sole desire and object has been to elevate and improve his character . . . and I can only hope no further unpleasantness may ever occur on his head.[20]

His enemies were not able to find any sufficiently incriminating evidence to unseat him but Hornby, having no doubt spent considerable time examin- ing all the rule books, came to their aid. In September 1875 he sacked Browning for violating the official ceiling on the number of boys he accom- modated in his house.[21] Curzon was disconsolate: 'I do miss you so much here, though I did not see very much of you for the last year or so, did I? Yet the place seems strange without you and I often wish you were back again.'[22] The boys in his own house were equally saddened by his sudden departure and clubbed together to present him with 'a silver cup, in which an inscription was engraved saying that it was given to me in grateful remembrance of my kind- ness and care to those who were members not only of my house, but of my home.'[23]

If the moralists hoped that Browning's dismissal signalled the end of inti- mate tutor-pupil friendships they were soon proved unduly optimistic. Brownings' downfall may have represented a victory of sorts. He had no suc- cessor at Eton who ever attained the same degree of influence nor was any sub- sequent Eton housemaster ever to host quite such an extravagant series of schoolboy dinner parties, but as a self-confessed befriender of boys he was by no means the last of his kind.

Several Eton housemasters continued the tradition of inviting boys to dinner. Lord Chandos, reminiscing about such occasions, recalled that the food was always outstanding, accompanied by 'a sound claret' and rounded off with 'a little good brandy'.[24] Alcohol was always a great remover of in- hibitions. It smoothed conversation, allowing boys to forget their homework, and housemasters their age. One of Eton's most famous provosts, Lord Quickswood, used to hold soirées in which he would regale his young guests with stories of medieval torture, while Tucker, his butler, constantly uncorked bottles in a vain attempt to keep glasses topped up. Occasionally a boy would subside into his chair only to leave in an ungraceful hurry a few minutes later, but his lordship was either too indulgent or too inebriated to notice.[25] Another Etonian who was a firm believer in befriending his boys was Henry Luxmoore who, basing his judgement on many years of housemastering, wrote in 1918:

Of the tutorial system the gist is this: from entrance to leaving the boy should be attached to the supervision of one master *in loco parentis*. The tutor and new boy, working together many hours daily, get to know each other pretty thoroughly, and, if each be a good sort, they become real friends. Then, all through the school, the tutor would supervise his pupil's work and have charge of his literary training.[26]

Sometimes these friendships created jealousy in tutors who, whether from laziness or sheer lack of skill, had been unable to win the companionship of boys in their own house. This was particularly the case if a teacher witnessed a friendship blossom between one of his 'own' boys and a master from another house. One such incident arose at Wellington College after a tutor suggested to a sixth former that he bring his prep over to his room one evening. It was shortly before the scholarship exams and the teacher was not unnaturally eager to give boys any extra tuition he felt necessary, but he was astonished when the lad turned up at his door declaring, 'Mr Ramsay [my housemaster] told me to report to you at the time you asked for me: and I'm to tell you that he does not approve of his boys associating with junior masters in the late evening. I am not to stay.'[27] At Charterhouse a similarly benevolent teacher, Harry Iredale, also became distinctly unpopular with housemasters. He used to go to amazing lengths to court the companionship of boys, even going to the extent of constantly cultivating a small flowerbed which lay beside the route between the classrooms and the playing fields. Whenever a master passed he was always to be seen furiously weeding, but moments later he would be waylaying boys again on their way to or from games. But what really annoyed housemasters was not so much his wasting boys' time as the indirect effect of his own generosity on theirs. He was always encouraging students to bring their problems to him. This infuriated housemasters who did not want their workload, already increased by the necessity of constant surveil-lance, made more burdensome, by any obligation to help boys with their studies outside class. But Iredale's indiscretions, however exasperating, were never of the same order as Johnson's or Browning's had been, and the staff at Charterhouse were not quite as ruthless as their Etonian colleagues. Though some housemasters banned their boys from visiting Harry, they were never able or sufficiently willing to intimidate him into submission or resigna-tion.[28]

If staff room loyalties could soon be lost when a tutor was too friendly with his pupils, the gratitude of the boys themselves was more enduring of the test of time. Such was the normality of boarding school brutality and sadism that a kind master stood out like a beacon of light in the night. Peter Fleming, later to become a famous travel writer, explained to his mother:

> My food consists of calvesfoot jelly and custard pudding . . . Mas [the matron] was beastly at the beginning but she's getting a little better. I dunno what I should have done without Maniac [Basil Maine, one of the masters]. He's been up here every minute he can spare reading to me and jawing and telling ghost stories, and he lent me stacks of books.[29]

At Haileybury a boy called Stephen wrote an enthusiastic description of the eccentricity and generosity of his drawing master to his parents:

My dearest Mummy and Daddy, I like Haileybury so much that I am already looking forward to coming back next term . . . There is an awfully nice drawing master here, Mr Blunt, a great tall man with a high forehead who wears pyjama-like shirts and ties of all colours in the rainbow and out. He took us [the people who do extra drawing with him] up to London yesterday to the Tate Gallery. Of course we paid for ourselves but he treated us to tea at Lyons and we had a gay time and we got some glorious warm chestnuts! It was great sport and he is awfully nice. I took extra drawing because I knew you would like me to . . .[30]

Later, after Stephen had left school, he went on holiday with Wilfrid Blunt to Venice. Their close companionship continued for years until it was suddenly cut short by Stephen's death in the Second World War.[31]

Another life-long friendship was that between George Curzon and Oscar Browning. After the headmaster banned the boy from visiting Browning, George wrote what at first reads like a final if loving adieu:

I can't say how distressed I am to think that I am prevented from seeing you, and all through the unkind, ungentlemanly and obstinate conduct of my tutor, whom I detest the more I see him. But I must thank you with my whole heart for all the inestimable good you have done me, for you have always been open to me as the best of counsellors, and have opened my eyes to the company by which I am surrounded and have warned me against evil companions.[32]

But, though temporarily handicapped, their friendship never faded. 'I want to ask you something,' Curzon requested in one of his many letters to Browning, 'please will you send me a photograph of yourself, one of those delightful ones? Vignette. Side face looking to the right – done by Hills and Saunders.'[33] When Curzon moved on to Oxford he invited Browning up to his rooms for dinner, and his former tutor stayed on for a further two days. 'I can't tell you how I enjoyed your two days at Oxford: It was the first time and it shall not be the last by a very great many that I have stood in the position of a host towards you and it was very pleasant.'[34] Curzon kept his word and many years later he was able to invite Browning to the more splendiferous surroundings of the official residence he had as Viceroy of India. 'Whatever I am,' Curzon informed his wife, 'I owe it all to Mr Browning.'[35] In later years he sent

Browning £100 so he could complete his history of the world and as a cabinet minister obtained for his ageing former tutor a most prestigious present. Oscar Browning was delighted. He now had an OBE.[36]

Oscar Browning's own mentor, William Johnson, was equally enthusiastic to preserve his intimate friendships with boys. Many a late night he would spend either writing to his former pupils or going over his diary reflecting on distant but undimmed memories. 'At Surley corner [on the Thames] was a regular picture, a barge laden with wood, with the slenderest, straightest thread of smoke at each end, one horse pulling it down stream, the poplars behind, Myrtle [a pony] and her glowing young rider in the foreground.'[37] Johnson later described the young rider, his pupil Frederick Wood, in a glowing tribute: '[He] has been my companion, the constant helpmate in my troubles.'[38] But his love was rarely unreciprocated and despite the cloud under which he left Eton, there was a constant stream of appreciative old boys visiting him at Halsdon House – his retirement home. One of them was Francis Elliot, a friendship Johnson cherished:

> I have always relished and worshipped his mere mind, besides the character: his exercises have been treasures to me, and I am proud of having my perseverance overcome his singular shyness. Not being afraid of him as some men would have been, I set to work when he was young to read Italian with him and my room was his refuge . . . The more I think of him, the more sure I am that his Eton life has been unique, incomparable, a spring of happiness, and he himself the flower of boyhood, the glory of Eton, the ideal and quintessence of virtue . . . No low passion to mar the loftiness of his mind . . . There has never been a time when his intellect has not been to me a kind of music.[39]

Another keen friendship, based on an intellectual rapport between tutor and pupil, was that of Dr Vaughan (headmaster of Harrow 1846–59) and Henry Butler, the boy who he considered to be the most promising of his Harrovian pupils and who eventually succeeded him as head in 1860. The two corresponded for years but sadly Vaughan's *in articulo mortis* was that all his papers and letters be destroyed, thus depriving future biographers of a veritable gold mine. What is known is that while Vaughan remained headmaster, Butler used to visit him virtually every vacation and that, even as the years passed, his admiration for his former tutor never waned. When Vaughan died in 1897 Butler paid this tribute to his memory:

> At Harrow – how can I recall those days which are so clear and so bright to some of us? We all knew that we had at our head a strong ruler who could

not be trifled with. His softness of voice and manner, at first almost startling, never left any illusion with boys or masters as to either his penetrating insight or his resolute will. But he was very gentle with us, more and more so as his time of office drew to its close.[40]

Some tutors had a sixth sense by which they unearthed and cultivated the talents of boys who later became eminent politicians. Oscar Browning's recognition and encouragement of Lord Curzon's abilities is only one, if perhaps the most striking, of many examples of this. When the Earl of Gowrie joined the Thatcher Cabinet in 1979 he was surprised to receive a letter of congratulations from Robert Birley, who a quarter of a century earlier had put aside all his obligations as a busy Eton headmaster (1949–63) to drive the young earl down to Oxford to convince him he would like it. In fact, the earl was not the only friend of Birley's in the Cabinet, for when Birley had been head of Charterhouse (1935–47) he had esteemed Jim Prior as something of a child prodigy. Now, years later, two men Birley had once held dear to his heart worked together at the highest level of government.[41]

Even when in some of the remotest parts of the world Old Boys still felt obliged to send an occasional letter to a kindly schoolmaster. One Old Sherbornian, while fighting the Japanese in the Burmese jungle, wrote wistfully

> I always remember those Sunday evenings with the chinwaggers in your study. The arguments we used to have and coffee and cake . . . I often find my thoughts drifting back to those days, even when ploughing through mud during a monsoon, and I thank God that I had the opportunity to share in it all.[42]

Sometimes even presidents were not immune from the obligation to make time amid their hectic schedule to write to their former tutors. The headmaster of the Gorton Boarding School for Boys sent Franklin Roosevelt a birthday card in each and every year after Roosevelt's final term in 1900. As president some thirty-six years later, Roosevelt wrote to him, 'If you had not sent me a birthday card I should have been really worried! Do you know that I have every one of them that you have sent me since the earliest days after I graduated.'[43]

Boys of a caring disposition never forgot the early attentions of a devoted tutor. They invariably recognized his untiring aid and encouragement for what it was – a labour of love. To his adult critics, however, the affectionate tutor had wandered beyond the bounds of his responsibilities. His devotion to those who showed interest and intelligence, and to others whose scholarly or personal problems drew his sympathy was labelled favouritism; a somewhat blinkered judgement but one which often proved fatal to a teacher's career. To boys these men seemed like guardian angels, but to school authorities they were at best dangerous fools, at worst sexual fiends. Of course in retrospect it is easy to see that they were neither saints nor devils, but merely compassionate and chaste individuals with a soft spot in their hearts for the company of boys.

DREAMS AND DESIRES

It is a demanding task to decide which relationships between tutor and pupil can be classified as close friendships and which have such an intensity of feeling by either or both participants that they can be defined as infatuations. The friendships considered below are those initiated by the teacher in which he became besotted by some combination of a boy's character, charisma and good looks.

While at times a tutor realized that he was drawn both by a boy's personality and sensuality, at other times he was often not aware of any degree of sensualism in his passionate interest in a pupil's progress. The drawing master Wilfrid Blunt was franker than most would ever dare to be when he described the blend of boyish attributes that attracted him while at Eton: '[They] were of exactly the same kind as those who had attracted me at Haileybury, though now sometimes in an older age group; bright, eager, vivacious, naive, slightly pert, and usually, but by no means always, reasonably good looking'.[1]

Many tutors were captivated by a boy's early signs of brilliance. One such bond grew up between the vivacious William Johnson and one particularly promising pupil, Lord Dalmeny, the future Lord Rosebery (Liberal prime minister 1894–95). When Dalmeny was taken ill in his second year at Eton, Johnson was already sufficiently attached to request his father that the boy should return as soon as possible, emphasizing that his contributions were sorely missed: 'He has twice made a speech in our debating society with singular fluency, spirit and wit.' Johnson also explained how 'his influence, although unconsciously exerted, has quite reformed one boy, and has done a great deal of good to some others.' To Dalmeny himself, he wrote 'Good and dear friend . . . come back soon, as well as possible; for I miss you.'[2] The following year Johnson wrote to a friend that: 'He [Lord Dalmeny] has the finest combination of qualities I have ever seen . . . I am doing all I can to make him a scholar; anyhow he will be an orator and, if not a poet, such a man as poets delight in.'[3]

A similar bond grew up between John Galsworthy and his Harrow house master. The school's headmaster had singularly failed to recognize any spark of talent in the lad, latent or otherwise, claiming later that the prospective Goliath of English literature had not afforded 'any notable promise of distinc tion in after life'. But his more discerning housemaster had held a more favour able opinion, appointing the boy head of house. When Galsworthy left he was disconsolate. 'I can honestly say to you,' he confided in a letter to Galsworthy, 'that I never expect to be able to replace your loss; and I have never had among many good heads one who was at once more easy to work with than yourself, and so completely to my heart in every respect. I shall always look back to you, therefore, as my ideal head, without exaggeration.'[4]

At other times masters were drawn to the boy in difficulty. William Johnson wrote to his successor at Eton, C.H. Everard, explaining that there was one of his pupils who 'has great trouble with his verses, and often has to come for help like a lower boy.' Johnson begged Everard not to be impatient and to give the lad particular attention as he had recently lost the services and guidance of his maid who had helped him more than 'any dame or tutor'. For Johnson his friendships with boys were not about fostering a cloistered clique of boy prodigies. They were merely unconditional acts of 'homage to the simple sweetness of good boyhood'.[5] Though separated in time by almost a century, the Wellington master T.C. Worsley was a kindrid spirit. He became infatuated by a boy from a fractured family who had a distinctly delicate constitution. This condition was not alleviated by his mother who, during the holidays, always took him along on her wild whirlwind tours of provincial night life, depositing him along with her other baggage in a dizzy succession of grand hotels. Worsley was the only adult with whom the boy was able to strike up a rapport. The young master was deeply taken by the lad's 'shy friend ship'. But one day the boy's jealous housemaster, Jenkins, did his utmost to undermine the friendship. 'I suppose you know about young Kirkpatrick, don't you?' Jenkins asked Worsley with mocking casualness. Then, as if to clarify what he meant, added, 'He's not the kind of boy to get attached to,' and paused purposefully in order to lure Worsley into making the somewhat com promising rejoinder, 'Why? What's the matter with him. He seems to me quite innocent', before delivering the final *coup de grâce*. 'He has about six months to live. Leukaemia.'[6] Understandably Worsley was devastated, but the grim situation only served to intensify his attachment to the fragile boy. After Kirkpatrick's death he penned a short poem in his memory which ended with these words:

> If foolishly when sense and manners want me
> to join loud talk of little things I'm rude –
> You won't despise my sentimentalizing:
> Out of your stillness you'll have time to grant me
> The fond indulgence of a sadder mood.[7]

But while the death of a pupil was an infrequent torment for tutors, there always came at the end of each summer term that dreaded moment when senior boys took their final leave of the school. A.C. Benson put the tutor's predicament lucidly:

> I am here, a lonely man, wondering and doubting and desiring I hardly know what. Some nearness of life, some children of my own . . . But . . . these boys who are dear to me have forgotten me already. Disguise it as I will, I am part of the sordid furniture of life that they have so gladly left behind, the crowded corridor, the bare-walled schoolroom, the ink-stained desk . . .[8]

The sociologist Mattha Vicinus explained the 'inevitable teacher-student dilemma' in more abstract but equally eloquent words: 'The teacher is static, remaining in one spot, growing older but not altering in his or her role, while the student is in flux, bound to leave at a certain time, and is expected to flower and grow in a larger world.'[9] The effect could be devastating when masters had cemented very close attachments to their boys. Johnson, having said farewell to one promising pupil, lamented, 'I cannot bear to think that he is lost.'[10] Another Etonian master, H.E. Luxmoore, poured out his grief in a letter to a former pupil:

> As I have told you before, failing in so much I want and wish to do, it is an unspeakable consolation to have your friendship and affection, and to feel that opportunity has not been all lost. Reflection whispers that it is little credit for a schoolmaster to have 'got on' with his best boys, who would indeed have got on with anyone, but it still remains a tangible consolation and happiness, and what I shall do without you I don't know.[11]

The letter was often the only way in which a master felt he could spell out his infatuation to a boy in considered words that would have inevitably failed him had he struggled to define his devotion face to face. But such methods also carried grave dangers should another teacher or parent discover the letter, or if a boy disclosed a letter's contents to others. The indiscretions of such *passions de la plume* proved the undoing of Dr Charles Vaughan, (headmaster of

Harrow 1844–59). In January 1858 one boy revealed to another, John Addington Symonds, a bundle of amorous letters written to him by Vaughan. Symonds was later to become an early campaigner for the rights of homo-sexuals. Then, he was disgusted by what he read, but later confessed, 'to com-plicate matters, I felt a deeply rooted sympathy with Vaughan. If he had sinned, it had been by yielding to passions which already mastered me. But this fact instead of making me indulgent, determined me to tell the bitter truth . . .'[12] Eventually Symonds mustered the courage to tell his father who, as soon as he had seen the letters, determined that Dr Vaughan should abdicate his headmastership. He wrote to Vaughan revealing that he held copies of his letters to his son's friend, Alfred Pretor, and assured him that he would remain silent if Vaughan immediately resigned. A few days later Mrs Vaughan arrived to see Symonds and begged him to be merciful, but to no avail. Vaughan was left with no alternative. He announced his sudden retirement, declaring that fifteen years was the maximum term that he thought it wise to continue a headmastership and hinted that a new head would benefit the school by introducing fresh ideas. His farewell audience, having no knowledge of the letters which had caused his downfall, was bewildered.[13] It was William Johnson's only fortune in his battles with the moralists on the staff at Eton that none of his many letters were similarly discovered, for he was never one to mince his words, whether verbal or written. In a typical burst of impetuosity he wrote to the fourteen-year-old Lord Dalmeny:

My Dear Dalmeny, what is the matter? . . . I have been unhappy for a week without you, though too proud to say so, till the gentle influence of Sunday and the peace-making Mouse [another boy] prevailed. On Wednesday night I had no companion but the dog Rabe and I was sorely tempted to remonstrate. If I did not show sufficient joy at your appearance on Thursday night, it was out of pride, which you ought to make allowances for: I was really very glad when you came in and began to romp – W.J.[14]

Even today such letters could be considered improper if written by a boarding school master to a boy. Dr John Rae (headmaster of Westminster School 1970–86) explains in his autobiographical *Letters from School* that 'If the letter was emotional but not explicitly erotic I think I would give the teacher a written warning that his action was unprofessional and that any repetition would raise the question of whether he should remain at the school.'[15] Although Rae uses the term 'love letter', it is not clear when a letter would fall into this category, but by stressing that such letters need not be explicitly erotic it would seem that any letter which was unduly affectionate might meet with his censure.

An easier way for masters to pursue their relationships with pupils, if either they or their boys' parents could afford the expense, was to invite their protégés to join them on holidays on the continent. The indefatigable Johnson frequently took a coterie of boys to Italy or France. Naturally, one of the youths he invited was the much favoured Lord Dalmeny, fifth Earl of Rosebery. The fifteen-year-old Lord was able to enjoy the pleasures of Rome. With time in hand it was a matter of looking round the Coliseum before sauntering through St Peter's on a visit to 'the old woman' (Pope Pius IX). And then it was on to Paris. Johnson was delighted by Dalmeny's intelligent company. 'He must be,' the Eton master rejoiced, 'the wisest boy that ever lived and full of fun too.'[16] Oscar Browning may or may not have been one of the favoured few who accompanied Johnson on his European tours, but after he returned to Eton as a member of staff he enthusiastically continued the custom of having tutees as holiday companions. On his final Eton summer vacation, Browning chose his beloved Curzon to accompany him on a holiday to Greece where together they climbed Mount Parnassus, a mountain that had once been held sacred to Apollo, the Greek god who symbolized male beauty.[17] On a subsequent holiday which Curzon took in Paris with another companion, he missed Browning's company: 'Very often, as we passed a tempting looking cafe, I fancied you by my side dropping in for a dozen *huîtres* and a glass of vermouth.'[18]

The Shrewsbury master J.B. Oldham had a particularly bizarre notion of what constituted the perfect European holiday. Taking with him a band of boys he would insist on maintaining the more masochistic elements of school rules such as the cold bath, into which he was the first to plunge every morning of the holiday. Then, after his bath, and apparently oblivious to any embarrassment, he would shave attired only in socks and boots.[19]

Other opportunities of getting to know pupils were provided by organized excursions. The Labour politician Woodrow Wyatt remembered fondly how his form master had driven 'a select group' of boys to dress rehearsals at Glyndebourne. Wyatt hated opera but he was elated at the opportunity of even momentarily escaping school: 'On the way home we would stop at a wood he knew and wait for the nightingales to sing. Not only the birds were happy as they sang out on a soft summer night . . .'[20]

But for every master who self-confidently consorted with favoured boys there were many others who were more quietly infatuated. One such man was the Etonian drawing master Wilfrid Blunt who was captivated by the charms of Z, a boy whose roguish smile reminded him of Frans Hals' oil sketch *Boy with a Flute*. Blunt remembered how '[Z] remained totally unaware of my feelings for him throughout the brief weeks my infatuation lasted.'[21]

There were also times when masters tried in vain to win a boy's affections. The problem was that a boy often retreated deep into a shell once outside the familiar context of the classroom. However cosy and homelike a housemaster tried to make the private side of his house, it often proved impossible to construct a truly casual atmosphere and consequently invitations to tea often proved disappointingly unfruitful, as one Winchester housemaster discovered:

I am irresistibly led to ask lonely pedestrians to tea, even when they are not members of my form, set, platoon or game. I nearly always repent. They invariably accept, and accept with alacrity; but outspoken and natural as they appear as they wriggle along by my side down into the town, they become tongue-tied and nervous within doors in the presence of my wife, and during tea do nothing but eat as if they were about to die of starvation . . . They will discuss revues, musical comedies, and the latest plays generally, varied occasionally by the shortcomings of politicians; but they fight shy at once of topics of real and lasting interest, however tactfully these are introduced. They are not the same boys we know and grow to love so well in form; all at once they seem to have become gauche, grotesque and out of place. This must be the reason why the majority of men invite the same boys over and over again and neglect the great majority . . .[22]

Masters who focused their efforts on a particular boy could find a reluctance to reciprocate most frustrating. The poet Edward Thomas remembered one master who tried all manner of means to win his affections, but with no success. 'I had no particular liking for him,' Thomas explained, 'or gratitude for his liking for me.' When he left the school, the kindly master wrote him a succession of letters, but after replying to the first, Thomas allowed subsequent letters to go unanswered.[23] The Etonian housemaster A.C. Benson tried equally hard to win the attentions of a boy, with whom he was hopelessly infatuated, but his exertions were also unrewarded:

I have had the feelings of my disabilities brought home to me lately in a special way. There is a boy in my house that I have tried hard to make friends with . . . I have lent him books; I have tried to make him come and see me; I have talked my best with him, and he has received it all with polite indifference . . . The advances are all on my side, and there seems a hedge of shyness through which I cannot break.[24]

But such failures have to be placed in perspective. Affectionate gownsmen often had a tendency to fret excessively over boys who cold-shouldered their

efforts. It was far more usual for boys to be grateful for the attentions and kindness they received from such teachers. The more obstinate opponents of the
overly familiar tutor were generally to be found in the staff room.

THE TEACHER AS HERO

While it was rare for a master's affection for a boy to go unrequited, a boy's
fondness for a tutor was normally met with an equanimity bordering on
indifference. Edward Carpenter, who later became an early campaigner for
homosexual rights, remembered at his mid-Victorian boarding school that,
'Even to one of the masters . . . who was a little kind to me, I felt this unworded
devotion; but he never helped me over this stile, and so I remained on the
farther side.'[1]

Sometimes a boy would make his own task even more formidable by falling
for a master who taught another form or for an even more distant and majestic
figure – the headmaster himself. Somerset Maugham described his hero, the
headmaster the Revd Thomas Field (1886–96), in the character Tom Perkins
in *Of Human Bondage*, relating how his compassionate and progressive
approach to education alienated most of the school staff. When Maugham
returned to King's School, Canterbury, years later, he was asked to pinpoint
his own position amid the vast pyramid of ranked boys. He declared that he
was bound to be somewhere close to the headmaster, and sure enough, he was
found sitting sheepishly between Field's legs.[2]

Other boys were not content merely to dream about their teacher heroes. 'I
tried to seduce them all the time,' remembered Quentin Crisp, who was silent
on whether his attempts were duly rewarded.[3] Invariably such efforts, however
skilful, were somewhat disappointing in their results. But a boy's hopes were
difficult to subdue, until the day he finally realized he had not been competing on a level playing field. The writer Hallam Tennyson recalled the sad
denouement:

> At school my real hero was my classics tutor, a man in his mid-thirties,
> short but well built with hairy wrists and a crisp, slightly sarcastic manner.
> When he made a later marriage with an attractive pre-Raphaelite girl,
> younger than himself, I felt sadly let down.[4]

Often the hero worship of a teacher blossomed in response to kind treatment,
especially in a school where such humanity was normally in short supply.
Such admiration cannot always be dismissed as merely the gratitude of a

teacher's pet, for sometimes a form master's charity and encouragement was thinly but equally spread across a large class and yet still found a powerfully emotive response in some boys. The Nobel Prize winner Hermann Hesse never forgot the charm and charity of his grammar school headmaster:

> I who had always been a sensitive and anti-authoritarian pupil accustomed to fighting tooth and nail against the smallest suggestion of subservience or dependence, was now completely captivated by this mysterious old man simply because he appeared not to notice my immaturity, bad behaviour and follies.[5]

Sadly, in other cases a lad's respect for a teacher was induced by flattery and favouritism. The painter Augustus John, who was a pupil at St Catherine's at Tenby in the 1890s, was one such victim. The headmaster advised the other boys in the class that they should look on John as an inspiration and even went as far as to compare him with the Colossus of Rhodes, one of the Seven Wonders of the World. His biographer, Michael Holroyd, comments that 'to these encomiums, which might have embarrassed another boy, Augustus responded like a bud in the sun.' But, for the headmaster, the lad was merely a tool with which to motivate the rest of the class, and like most tools he was disposable. As soon as their friendship became the subject of the usual cynical speculations, the headmaster's mood took an about-turn and the young 'Colossus' was suddenly cold-shouldered.[6]

In the end it was the fog of suspicion which enveloped boarding schools, permeating every corner from the staff room to the playing fields, that stifled all warmth and sentiment between boys and their teachers. Kindly schoolmasters were coerced into holding back their affections while unkindly teachers were able to cultivate favourites by treating boys with unequal cruelty. In such an atmosphere a boy's dog-like devotion was at best met with indifference, for any more charitable response always attracted jealousy and suspicion.

LIVING DANGEROUSLY:

HOMOEROTIC FRIENDSHIPS BETWEEN BOYS

*I shall be careful to mortify my feelings severely, keeping them
within the limits of Christian modesty; especially shall I
discipline my eyes, which St Ambrose called insidious snares,
and St Anthony of Padua thieves of the soul.*
Prayer of boys at a Catholic seminary in Bergamo, Italy

LE COUP DE FOUDRE

As opposed to ordinary friendships which usually evolved slowly, a boy 'crashed' into a 'crush'. The realization of a new burning obsession came suddenly and had about it a delicious sensation of phenomenal import. Of course this attack could occur anywhere, but among the most likely locations was the chapel. Perhaps there was something mystical about the religious rituals which aroused instinctual desires. In any case, it was often during the silence of Sunday service that the bonfire of hero worship ignited.

A.C. Benson would always remember watching in awe as a senior boy strolled late into Eton Chapel nonchalantly swinging his cap. His instant reaction was, 'Who could this hero be?'[1] Michael Davidson remembers a similar infatuation:

> It began in the cloisters; but it was in chapel that the sudden tidal wave of worship hit me and knocked me head-over-heels. I haven't the slightest idea why: I suppose it was some angle at which I caught his face, some light and shade upon it, some tilt of the head – all I know is that my spirit soared with those fluted pillars into the gothic height, and I walked out of chapel feeling as I didn't know human beings could feel.[2]

And it is notable that John Betjeman's memories of youthful love at Marlborough also focus on the chapel:

> Here, twixt the church tower and the chapel spire,
> Rang sad and deep the bells of my desire.[3]

More obvious locations for the ignition of homoerotic desires included the playing fields, the fives-courts and the gymnasium. Whether it was the half-nakedness of football players with their rolled-down socks and high-cut shorts, or the elegant grace of movement on the cricket field or the indecent posture of the tennis player with bum protruding, games-time provided ample opportunities for infatuation. School sports were an essential ingredient in the manufacture of hero worship. In fact the recounted memories of such moments often read just like the script for a commercial. This account, for instance, by ex-Barnardo boy Frank Norman might have been profitably used by Reebok:

> Suddenly the Spanish boys appeared in the doorway . . . Then without warning one of them who was about the same size and age as me stepped forward and, taking a firm grip on the thick rope . . . shinned up it like greased lightning . . . His dexterity was such that he put even the best of the school athletes to shame as he swung from one bar to another with wonderful grace and precision . . . After a while the Spanish boy, having made his point, slid down the rope to the floor, his face gleaming with sweat and wreathed in smiles. Then as though to add insult to injury he ran several paces, leapt off the ground and did a somersault in mid-air. He landed lightly on his feet like a panther, grinned at his astonished audience, caught my eye and winked, then proudly joined his compatriots and strutted out of the door. I resolved then and there that this was someone whose friend I was going to be.[4]

If there was ever a moment when a boy instinctively felt that he was in imminent peril of experiencing a crush, it came as the bell sounded for sports, a Pavlovian reaction to accumulated past experiences. There was no knowledge of who the loved one might be or indeed any certainty that anything extraordinary was about to transpire. It was nothing more and nothing less than a vague and ill-defined anticipation. Yet again, John Betjeman's poetry expresses such feelings better than any prose can:

> Along besides the five-courts pacing, pacing
> Waiting for God knows what. O stars above!

> My clothes clung tight to me, my heart was racing:
> Perhaps what I was waiting for was love![5]

But a crush did not necessarily require any conjunction of specific circumstances for it could strike at the least likely moment. For the future *Guardian* film
critic Derek Malcolm it came while eating apple crumble in his Eton house
dining-room:

> The apple crumble was delicious – and I can remember another beautiful
> boy, with the most beautiful bum in bum-freezers, going up to ask for a
> second helping . . . I was eating the crumble, just watching him and think-
> ing what bliss to be eating the crumble and going to bed with him at the
> same time . . .[6]

Sometimes it was just a chance meeting in a passageway as boys hurried from
one class to another with their books; a superficially trivial corridor collision or
conversation that was nevertheless sufficient to trigger an infatuation. Old
Etonian Jeffrey Amherst recounted one such encounter:

> It must have been not long after I had first come to Eton that one morning
> I happened to be coming out of the boys' entrance of M'Tutor's when I was
> confronted by a tall slender, athletic figure. He had yellow hair, a thin rather
> finely chiselled mouth. He was coming to study maths at M'Tutor's Pupil
> Room. Elegant with a hint of arrogance, piercing blue eyes that twinkled.
> For no reason that I can think of we both burst out laughing. What we said
> I do not remember. He went his way into the house to find M'Tutor and I
> went on down the passageway to the street. We subsequently saw a lot of
> each other . . .[7]

Sometimes a new boy finding himself isolated and routinely bullied would
attach his affections to the first kind Samaritan who passed his way. Everlasting
gratitude could spring from an incident in which a senior boy casually lent a
helping hand. Usually it was just an instinctive act of human sympathy, but it
could still be an event never to be forgotten by the rescued victim. Through
such incidents the seeds of hero worship were often sown. Ex-orphanage boy
Reg Ferm later wrote about one such moment in his autobiography *Ice Cold
Charity*:

> I've forgotten the initial cause of the trouble but an older boy was hitting me
> with a stick in the wash house. I had only my hands to defend myself with

and wasn't having much success. Mayes, a big lad of thirteen came in. He grabbed the other boy and wrenched the stick from him . . . 'If he touches you again, come and tell me,' said Mayes, and walked away. I wasn't troubled again. Mayes was my hero until he reached the ripe old age of fourteen and left the orphanage a few months later. I was too small for him to bother about but I admired him from afar.[8]

Sometimes even a passing smile from a senior boy was sufficiently unusual to capture the unrelenting gratitude of an emotionally starved junior. 'I shall never forget it,' confessed one such boy in Vachell's *The Hill* (1905), a novel based on life at Harrow. 'You were standing near the chapel. I was poking about alone, trying to find the shop where we buy our straws . . . You smiled at me, Caesar. It warmed me through and through. I suppose that when a fellow is starving he never forgets the first meal after it.'[9]

There was something almost magical about the instant when the monotony of school routine was transformed by sudden and rapturous adoration. The Labour politician Tom Driberg remembered being amazed by the speed of it all. He was gazing idly across the quadrangle when someone caught his notice:

> What a topping boy that chap there looks!
> 'Who is he?' Just then he dropped his books.

The next moment Driberg found himself half-helplessly rifling through the books in a desperate attempt to find out any crumb of information about his new hero.[10]

The thirst for knowledge about a new deity was impossible to satisfy. What was his name? Which was his house? Who were his friends? In what teams did he play? Who was his tutor? Which of the high-street shops did he frequent? Break times were no longer boring. There was important detective work to be done. Michael Davidson, who, like Tom Driberg, was engaged on a time-consuming surveillance operation amid the cloisters of Lancing College, was later amazed by the absurdity of it all: 'I can't think how much time I lost over lurking, waiting, prowling, in the hope of a glimpse of Mason; what an economy it would have been if I could have met him openly and licitly – and, then, how quickly probably the infatuation would have been over!'[11]

Ironically, despite all the effort put into gathering intelligence, the accumulated information was something never put to effective use. Perhaps this reflected the difficulties of arranging a rendezvous. It was easy to watch from afar as one's favourite traversed the quad or strolled down the high street, but to put one's dreams into motion required an almost insane degree of courage in the highly segregated society of boarding school. But there were also some who were more than prepared to run the risks.

THE ENSLAVEMENT PARADOX

Boys were able to convince themselves that they had really crashed on someone only when they accepted both the dangerous challenge of initial communication and all the frustrations of courtship. A refusal from a beloved one was a gauntlet thrown down to one's emotions, to give up was evidence one was a mere opportunist – a sort of tart's punter who could not stomach the rollercoaster of real love.

No better example of persistence can be found than that of William Burroughs, the author of *Naked Lunch*, who from 1929 to 1932 was a pupil at an Englishstyle boarding school at Los Alamos in New Mexico. For a while his hero was friendly towards him, but after a while he refused further overtures. This just made Burroughs all the more abject in his unfruitful petitioning. But his selfabasement was rewarded only by taunts from and whispers between his beloved's friends. Yet the hurtful rebuffs only inspired Burroughs to greater acts of humiliation, a torment which he was able to share only with his diary.[1]

Sometimes a boy would even invite refusal, for at least in that way he could escape the humdrum of cordial chatter and prove the extent of his adulation. One pupil driven to such drastic brinkmanship was the Etonian Cyril Connolly who told his loved one that their friendship should be 'all or nothing', only to receive the perhaps deserved response, 'Very well, I choose nothing.'

> After a day I tried to make up. 'Nothing' was not having the effect I hoped for. Nigel was brutal and called me a dirty scug (boy without a colour). I left him in a hysterical mood and went and broke a chair in Upper Tea Room. Then I rushed to Freddie and Denis for sympathy. I was fond of Nigel and fond of myself, and he had injured both these idols.[2]

Another test of the devoted was whether he received a response other than complete rejection with anything less than grovelling gratitude. For the real Romeo even the slightest nod of recognition was treated as a sure sign that one's god acknowledged and accepted one's penitent devotion. Wilfrid Blunt, brother of spy Anthony Blunt, was always to remember one small gesture of his beloved, Paxton, at Marlborough. Wilfrid had stolen a Pink from the commonroom garden and Paxton, without a moment's premeditation, seized the flower and pressed it into Wilfrid's button-hole. In his autobiography, *Married to a Single Life*, he confessed, 'I have it still. Pressed under glass in a little sealed-box with a perfectly ghastly poem behind it. Yes — it was as little as this; but it was enough to transform a whole year of my life.'[3] It is amazing how boys in love managed to fantasize even over the most manifestly trivial gestures. One Eton pupil, who later returned to become an Eton housemaster, confided in his diary:

> Today I received the greatest pleasure that for many days I have received, indeed a noble birthday gift, an hour of Prothero's society. For the last three weeks have I prayed to God that his heart might have changed and he might love, and my prayer has been answered. For today I met him and walked with him. I told him that it was my birthday, and his lips wished me many happy returns of the day. Surely God will receive that prayer, surely I am blessed in that wish.[4]

Frequently, a boy felt that the only way to come to terms with the intensity of his feelings and the near impossibility of their realization, was to compose a eulogy by which at least someone, perhaps even the desired one himself, would recognize the authenticity of his devotion. The young Rupert Brooke was bolder than most. Drunk on adoration, he declared in a letter to his young 'Hyacinth': 'The Greek gods lived that you might be likened to them: the world was created that you might be made of gold and ivory: the fragrance of your face is myrrh and incense before the pale altar of beauty.'[5] Similarly besotted, one St Paul's boy, later famed for his writing and gigantic stature, used to end his letters to his beloved Bentley, 'I am your grovelling serf, villein and vassal, G.K. Chesterton.' When many years later Chesterton died, Bentley confided to his widow that it had been 'a friendship which meant more to me in my youth than I can say.'[6]

There were, however, some boys who never came to express such passion in words. This was usually because they were the type who felt that the sanctity of worship made such open avowals indecent and unworthy of the pureness of true love. Nevertheless, such quiet believers were often just as deeply besotted, but since they never committed their sentiments to paper, we need to turn to literature for sometimes it is possible to find, in an author's observations, a confession in the guise of fiction. Here, for example, is E.F. Benson's amazingly convincing depiction of a young boy's adulation of a senior:

> It was quite sufficient then that Maddox, the handsomest fellow in the world, the best bat probably that Manchester had ever produced and

altogether the most glorious of created beings should have noticed him at all; indeed that was more than sufficient; it was sufficient that Maddox should exist.[7]

There were also other reasons why some boys felt that words alone were not enough, for how could one genuinely proclaim one's servility without first humbling oneself in time-consuming hard labour for one's beloved. Sometimes it could even work the other way round with hard labour inducing a hero worship for one's work-master. So, as perverse as it may seem, a fag could be overtaken by a desire to outdo even the humiliating and laborious tasks already allotted to him, simply to please a prefect. One Harrow boy later confessed to having had such an obsession:

> I just wanted someone there so I could lie in their arms and be comforted. But who? Bennett. Why not Bennett? I'd been doing Bennett's private fagging, but how could I ask him that? I loved Bennett. He was so strong and handsome and had a deep, deep voice. I used to polish his shoes until they almost wore away. I bought the finest polish I could find to buff up the leather . . .[8]

But what was it all for? Such love was invariably unrequited. So why did boys expose themselves to such pains and ridicule for so little reward? Perhaps it was a way of self-assertion in a spartan, uncaring institution. Perhaps it was the love of striving for the unattainable, a reflection of the public school stress on heroics. But whatever the motivation may have been there can be no questioning the sentimentality and impressionability of these supposedly toughened boarding school boys.

THE INCONGRUITY PARADOX

Throughout the late nineteenth and for most of the twentieth century there was no freedom to mix socially at boarding school. A boy's friendships were confined to his year group and his house. They were often further limited to those who also shared his dormitory and class. But the crush recognized such boundaries only by its propensity to violate them. The artificiality by which boys were kept apart created a tempestuous tension that was only ever released in lightning-like surges of hero worship.

Of all the artificial structures of segregation, perhaps the most blatant was a boy's house, to which most of his after school hours life was confined. Often a boy was forbidden, at least in his junior years, from even talking to boys of similar age if they belonged to another house and as for actually entering through the door of another house, such an act was unthinkable. So, given that a larger boarding school often contained a dozen or more such houses, it was almost inevitable that the desirable unknown with whom a boy collided in the passageway was likely to be forbidden fruit. If so, there was little if any possibility of casually striking up a conversation, so other tactics had to be employed. One of the most popular methods of establishing first contact was the letter or note that could either be deposited in the desired one's desk or given to someone who had legitimate access to the hero's house or dormitory.

Of course there was always the awful risk that the messenger might mislay a love note or that some prying master might ask to see what a boy was so protectively carrying. To minimize such risks notes were normally written in code. Sometimes a particularly cautious boy would send a coded anonymous note, hoping against hope that his identity might remain hidden or be discovered, depending on the recklessness of his passions.

The television presenter Ludovic Kennedy, when a schoolboy, sent several such notes. One read 'Hymn 147, verse 2, last line' and if his red-haired hero had looked it up he would have found the words, 'The secret of my love'. Kennedy, however, was far from certain that he wanted to be found out. 'I think,' he confessed, 'I would have died of embarrassment had Dunston ever got to know who had sent them . . .'[1]

It could certainly prove embarrassing if one's note was intercepted. Usually however, messages didn't contain quite sufficient information to conclusively incriminate the sender (see for example Quentin Crisp's contribution in part two). Occasionally however, valour won over discretion and boys sent more daring and explicit notes such as, 'May I hold your hand?'[2]; sometimes even arranging for such messages to be passed from boy to boy across a dining-room or classroom. The note was normally returned with an equally brief message, usually 'no', written on the reverse side.

Perhaps the greatest risk was taken by those eminent seniors, particularly prefects, who attempted to give reality to their desires by dispatching a note to a winsome boy several years their junior. In the hierarchical society of boarding school it was almost impossible to justify such unorthodox behaviour. The sender might try to phrase the letter carefully so as to avoid any impression of indecent intent, but unfortunately these same protestations often served only to emphasize his own feelings of guilt. One Eton boy, Alfred Lyttelton, son of Lord Lyttelton, a senior of high social standing and a cricket hero, had a particularly uphill struggle in justifying his request for a portrait photograph sent to a boy four years his junior:

Perhaps it may have seemed odd to you that I, who have had so very slight a claim to be considered as one of your acquaintance, should have asked so coolly for your likeness, and I should like to give you an explanation . . .

I have heard a good deal about you at one time and another from Oscar Browning . . . What he told me and what I have been told by other people could scarcely fail to awaken in me a considerable interest in a boy of your position . . . (But) I well know the sort of view which the world takes of any big fellow hemmed in by the social chains of being what is called a swell, taking any notice of one younger . . .

[Such] considerations induced me against my will, but out of regard for you and the harm it might do to others if I was incautious, to keep aloof and behave as you may have thought rather oddly in this matter. I could not help, then, making an effort to carry away with me something to remind me of one who has occupied a considerable share of my thoughts giving me cause now and then, but seldom, for anxiety and always for feeling much interest.[3]

In the end Lyttelton may have felt the correctness of his interest vindicated for the young boy later became Viceroy of India, but incriminating evidence that this self-acclaimed letter of pure intent was in fact a declaration of desire came in the postscript. 'It is needless to say' – although nevertheless he felt driven to say it – 'I should prefer this being kept private.'[4]

Many boys never got beyond the stage of the furtive glance. Such was the stigma attached to a student consorting with another of dissimilar age that a quick look was as far as a more timid boy would dare to venture. A lad of less nervous disposition might attempt to smile as meaningfully as possible, but he often discovered that a puzzled look or angry scowl was his only reward. An unknowing observer might consider such a result a somewhat pathetic frui-tion of a boy's desires, but even in those instances when the lover's devotion passed completely unacknowledged and unnoticed, yet he could still feel that he had been rewarded a thousand times just by having been able to be near his heart-throb. Here is one such account:

My delight in this boy's loveliness was so intense that when I stole timorous, nervous, furtive, and yet ardently staryish glances at him, as having undressed at my side he stood for a moment in his bathing-drawers medi-tating his plunge into those blue-green waters, I was totally lost to the world. The boy himself was completely oblivious of me. I never in my life spoke to him, though I must have undressed by his side a hundred times. But it was so delicious a paradise to me merely to snatch quick glances at his lively form that I altogether forgot that such an unpleasant phenomenon as 'ducking' existed anywhere on the earth.[5]

Even a boy's dreams about his hero often appear somewhat pitiable in their limitations. But it is perhaps this very modesty of love's ambition which makes these stories of boarding school romance so touching. The passions were so hesitant and humble in their objectives and yet so potent that it was almost impossible for the uninvolved to understand them. Even some of the boys found, or at least pretended to find, the confessions of their friends ridiculous. 'I remember,' wrote television presenter Arthur Marshall, 'one of the impressionable boys above mentioned, when firmly crossquestioned as to his ideal last day, blushing painfully and annoucing that he would "like to go for a walk with Pendleton." Loud and scornful shouts of "Boo!", though some shouted more loudly and scornfully than others . . .'[6]

But there were some boys who were not at all timid, and for whom the obstacles of age and house status were simply rivers that had to be crossed. In fact sometimes these very difficulties could be put to good use, as by overcoming them the Romeo could prove his devotion. It was in such a spirit that the young Anthony Hopkins crept up the stairs to another boy's dormitory, and lay down doglike beside his hero's bed.[7] How Hopkins would have explained his presence had he been caught it is impossible to know. It is unlikely that any master would have believed his protestations of innocence. Not surprisingly most boys tried to circumvent such obvious dangers.

The largest loophole in the regulations on friendship were the exiats and holidays. Providing a boy won the permission of his parents, he could invite home whoever he desired. It was a golden opportunity for him to strike up an acquaintance with a passion with whom he was unfamiliar, for he could disguise his plot as an act of gentlemanly charity to some fellow who might otherwise have been abandoned alone at school for the weekend. 'Could you, I mean, will you come out with my parents tomorrow?' and then hopefully that blissful reply, 'Thanks awfully – Are you sure that's all right?'[8] The other advantage was that any initial difficulty in striking up a conversation could be more than made up for by a myriad of exciting distractions on offer once outside the bounds of school. A lad of wealthy parents could also hope to impress his hero, especially if Momma and Papa arrived in style, driving across the playground in a Jaguar or RollsRoyce. But there were risks to such machinations. What if father referred to mother as 'Mummy' or if mother, or worse still father, insisted on giving one a sloppy kiss and hug? The writer Robin Maugham recalled one such moment:

When we settle down to an enormous lunch in the restaurant, I notice that he is impressed by the menu. Suddenly my mother says: 'By the way, Robin, I forgot to tell you – Nanny sent you her love.' There is an awful silence. She has uttered the unspeakable. Haines will never realize that my parents have kept on Rose to do sewing and mend clothes. He knows I'm the youngest of the family. The rumour will go round the school that Maugham still has a nurse . . . That night as I enter the dormitory, they all chant in chorus: 'Maugham's got a Nanny . . . Maugham's got a Nanny'. . .[9]

Another way of meeting, for boys of disparate age, was to arrange a tryst outside the school bounds at some country landmark or in one of the high street shops. The young Lord Drogheda, the future Managing Director of *The Financial Times*, conspired to meet another Eton boy and future governor of Malta, Bob Laycock, in the town's gramophone shop,[10] and the writer Michael Davidson once arranged a rendezvous with his hero at the Ring, a pleasing roundel of trees on the Downs.[11]

At other times a god and his devotee would be brought together unexpectedly, perhaps during a school organized expedition, or as neighbouring patients in the sickroom during a flu epidemic, or just as the result of some accidental meeting outside the school bounds. The diarist A.C. Benson described one such incident:

I adored him at a distance when I was at Eton. I was fifteen and he I suppose eighteen. His room was opposite mine and I admired the artistic quality of all he had. Then his pale abstracted face, aquiline nose, mobile and scornful underlip were beautiful . . . But I never spoke to him till the blissful day when I had gone to Henley, and tired of heat and noise, made my way to the station to return. He got into the same carriage and told me ghost stories. I hoped it would lead to acquaintance later but it did not.[12]

It was perhaps because of all the petty but real obstacles to association that the realization of a boy's dreams depended so much on just one tiny opportunity and if he failed to strike then, all too often further opportunities proved elusive. So while the impatient often met with rejection or suffered exposure, embarrassment and sometimes even expulsion, for the timid the moment would arrive all too soon when either they or their beloved left the school, and with that vanished all chance of reciprocated love. It was this dilemma which made hero worship a difficult and delicate balancing act, in which only the unlikely combination of calm confidence, charm and lucky coincidence could

construct a bond of comradeship across the chasm of public school conven-
tion and tradition.

THE RELUCTANT HERO PARADOX

It may seem a mathematical absurdity which defies the laws of proportional-
ity, but almost without exception each boarding school, whether it was large
or small, produced every year exactly one boy of exceptional magnetism who
became a legend. This hero was not, like many others, merely the jealously-
guarded secret desire of one or two boys but rather a cult figure whom almost
all boys adored. He was invariably of exceptional good-looks and an outstanding sportsman. Sometimes he was also academically brilliant. More often
he was academically average, but of greater import was his charm, his
charisma and his apparent indifference to success; a convincing combination
of character traits that could win over even the most cynical of minds.

Old Marlburian E.F. Benson captured the essence of such hero worship in
his fictional *David Blaize*:

> 'Oh, go on, tell me about Maddox,' he said, 'I dare say you'll see him. Sure
> to, in fact. He's not very tall, but he's damned good-looking. He's far the
> finest bat in the eleven, and the funny thing is he says cricket's rather a waste
> of time, and hardly ever goes up to a net. He's editor of the school paper and
> played racquets for us at Queen's last year. But what he likes best of all is
> reading.'[1]

The school hero had to be a great all-rounder and could never be seen to try
too hard. He had to be the casual collector of trophies, someone who played
any sport with a refrained but skilful grace:

> His running between the wickets seemed lackadaisical, the state of the game
> seemed no concern of his. He did not strike the ball; he did nothing with
> violence or haste. Yet somehow the ball that was not hit was picked up by
> his bat and played beyond the distant boundary.[2]

At Rugby one might glimpse

> his slim figure stretching easily for a pass, his body angled to the ground so
> that balance seemed well-nigh impossible, treading the earth as if it were
> precious and moving forward easily, slowly, so it seemed, yet miraculously
> he outstripped his bustling opponents.[3]

Most boys were glad just to have the privilege of observing such a legendary figure from a distance. Invariably his presence on a school team drew a crowd of onlookers more interested in the hero's performance than the outcome of the match. But despite being the focus of such enthusiastic attention the king of heroes always retained that essential composure that distinguished him from lesser gods. The diarist A.C. Benson recalled one such legend:

> [He was] the unquestioned, undisputed king of the place, last of a long line of well-known brothers, and the most famous of all. One saw him about the streets and playing fields, in glimpses and vignettes, always talking and laughing, or splashed and stained with mud in the football field, or striding to the wicket in his blue cap and sash; always the easy centre of every scene, perfectly natural, unembarrassed, serene. I remember his great shouts and his huge laughter on the football field; he never blamed his team but always encouraged and applauded every bit of creditable play; the only boy who might do exactly as he liked and about whom, in every relation of life, there was never a word said except in praise.[4]

While it might sometimes be dangerous for a boy to confess a crush on some relatively obscure senior, or worse still junior, the hero worship of a school legend was something which was always shared. It was the one instance when school boy adulation invariably took on a public, almost ritualistic, form, which one writer, John Lehmann, described as akin to a communal outbreak of homoeroticism:

> Sometimes, at a school like Eton, a boy appears of such exceptional beauty and sexual fascination that he becomes a legend . . . It happened while I was there. The boy's name in this case was Sandy Rogers . . . Everyone was talking about him, and most were lusting after him . . . Besides his unearthly beauty, he also had a great gift as a footballer, and when he was on the field with his house eleven, older boys from other houses would often gather round just to watch his exquisite flying figure, groaning with longing as he tossed the tarnished gold of his hair back from his forehead, or charged into the scrum with arms flying . . . He appeared to have the unconscious power to uncover a hidden vein of pederasty in the breasts of the most normal seeming male[5]

Sporting success, good looks and calm composure were the essential ingredients of legend, although much could also depend on pedigree and other family attributes. At Charterhouse one deity was all the more acclaimed for his ability to casually drop famous names into the accounts of his exiats and not least for the famed beauty of his sister Barbara, who on her visits never failed to satisfy the onlooking boys by routinely displaying 'a generous quantity of pink silk thigh as she alighted from a low-slung Lancia.'[6]

But in the end good looks and charisma counted for infinitely more than one's ancestry and connections. One of the earliest-known public school legends, Beau Brummell, who rocketed to glory at Eton in the 1790s, possessed little in his blood to recommend him. His father had managed to scrape together the money for Brummell after years of hard work as a steward on a country estate. But Brummell more than made up for his lack of nobility by his good looks, sporting prowess and abundance of charm. As the top boatman and cricketer at Eton, he soon captured the attention of the Prince of Wales, the future George IV, across the river at Windsor, who sent for the schoolboy and was so pleased by his fastidious neatness and easy-going manner that he gave him a commission in the 10th Hussars. Unfortunately however, soon after joining, he was thrown from his horse at a grand parade at Brighton and broke his celebrated classical Roman nose.[7]

It is tempting to consider whether it might have been possible for a boy not quite matching Brummell's formidable array of abilities to have achieved similar acclaim. The problem however arises of separating fact from fiction in these stories of schoolboy legends. It was, after all, necessary for each school year to invent its hero, so it is probable that in many cases a myth-ology based on hero worship wrapped itself around whichever boy was least unqualified. However, such sober cynicism can never detract from the indisputable magnetism such boys exercised, captivating admirers with the same potency as a powerful night-light mesmerizing the moths that dance around it.

GÖTTERDÄMMERUNG

Perhaps the greatest paradox of the schoolboy crush was the ease with which 'undying' devotion died. An infatuation might last a lifetime in the right cir-cumstances. It could bring together boys who then recognized in each other similar interests, so that a mutual friendship superceded the inequality of hero worship. However, fate was not normally so kind. Frequently subservient adulation was met with contempt and when more successful it was, ironically, often killed off altogether when the suitor discovered that he did not desire the easy conquest he had won.

The daring, who were quick to make contact with their beloved ones and win their affections, were often victims of their own success. E.F. Benson used to change his heroes at Marlborough virtually every month[1] and Cyril Connolly's affairs were almost as short-lived. He used to compete with Eric Blair for the attention of this or that demi-god. He confessed that 'victory' was always a depressing experience:

> To say I was in love again will vex the reader beyond endurance, but he must remember that being in love had a peculiar meaning for me. I had never even been kissed and love was an ideal based on the exhibitionism of the only-child. It meant a desire to lay my personality at someone's feet as a puppy deposits a slobbery ball; it meant a non-stop daydream, a planning of surprises, an exchange of confidences, a giving of presents, an agony of expectation, a delirium of impatience ending with the premonition of boredom more drastic than the loneliness which it set out to cure.[2]

Suitors often never defined their objectives. This meant that, ironically, the infatuated boy could be far more priggish than his hero and this often had disastrous consequences. The diplomat Paul Wright, when at Westminster in the late 1920s, was 'something of a puritan', and he recalled:

> It was thus an appalling shock when, after some school play in which my hero and I had both acted, and flushed with the half-pint of beer allowed on such occasions to the senior boys, this God-like creature who occupied the centre of my small world attempted to give physical expression to our relationship . . . I was mortified, being convinced that it was somehow my fault that this terrible thing had happened. I wept for a moment in his arms, gasping out my shame and sorrow, and then fled, my pounding feet carrying me full tilt into adolescence.[3]

In those instances when a successful physical advance was made by the suitor, sex often diminished the passion of infatuation, especially if repeated. The Labour politician Woodrow Wyatt observed that after several such experiments with his god, 'the satisfying of my curiosity . . . damped down my fires'.[4] Such a response finds an echo in the response of Jean Cocteau to a fellow pupil at a French boarding school:

> 'Invite him out one weekend and take him behind the bushes. The moment you flatter him he does whatever you want.' Cocteau, in the grips of idealized puppy love, was not convinced. 'I didn't want to play with him for five minutes,' he wrote, 'I wanted to live with him forever.'[5]

In the end Cocteau did not score with his beloved Dargelos but continued to worship him from afar, and after leaving the school the image of the dark haired virile boy continued to haunt him. Cocteau appears to have forseen the dangers of consumating desire, a temptation that wrecked many another schoolboy crush. He knew already what others had learned through sad experience, that in the pursuit of the unattainable, its attainment often came as an unpleasant shock. The possibility of continued reverence was often destroyed by the familiarity of lust, and one's god perished in a sort of Wagnerian *Götterdämmerung*.

FROM COLD SHOWERS TO COEDUCATION:

HOMOSEXUALITY AND HOMOPHOBIA AT BOARDING SCHOOLS
1965–1995

To all outward appearances little of the old boarding school regime remains. Out have gone cold showers, corporal punishment, fagging and the perception of homosexuality as a highly contagious condition. In has come coeducation, carpets, central heating and (much to the chagrin of many parents) the occasional tacit acknowledgement of gay liberation.

Some schools have even invited lesbian and gay speakers and at Eton, often unfairly portrayed as a bastion of traditional public school education, the gay rights advocate Peter Tatchell was recently asked to address the school's Shelley Society. It certainly caused quite a stir. 'Some boys,' he recalled

> seemed to revel in the rebellious outlaw kudos that the assumption of homosexuality might give them. They enjoyed suggesting a sexual ambiguity. Several, including two who were almost certainly straight, bought 'Outrage' and 'Queer as Fuck' T-shirts, which they wore the next day with evident delight – perhaps partly as a gesture of solidarity and partly for the sheer joy of shocking their friends.

> I found it surprising that while no one ever came out as gay in the meetings I addressed, some boys were quite happy to later identify themselves by wearing a queer T-shirt in public. More amazingly, two who were straight did likewise, evidently unconcerned that others might think them gay.[1]

So is homophobia at public schools ebbing? Do boarding school boys today feel more free to express their sexuality than was the case fifty years ago? Unfortunately many of the changes in boarding school life have been more superficial than real. Some of the most blatant and intrusive measures of controlling same-sex sexuality have been dropped. No boy now faces the indignity of wearing pocketless trousers or having his pyjama bottoms inspected for marks by zealous matrons (though neither of these extreme measures were ever common in boarding schools) and boys are far less frequently interrogated by house tutors about their friendships and sexual preferences (a method of control which boys have always bitterly resented); but, that said, the most effective methods of policing sexuality remain firmly in place.

DEMARCATION

There is no longer any need for headmasters or housemasters to lecture juniors on the dangers of forming friendships with older boys (although occasionally they still do). Age segregation is now inevitably engendered by the very architecture and ethos of boarding schools. Age-segregated dormitories and classrooms are not seen as Victorian inventions, but rather as part of the natural order of things. Neither boys nor parents would question what purpose they served for few are aware that a different system of boarding school education ever existed.

The result is that many boys see it as 'natural' that they restrict their friendships to boys of their own age. Of course there is still a temptation to solicit friends of a different age but this is checked by the fear of such a relationship being labelled 'queer'.

Boys have become far more conscious of the sexual labels used by the outside world and this has led to a new form of demarcation far more effective and permanent than any strategy concocted by Victorian headmasters. Individual boys are now frequently derided as 'poofter' or 'queer' by their peers. This is rarely because the boy has 'come out' but is normally the result of either a boy's behaviour being stereotyped as gay or of some chance discovery such as a love letter, diary confession or overheard conversation. The resulting isolation and name-calling can prove unbearable and several young people have told me of cases of suicide when their friends felt overwhelmed by what was often an ineffacable stigma. It is the tragic flip side of the otherwise positive inroads into the public consciousness made by the lesbian and gay movement in the last twenty years.

Homosexuality is no longer seen simply as a result of moral weakness, a temptation waiting to entrap the unwary, but rather it is seen as a congenital condition. Most people now believe, rightly or wrongly, that everyone is born with either a fixed or at least a predisposition to a particular sexual orientation

– whether heterosexual or homosexual. One unfortunate consequence is that early in a boy's school career his sexuality is often defined for him by his colleagues who, given the prejudice of many of their parents, understandably wield the labels 'straight' and 'queer' with an arbitrary brutality.

The other effect of such a shift in perceptions has been effectively to stigmatize homosexual behaviour as being incompatible with a 'healthy', 'normal' heterosexuality. Homosexual experimentation is no longer seen by boys as a natural if subversive outlet for their sexual desires. Instead, it is seen as evidence of being intrinsically 'different' and meets with attitudes varying from a cautious tolerance ('I don't mind if you're gay but I'm straight') to outright condemnation ('Fuck off, you queer bastard!').

Even in the more progressive schools the primary desire of the school authorities is often to diffuse the resulting tension rather than help the victim. I asked one housemaster at a Quaker school how he thought such bullying should be tackled. He replied that it would be 'best dealt with by talking to both parties and attempting to get both bully and victim to modify their behaviour so that the former desists from bullying and the latter gives less cause in future for potential bullies to find him attractive as a potential victim.'[2] He said nothing about comforting or reassuring the victim and his response implied that he felt that such pupils were as much to blame as the bullies.

DEMONASTICIZATION

In the first half of the twentieth century boys were seldom allowed to leave the immediate vicinity of the school and only rarely did boarding schools permit any socializing with girls from neighbouring schools. In the opinion of many critics this created a hothouse atmosphere which encouraged homosexuality and frustrated all attempts to improve 'the tone' in schools. So gradually headmasters began to allow more weekend exiats and introduce supervised dances in the hope that increased contact with girls would heterosexualize the pupil culture. In the opinion of two headmasters I contacted, this demonasticization of schools transformed boarding life. This is what they said:

My impression is that homosexuality in independent boarding schools was already declining before coeducation. By that I mean there were fewer 'cases', there was less discussion and anxiety among adults responsible for the pupils and so on. My guess is that the reason for the decline was the greater openness of the boarding schools; pupils were no longer shut away from the outside world for weeks on end. This – more than co-education –

removed the hothouse atmosphere that had created the circumstances in which homosexual fantasies and activity had flourished.

John Rae (headmaster of Taunton 1966–1970 and of Westminster 1970–86)

In the past, many schools were virtually all boarding and there was very little opportunity for pupils to be away at weekends . . .

Today, most boarding schools have a considerable number of day pupils and many, like ourselves, allow pupils to go home at weekends as little or as often as they wish. As a result, the atmosphere in school is quite different and, I believe, has led to a decline in homosexual practice.

Headmaster of a leading southern independent school

DIVERSIONS

Restrictions on a boy's free time through participation in arduous sports were never an effective means of controlling homosexual passions and (as was argued in the first chapter) seem to have encouraged a certain muscular hero worship which bordered on the homoerotic. School timetabling reforms, allowing more latitude and choice, are not symptomatic of a new indifference to sex between boys. No one now believes that games deter homosexuality, which has always thrived on the many opportunities generated during and immediately after compulsory games when teams of high-spirited boys crowd into the changing rooms. In fact even those who claim never to have been involved in physical activity often admit they were goggle-eyed spectators. One boy later recalled that he was 'dumbstruck by the Parthenon frieze of heroic male flesh parading to the showers after practice'.[3]

In the past school authorities were often unable to segregate boys of different ages in the confined space of the changing rooms and there were sometimes occasions when older boys exploited the circumstances to seduce or rape juniors. One former pupil explained to sociologist Royston Lambert that 'It was a regular thing to be gang-raped in the showers or changing rooms during the session (swimming lesson) or at the end of it.'[4]

Sports never succeeded in depriving boys of opportunities for sexual mischief and the decline in the emphasis on sports is not because schools are no longer worried about homosexuality. Indeed, one factor working in favour of such changes has been the recognition that reform would undermine one of the essential underpinnings of schoolboy homoeroticism and romance in the old regime – the athletocracy.

COLD SHOWERS OR COEDUCATION?

Similar conclusions can be drawn from the demise of the masochistic machismo of the cold baths variety. Such tortures have long been abandoned, not so much because their use implied that the school authorities were sadistic (though such inferences were doubtless embarrassing and themselves carried homoerotic overtones), but because no one continued to believe that the *douche froide* could liberate boys from homosexual desires. That schoolmasters once thought so now seems absurd.

Boarding schools have looked instead to a more obvious, if at first glance unplanned, solution – coeducation. More and more public schools have chosen this option in the last thirty years, leaving a minority still swimming against the tide (see tables A and B in the appendix), and even here social con, tacts with girls' schools have become far more common. At the same time the proportion of women working full, time on the staff of HMC schools[5] has risen from nine per cent in 1984 to twenty, one per cent by 1993 (see table C in the appendix).

As early as the late, nineteenth century some of the public schools had con, sidered introducing coeducation as an antidote to the 'problem' of homo, sexuality, with even the headmaster of Harrow acknowledging in guarded language that the lack of contact with girls encouraged homosexuality and confessing that 'the remedy, then, for these evils will be in restoring the life of boys, as far as possible, to its natural conditions.'[6] But then such schools lacked any palatable explanation or justification for such a transition. Any public admission that homosexuality was rampant in their schools would have been suicidal, and they could not find alternative excuses. Coeducation was cer, tainly not a vote winner with fee, paying parents who did not want their brawny rugby, playing sons effeminized by girls. Neither did they desire their daughters distracted from the goals of marriage and motherhood by boyish ambitions.

It took the women's movement, two world wars, decades of rapid eco, nomic change and the emergence of feminism as a potent political force to change such views. Even then it was only gradually that the presence of girls came to be seen as less of a threat and more as a 'civilizing influence' (not a label that can have pleased the feminists), and it was equally tenta, tively that parents crept towards the notion that their daughters might have an equal right to the opportunities of economic independence. But from the late 1960s several boys' schools (starting with Marlborough in 1968) began to claim that they had been won over by the logic of gender egalitarianism, though some members of staff continued to hint that they were rather more preoccupied with the 'unhealthy atmosphere' of their schools. When pressed to give an opinion one teacher commented, 'I think that one disadvantage of this type of school is that they are always in the presence of males. And I think that's . . . I'm not really sure that's healthy . . . It's not always good . . .'[7]

But it is the more vociferous voice of many parents and boys that mixed education is more 'natural' which is the more revealing, hinting that fear of homosexuality has played a considerable but unquantifiable role. One thir-teen-year-old boy at a state boarding school answered a question on coeduca-tion put by sociologist Royston Lambert with the simple but thought-provoking answer: 'Boys and girls together: it's natural, it's life, isn't it?'[8] Even headmasters sometimes resorted to similar rhetoric. John Buchanan, who brought coeducation to Oakham, explained:

A monosex school, because it is operating counter to life, is basically an unnatural institution . . . The simple lesson which a monosex school learns on becoming coeducational is the rediscovery of a relaxed normality: one is no longer struggling to operate an inherently abnormal community.[9]

It seems much easier to believe that headmasters were concerned more with parents' perceptions of their boys' social and sexual development than with a real determination to improve the educational opportunities for girls. John Rae, elected chairman of the Headmaster's Conference in 1977, remembers 'The headmistresses of girls' independent schools were convinced that the headmasters' motives had little to do with educational philosophy.'[10]

Some sceptics attribute the transition to the overwhelming attraction of extra fees, but this does not explain why Marlborough, which in the 1960s under John Dancy was one of the most successful schools, should have been the first to have made the leap nor why the admission of girls at Marlborough and other schools was limited initially to the sixth form. Dancy was able to claim, 'Marlborough remains a boys' school,' though he added, 'I am con-vinced it's a much better boys' school for having some girls in it.'[11]

It was obvious to anyone who looked beyond the claims of school prospec-tuses that girls were being introduced because the school authorities felt they would benefit the boys. Indeed it would seem that while the newly coeduca-tional public schools claimed to be championing equality of opportunity between the sexes, their real concerns were with how to use girls to hetero-sexualize the boys.

DETERRENCE

That the new public school liberality is more rhetoric than substance can be seen from the fact that the maximum penalty for homosexual behaviour remains unchanged. Expulsion. Admittedly in the more liberal schools expulsion is not always automatic. The headmaster of one London inde-pendent school assured me, 'I certainly do not believe in instant expulsion, rather in getting to the root cause of any problem.'[12] But the alternative solu-tions are often almost as painful to those caught. One fifteen-year-old boy explained: 'If they find out, they have your parents up and interview you in front of them. I would rather die than face that.'[13]

The stigma on homosexuality still runs deep and when boys are expelled for homosexual activity their parents rarely dare challenge the decision (for fear of attracting public attention) even though such disputes are not uncommon in cases of pupils sacked for heterosexual activity.[14]

DETECTION

Today, there is not the need for vigilance that there was thirty years ago. Not only do school authorities claim to be more liberal but (conveniently) boys have become more willing to police their peers' sexuality. Today, it is the boys themselves who have come to question close friendships between those of different ages, whereas thirty years ago such romantic affairs would often have received popular approval. So some of the burden of detective work has passed from the school staff to the pupils themselves and inevitably boys are always more aware of their friends' interests and activities than distant house tutors could ever have been.

DENUNCIATION

Superficially many of the teachers at boarding schools now exude a more liberal attitude to homosexuality, though very few would dare come out as gay. Indeed some schools now make it blatantly obvious in their promotional liter-ature that only married family men or (very occasionally) women are taken on as house tutors.

A bachelor status, which was once seen as an essential prerequisite for a housemastership, is now looked on with suspicion. A typical example of this sea change is Haileybury, founded in 1862. In the whole of its first fifty years only three housemasters had ever been married, but by 1967, the headmaster, William Stewart (1963–75) was able to host a dinner party to celebrate the fact that, for the first time in its history, Haileybury had not even one bachelor housemaster.[15]

When it comes to acting *in loco parentis* the only acceptable lifestyle is an unequivocal heterosexuality. This rule applies particularly to house tutors, but in some schools extends to other members of staff. One teacher explained:

> I was appointed to the preparatory department of a prestigious independent grammar school. I was a conscientious and dedicated teacher and sub-limated my emerging sexuality in running, listening to music and cinema ... In 1981, unable to 'come out' openly in [the local town] ... I came over to London and established a friendship which, at the end of that year, encouraged me to try to 'come out' as a teacher in school . . . [However] having spoken to the school chaplain and explained the nature of my new relationship, I was summarily dismissed by the headmaster the following day.[16]

I know of only one boarding school, Mott, a Quaker boarding school in the United States, where a member of staff has come out as gay without adverse consequences. Amazingly she was eventually successful in persuading the headmaster to allow her lesbian partner to live with her on the campus. The head defended his stance, arguing that the school had an obligation

> to help people struggle with the pain in their lives and do it in a way that . . . produces wholeness rather than more brokeness. Anybody in this society who's gay has got a little more struggle than someone who's not, and anyone who has the courage to struggle publicly needs to be supported by the people who care about them. So then that's what the school is all about.[17]

Such liberalism does not however necessarily herald positive changes in atti-tude throughout the boarding school system. Quaker boarding schools are organized according to Quaker tradition, which stresses both the importance of individual conscience, whereas other boarding schools, particularly those of a more traditional character, still focus on an external and usually somewhat conservative code of moral behaviour.

Openness about sexual orientation would certainly not be encouraged in most English boarding schools. But while such schools do not wish to be accused of championing gay rights, neither do they wish to be depicted as actively homophobic and while discretion may be forced on the most liberal

exponents of gay rights among the staff, the same demand for peaceful consensus ensures that the bigoted exponents of Victorian values are also discouraged
from being too outspoken. The result is often an unhappy consensus, where
staff prejudice is usually kept private or at least polite, and heterosexism is
masked by a language which appears and indeed often is honest and heartfelt.
Typical of such well-intentioned heterosexism is a letter I received from J.H.
Arkell, headmaster of Gresham's since 1991:

> If I were to come across it [a boy being bullied because of his sexuality] I
> would treat it very seriously and do my utmost to encourage sensitivity and
> care of the person who had been bullied. I would do my utmost to help
> such a person overcome his homosexual tendencies . . . In certain circum-
> stances that is not going to be possible, but I believe at present in society
> there is too easy an acceptance of people who are gay, in the sense that the
> undesirability of that state is not underlined. It is so extremely sad if the
> natural and normal joys and happiness of life, discovered through children
> and grandchildren etc are denied a boy or girl. I therefore think that every-
> thing should be done that can be done to help those people who are perhaps
> wavering between the two worlds to manage to exist happily in the 'normal'
> one. Having said that I believe sympathy for those who cannot exist in that
> world must be manifested, and encourage all those in my school to have the
> same.[18]

The reluctance of schools to openly embrace gay liberation has had a negative
influence on the boys themselves who, with a natural tendency to controversy
and polarity, have often made those rightly or wrongly identified as gay the
unfortunate victims of classroom prejudice. Not surprisingly gay youths at
boarding schools rarely make themselves visible. Gay activist Peter Tatchell
recalls of his recent talk at Eton:

> It was notable that even in the supportive atmosphere of the progressive
> Shelley Society meeting, none of the half a dozen fairly obviously gay pupils
> felt able to be open about their homosexuality. Afterwards, at a small private
> gathering over drinks in the master's lodge, one or two boys hinted at being
> gay, but did not dare be explicit about it. That speaks volumes about public
> school hypocrisy concerning homosexuality. Everyone knows that queer
> sex is quite commonplace, but no one is supposed to talk about it.
> Homosexuality exists in a context where it is invisible and unspoken. The
> public school code of silence means that gayness is still the love that dare not
> speak it's name.[19]

Boys think twice about standing up for a gay friend in case they too be labelled gay. The only exception of course is when the defence of a friend can be based on outright denial. 'Gay' and 'queer' are seen as labels to steer clear from. Boys have to hide any homosexual desires from both staff and friends. Ironically therefore same-sex desires have become far more effectively policed in the modern boarding school than they ever were even in the most rigorous of Victorian educational institutions.

PART II

TALES OUT OF SCHOOL:
OLD BOYS REMINISCE ABOUT HOMOSEXUALITY
AT BOARDING SCHOOL

Compiling the recollections for the second part of this book was a labour of love. For months I placed adverts in various gay papers asking for former school boarders to contact me. My telephone was constantly ringing and I spent many a happy afternoon and evening travelling to meet other gay men to chat about their memories of schooldays. It was particularly gratifying for me as a gay Old Boy to interview men who shared the same love–hate recollections of school. Like me, they could remember all the irksome and petty regulations which made the typical day so frustratingly uneventful but also the occasional untypical day in which a new sexual encounter or romance was savoured. At such moments it was the furtive planning of the rendezvous and the dangers of discovery which amplified the tension and excitement of the encounter. This is the spirit which pervades some of these accounts.

I was also eager to obtain recollections from another spectrum of the population, many of whom would be primarily or exclusively heterosexual. So I wrote to five thousand *Who's Who* and *Debrett's* names listed as ex public school boys. In the most respectful and deferential language I could come up with, I asked them for their recollections of homosexuality and intimate friendships at school and explained that I was writing a book on the subject and that I hoped to include a range of comments, by letter and interview, from Old Boys.

But whereas gay men were generally very willing to talk frankly and openly about sex at their old school, many of those listed in *Who's Who* and *Debrett's* were annoyed at my presumption that there might be anything, whether serious or amusing, to contribute and several returned my original letter with marginal notes such as, 'Bugger off!' and, 'You prurient shit. At my school you would have been done!' Fortunately, others were a little more forthcoming.

Even among the several hundred who sent in contributions, both opinions and recollections were divided. Some seemed anxious about their school's reputation and insisted that homosexuality simply did not exist while a few

THE CONTRIBUTORS' SCHOOLS

FETTES

SEDBERGH

STONYHURST

LINCOLN CATHEDRAL
SCHOOL

REPTON

SHREWSBURY
WREKIN   GRESHAM'S
                    UPPINGHAM

                              OUNDLE
              RUGBY

        CHELTENHAM
                      STOWE
                      •ALDENHAM
              ST EDWARD'S
CLIFTON   HARROW HAILEYBURY
              RADLEY   ETON

MARLBOROUGH   BRADFIELD
DOWNSIDE   WELLINGTON
                      CHARTERHOUSE
SHERBORNE   WINCHESTER
                      CHRIST'S HOSPITAL   •KING'S,
                                           CANTERBURY
BRYANSTON   CHURCHER'S

              LANCING

                      EASTBOURNE

appeared more concerned about their own good name than the school's and claimed that they had been 'too naive to notice'. And yet, many others, some-times of the same age and from the same schools, said that at least some forms of homosexuality were very popular and that the schoolboy crush was one of the common denominators of everyday conversation. Similarly, while some maintained that homosexuality at school was nothing more than a temporary outburst of physical lust, others were adamant that it was confined to passionate but *non-physical* friendships, and while a few recollected that 'homo-sexual' boys were an isolated faction despised and avoided by the majority, an Old Etonian remembering that at school 'one avoided them like the plague', many others recalled that homosexual encounters were a popular pastime, the commonly shared experience of most boys. Certainly the gay men I inter-viewed all seem to have been sexually active at boarding school and one or two, who left school in the 1950s or 1960s, said they were depressed by the relative lack of homosexual opportunities in the outside world.

From this mixed bag of responses I selected extracts from the letters and interviews of over one hundred Old Boys representing over thirty schools. Some of these had to be edited because of their length, particularly in the case of the interviews with gay men, many of which were over two hours long. In the latter case I often had to précis their accounts and have done my utmost to retain all the most pertinent facts. I hope that in the process I have not lost any of the pathos of their stories.

In the case of the letters, I retained some comments which readers may find uncomfortably heterosexist and at times even homophobic. This was done either because their stories provided an interesting illustration of how such prejudice influences school memories or because their recollections could be contrasted amusingly with other more honest accounts. Sometimes however they were included for neither of these reasons but simply because it was impos-sible to disentangle the odd heterosexist remark from an otherwise well-meant and constructive contribution.

Finally, after the difficult task of selection and editing was completed, I arranged most of the chosen contributions by school in alphabetical order and added anecdotal histories of the schools whenever possible.

ALDENHAM

Anonymous Contribution

I was born in 1939, the year war broke out in Europe, and at the age of a few months was shipped across the Atlantic with my mother to the relative safety of America, where she had obtained a job at the British Embassy, receiving and decoding important messages from London. We stayed there for four years, returning to England in 1944, just in time to experience the full brunt of Hitler's rocket attacks on London.

My father awaited us. He had had to stay behind as he worked as an engineer in the munitions industry, supplying and fitting ventilation equipment. I don't know what he must have thought of me as I had become a typical Yank, with a strong American accent and when I went to my day school I was teased mercilessly.

Fortunately, I had long lost any trace of Americanism when, soon after my eighth birthday, I started at Gadebridge prep school. As it was I was overwhelmed by the strange sounds and smells of the place, and I clung to my Mum until the last moment and then watched gloomily as my Dad ushered her into the car and they sped off down the school driveway. It was a little while before I was able to appreciate the full beauty of the school's surroundings. It was set in idyllic parkland with the river Gade cascading through it, teaming with trout, and I spent many a happy hour sitting on the bridge watching their quick movements. I loved nature and I suppose, if for that reason only, I was lucky my father had chosen to send me there.

My sexual awareness began to blossom at the large open air swimming pool which stood adjacent to the school changing room. By that time, aged nine or ten, I had become intrigued by the physique of the larger boys. I think I must have been a bit naive as I wasn't at all discreet and would stand spellbound just gazing at their bodies.

The first incident as such occurred when I was about eleven. The other person was a big boy about two years older than me. He had gorgeous dark hair, not just on his head, and I still occasionally steal a glance at our school photo and remember his alluring anatomy with an intense nostalgia. One afternoon he came up to me and asked if I would like to go with him to the school changing room. I immediately knew what he intended but was puzzled as to why he had chosen me as a fairly ordinary eleven-year-old. I suppose he must have seen me ogling at him, but at the time I didn't understand why I was so favoured.

I can remember every detail of the incident as though it happened yesterday. We went up there very surreptitiously and entered one of two lockable cubicles in the changing block. Neither of us really knew what to do, but after some fumbling I lay down on the floor and he rubbed himself along my back. I wasn't surprised when he ejaculated as I'd seen other older boys do it, but not of course in the same intimate circumstances.

Thereafter, every now and again, whenever he was feeling lusty, he would call on me and we soon developed a routine of going to one of two hideaways. The first was the trunk cupboard, a dark little room on the first floor of the main school, and the second was a more comfortable hideout behind the rug pile in the school changing room. Boys would only go there on inter-school cricket days to take their alloted rug to lie on while watching the game. Actually my eyes were seldom on the match as I was fascinated by the animals on the adjacent farm and when occasionally a boar and a pig began to copu- late there were very few boys whose attentions remained fixed on the cricket. Anyway, the rug pile proved useful as my older partner and I were able to build a nest of rugs behind it. I can't remember exactly the frequency of our trysts there but they were certainly too numerous to count.

The next two years proved to be a great age of sexual discovery. It was then that I began to make frequent, almost routine, visits to other boys' beds. Of course one couldn't be too blatant, but I don't remember any great fear of other boys seeing. I think the sort of sexual play I was engaging in was fairly common practice and none of my friends ever made any adverse comments. It was all very innocent and naive.

The masters took great pains to instruct us in the art of proper undressing. The correct way was to change gradually and pull on one's pyjama bottoms before taking off one's shirt. It was wrong to ever allow oneself to be totally naked and an even greater sin to be unselfconscious about one's nakedness. Any boy committing such errors soon became the butt of a master's derision. 'You're undressing like a new boy' was the scornful remark one master used. And that's about all I can remember of my prep school.

My public school was Aldenham. It stood on a hill in a beautiful part of Hertfordshire. The only thing it was really well-known for was fives. The boys played Eton fives and used to beat Eton at their own game. That I think was Aldenham's greatest pride.

Again I was fortunate in the school's situation as it enabled me to continue my fascination with the countryside. I used to spend hours walking through the fields. Fortunately I found another boy who had a similar enthusiasm and together we used to set rabbit traps and lay them everywhere, even behind the cricket pavilion. Once, on our way to inspect the traps, we came across some partridge eggs and we took them back to school where they hatched. We devoted hours to finding food for the fledgling birds. Some of them died but by some miracle three reached maturity.

You might be thinking, where does sex fit into all of this? Well, I idolized a boy who had recently attached himself to our excursions. He was slim with voluptuously smooth skin. For several days one autumn we went together, just the two of us, into the grounds of Aldenham House, where we would find a secluded spot to sit smoking and chatting. One day when we were both lying on our backs I casually moved my hand on to his chest from where it strayed unintentionally across his crotch, or so I hoped it appeared. However decep- tion hadn't been necessary as I discovered that he too was erect. From that moment on our relationship flourished and my school life became bliss. Even on bad days I could look forward to the evenings as we had adjacent beds in the dormitory and would fall asleep holding hands. Only if anyone suddenly opened the door would I quietly but quickly withdraw my hand. The other boy in our countryside trio was jealous. I think he fancied my partner but I was very possessive and although he was a close friend I certainly didn't welcome the few attempts on his part to intrude on our affair. Unfortunately this meant that we began to exclude him from all our country walks. It was quite brutal really. He loved nature and was such a good friend, but my passions exerted an even stronger influence.

It was about this time that I began to develop an interest in the more junior boys. My craving reached its peak soon after I entered the sixth form, when I would spend hours every day dreaming about this or that junior; but the only real crush I had was on H minor, the younger brother of my study companion. He had the most winsome smile I had ever seen. I never really spoke to him, partly because I was shy, partly because the school rules forebade older boys to talk to juniors; but even to this day his image haunts me. I thought I was the only one to be so enchanted until last year when I spotted someone of my own age wearing an OA tie in the Sainsbury's on Cromwell Road in South Kensington. A few days later I saw him again in Manhattans, a gay night club in Earls Court. We started reminiscing about schooldays. He had been in my house, just one year my junior, and when I mentioned H minor and asked whether he had noticed him, he replied, 'You think you were the only one! Why, the whole school lusted after him.' I felt a little embarrassed at my ignorance. I had never discussed my own interests with other boys. I don't think they would have reacted critically, but I was always discreet.

The only time I wasn't so cautious was with a sixteen-year-old Irish school maid. She used to watch me wherever I went and my friends used to nudge me. 'She's looking at you again! She's after you. I'm sure of it!' All the attention made me feel very cocky and one day I made an arrangement with her to meet behind the back of the Battleaxe, the local pub. I thought nothing would happen but I went all the same. To my surprise she was already waiting there. So we crossed a field and found a secluded sight. To me it was an exciting new world as I'd seldom even talked to other girls, let alone explored a female body so intimately. However, when I returned to relate my adventure to my friends they warned me that such exploits might get me expelled and I was never again brave enough to speak to her.

Perhaps all this is a somewhat nostalgic view of public school. I forget how bored I was most of the time, whether in class, in church or on the cricket pitch. But there certainly are happy memories of friendships and romance, and I often dwell on them.

BRADFIELD

Founded in 1850, Bradfield lies in a remote valley in the Chilterns. One of the earliest surviving letters from a Bradfieldian boy (written around 1860 to his sister) suggests a surprising degree of honesty about homosexual sentiment: 'Excuse this awful letter, but have got six docks (juniors) to lick, six to jaw and six to kiss.'[1]

The school soon earned a dismal reputation for sexual bullying. The Revd G.E. Tyndal-Biscoe (a pupil 1875–82) recalled:

On another occasion I was saved again as by a miracle. The bigger boys were intent on raping me. I of course fought furiously with fists and toes. As they bound me, I used my nails and finally when they forced me on the floor, and I thought all was up, the chief devil's leg came within reach of my mouth. I was just able to raise my head and with all my strength I got his calf between my teeth, and I am sure he carried that scar until his death.[2]

Sir George Hamilton (a pupil 1901–07) was also critical: 'Boys are commonly enough interested in one another's private parts, but here the interest was carried to excess.'[3] And it was at Bradfield that Lord Owen suffered terribly as a boy: 'The unpleasant part of the life there was that because I was a good-looking boy, other boys tried to tease me, calling me Dalia because of my initials, D.A.L.O. . . .'[4] He appears to have got his just revenge when as Foreign Secretary in 1979 he allegedly refused to write a piece for the centenary magazine.[5]

But it would be wrong to infer that sexual bullying and teasing stemmed from any indifference among the school staff to homosexuality. From the late nineteenth century a series of radical 'reforms' were introduced to limit the possibilities of inter-age liaisons whether based on abuse of prefect power or more loving passions. First, the school stopped admitting nine to twelve year olds. Second, every attempt was made to occupy idle minds. A quasi-military organization, the rifle corps, was established (1883) and two daily compulsory chapel services together with compulsory games further limited the time for casual flirtation. And third, stringent new regulations were introduced by which no boy was permitted to enter any classroom except his own, to talk with his seniors or juniors 'except in the fulfilment of his duties', or, on any account, to visit sixth form studies. But as John Blackie, the Bradfieldian historian, concludes 'this was all to no avail'.[6]

Contribution

TIMOTHY BARNES. Called to the Bar, 1968. At Bradfield in the late 1950s/early 1960s.

When I went away to board at my public school in 1958 the atmosphere was monastic. There were no females apart from 'skivvies' who worked in the kitchens and on the domestic side. The targets for romantic affection were other boys. There was great competition among house prefects to acquire the most beautiful of the crop of new boys as 'fags'. There was a certain amount of active homosexuality but more for want of anything better to do with exploding hormones than for any latent homosexual enthusiasm.

What we did know about homosexuality certainly did not come from any form of sex education. Our housemaster was a bachelor – and a delightful man – but as I recall the extent of the sex education which we received in our one talk with him was the provision of some Christian pamphlet which described ordinary sex in such guarded and opaque terms that one did not know what went where and what was the idea of the whole thing. As I recall the sex act was equated to something like the completion of a cross-country run, which did not make it sound that exciting. As for homosexuality, there was no suggestion that such a thing existed.

BRYANSTON

Bryanston perches two hundred feet about the river Stour in Dorset. Founded in 1928, some considered it an outlandishly avant-garde school. There was no fagging and there were no restrictions on friendships between boys in different houses. But even at Bryanston there were limits and as late as the 1950s the school still did not allow the boys to dance with each other or with girls from other schools during dancing classes. Rather, they had to choose their dancing partners from a stack of brooms.[1]

Contributions

DAVID DEAN. Author of several books on architecture and a director of the British Architectural Library, 1969–83. At Bryanston in the 1930s.

... In those days Bryanston boys wore a pleasant uniform of open-neck shirts, pullovers and shorts, all blue-grey and all made by the same supplier. This had the effect of cutting out sartorial distinctions between wealthy and poor, and also of allowing boys who elsewhere might appear as fetid and grubby black-jacketed scruffs to emerge as healthy and rather appealing (if perhaps a touch lederhosenish) youths.

The uniform did nothing to constrain an agreeably pervasive sexual atmos-phere. Sex among these sunburned barelegged boys was, so to speak, nearer the surface, and shorts offered only the slightest impediment to manual exploration of one another's genitals. There was a good deal of this, often very casual, far from always leading to serious masturbation. But I hardly ever recall hearing of, let alone coming across, instances of buggery. Sexual expression mainly took the form of self-display (with unearned acclamation for the well-endowed), and of genital handling ... It took one quite a long time to learn that the genitals were not the be-all and end-all, that sexual pleasure (at least with women) was a far more subtle, delicate and sensuous affair, and one far less crudely delimited ...

Sex was a matter of fervent interest, consciously or subconsciously. But it wasn't easy to distinguish a separately identifiable '*homo*sexuality'. I think we mostly recognized that, in a more or less closed single-sex society, sexual activ-ity would spill over one way or another. But even when enjoying practices which, then at least, would have had vicars unfrocked and scoutmasters jailed, we didn't think of them as 'homosexual'. They would do nicely, we felt, until the real thing had a chance to come along ...

This at least is my experience. I write of course as a heterosexual ... My account isn't quite what you want in its lack of example and anecdote. But I wanted to get across the fairly light-hearted pleasure, the lack of shame and guilt, and the comparative lack of real importance, that constituted sexual activity in one's teens.

HUMPHREY KAY. Professor of Haematology at the University of London, 1982–1984. At Bryanston in the late 1930s/early 1940s.

There were certainly plenty of physical and non-physical relationships in my time, many of which came to light in 1941 in a mass exposure caused, I think, by one highly promiscuous boy who expressed a wish to toss off the whole school . . . Mostly it [homosexual experimentation] was restricted to pairs of boys who indulged in mutual masturbation in studies or, as I remember well, after creeping across the dormitory to another's bed.

More interesting in a way were the earlier and more innocent relationships in the last year at my prep school. I was attracted to two boys of my own age with feelings every bit as intense and obsessive as those of adult heterosexual affairs, but the most that we did, I recall, was to meet surreptitiously behind the gym to exchange some furtive kisses. The second attraction came about when we were being taught English by W.H. Auden who remarked casually one day that the masters had been judging the boys in a beauty contest, and that the winner was a certain boy, X. I had not until then appreciated how beautiful he was: he had perfect features, a wonderful complexion like sun-kissed peaches, and a blissful expression which combined contentment with expectation. I transferred my affections almost immediately and was pleased to find them reciprocated, but then came a sad separation at the end of the summer term.

CHARTERHOUSE

Charterhouse is one of the most prestigious of all public schools. The 1991 Harpers and Queen *Good Schools Guide* suggested that a nostalgic portrait of the school might be obtained by reading Simon Raven's *Fielding Gray*, but it also advised 'though edit out the homosexual overtones'. Presumably the implication is that nostalgia can produce smoke *without* fire.

The same guide accurately described the school as 'one of the most expensive schools in the country . . . pots of money about.' It had been a different situation three centuries earlier. At the beginning of the eighteenth century, dormitories were so cold that Carthusians had to be assigned two to a bed.[1] Today, each student has his or her own study-bedroom.

The school was founded on the site of a Carthusian monastery on the edge of burgeoning early Stuart London. In its early days Charterhouse was renowned for its cruelty. If a fag failed to dress a monitor in time for 'first school', he was duly flicked by a gang of monitors armed with wet towels[2] and there are many nightmarish accounts of the suffering of junior boys:

. . . He was almost literally killed there by the devilish cruelty of the boys; they used to lay him before the fire till he was scorched, and shut him in a

trunk with sawdust till he had nearly expired with suffocation. The
Charterhouse at that time was a sort of hell upon earth for the younger
boys.[3]

When in 1872 the school moved to the Surrey countryside the system of
fagging was reformed. The most onerous duties were dropped but enforcement
of the remaining obligations remained strict. Fags who missed a catch at
cricket were 'cocked up', a painful procedure which involved a stump.[4]

Many famous Carthusians of different generations (including William
Thackeray, author of *Vanity Fair*, Osbert Lancaster, the writer and cartoonist,
and Gerald Priestland, who presented several television programmes on religious affairs) have recounted the homoerotic tendencies of the schoolboys.
These seem to have become more discreet with the passage of time. Thackeray
had barely arrived at the school when he received an order from a senior boy
instructing him to 'come and frig me.'[5] A hundred years later in the 1920s,
Osbert Lancaster's only experiences were 'limited to the occasional intrusion
into my trouser pocket of a friendly but alien hand and now and then
participation in a group wolf-whistle as the reigning beauty made his provoca-
tive way to the choir stalls in chapel . . .'[6] Gerald Priestland recounted no overt
experiences at Charterhouse in the 1940s, but did recall that 'housemasters
kept an anxious eye open for signs of buggery in the shrubbery or the early
symptoms of older boys buying younger boys raspberryade at Crown, the
school tuck shop.'[7] Robert Graves struggled against physical temptation in his
crush on another boy, Raymond, referred to as 'Dick' in *Goodbye to All That*.
Initially he was somewhat holier than thou about his friendship. One master
who had warned him of the 'dangers' of the relationship was reprimanded by
an indignant Graves who lectured him on the virtues of Platonic love. Later,
however, he came to realize the physical undercurrent to the friendship and
concluded, 'In English preparatory and public schools romance is necessarily
homosexual.'[8]

Contributions

*ALAN ELLIOT-SMITH. Headmaster of Cheltenham College, 1940–51. At
Charterhouse from 1918 to 1922.*

Incredible as it may seem today, when I emerged from Charterhouse the
only facts of life I knew, which I had actually known before I went, were
that babies came from Mummys' tummies! The school was not particularly

ignorant or innocent for I recall the new boys section of the O.T.C. (Officer Training Corps) being referred to as 'The Tarts Parade' and a young fair-haired blue-eyed boy was liable to be taken up as a 'bijou'. I myself attracted two senior boys but was blissfully unconscious, as I believe they also were, that the attraction was of course sexual. Then, later in my time, I was at a complete loss to know what my housemaster was on about when he said I should make friends with boys of my own age as he had seen me dictating lines to a small boy (who was actually very plain) whom I thought had been unfairly treated.

ROGER MARTYN. Master of the Supreme Court from 1973. At Charterhouse in the late 1930s/early 1940s.

... On one occasion when I went for a long cycle ride with a friend ... we got lost (there were no signposts or maps) and were late back. [A] bachelor, cricket-obsessed master was convinced we had been up to all kinds of unmentionable things when in fact it was all totally innocent. And when I say 'unmentionable', it is characteristic of the time that nothing specific was ever mentioned when he grilled us. I suppose it was assumed that we would know what he meant.

The only homosexual incident which was talked about for a short period (I don't recall any official action) was when some boys became annoyed by Martin [name changed]. Martin had some glandular disorder and was very overweight and not very intelligent. He was a weak bully and tended to brush his hands against younger boys thighs as he passed them. They took him into a hayloft, persuaded him to undress, and ran away with his clothes. I suppose they left them where he could find them as otherwise it must have come to the notice of authority.

CONRAD DEHN. At Charterhouse in the 1940s.

I do not recall any pep talks ... on the subject of homosexuality ... but I do recall it being reported that Mr Anderson, the junior school chaplain, known as the cycling Jesus, had said that we should all treat the boys in the choir as if there were circles of purity around them. This, needless to say, caused some hilarity.

I have ... only one story, and that the notorious one of Simon Raven's expulsion in the autumn of 1945 [during Robert Birley's headmastership]. I say notorious because of the publicity he himself has given it, in particular in his novel *Fielding Gray* and autobiography *Shadows on the Grass*.

Simon, who was the top scholar of his year and had by 1945 won a scholarship to King's College, Cambridge was in the First XI cricket team and was a monitor. He was one year junior to me but in the same house. I had left in April 1945 to go on a course at Oxford for potential army officers. In May the boy on whom I think Simon in his *Alms for Oblivion* series based his character, Max de Freville, an exact contemporary of mine, who had been head monitor of Saunderites for the previous two terms, became head of the school as well. In July 'Max' left, to be succeeded by James Prior in the first post (head monitor of Saunderites) and William Rees-Mogg in the second (head of the school).

In the autumn, together with George Engle (Max's predecessor as head of the school and the top scholar of our year) and another Carthusian contemporary, I was doing my primary military training near Winchester. I recall the news reaching us that a scandal had been uncovered at Charterhouse, that Simon had been expelled, that Max had been forbidden to revisit the school, that James had fought to save Simon but that [others] . . . had insisted on his expulsion and prevailed, and that Birley's hair had turned white overnight . . .

Max [had been] . . . a scholar, in the First XI for both cricket and football, Under Officer in charge of the JTC (Junior Training Corps), and a charming, courageous, efficient, ambitious and popular boy. I would never have guessed he would get mixed up in anything like that, particularly whilst in a position of authority. I remember not knowing how to write to him, and then receiving from him a postcard bearing nothing but a large question mark and his initials, after which I wrote him in terms I can not now recall but I hope and believe were supportive. The incident did not appear however to do him any harm. He went up to Cambridge, did well, inherited a publishing company, married and then died tragically young, I believe from a heart condition that had always dogged him. The sentence of banishment did not I think remain long in force and though I lost touch with him I have no reason to think he indulged in homosexual behaviour afterwards and doubt if he had done so often if at all before. He was certainly active heterosexually after leaving school.

So far as Simon was concerned, I believe that Birley had on some earlier occasion given him one more chance but this was it. Birley never I think forgave Simon, on whom I think he had lavished much care and concern. George and I later organized a dinner to celebrate Birley's seventieth birthday, to be given by a number of Carthusians of the 1941–42 vintage, including James Prior, William Rees-Mogg, Gerald Priestland, and Dick Taverne. I wrote to Birley to say we wished to invite Simon and hoped he had no objection. He replied that he had not. After dinner I made as if to reintroduce them to each other and remarked that Simon was in the course of adapting the Palliser novels for TV. Birley, recently back from South Africa where he had been a professor at Witwatersrand University, said simply, 'I remember meeting a chief of an African tribe in the bush who told me his favourite author was Trollope', and moved on.

CHELTENHAM

Founded in the same years as Britain's Opium War with China (1840–42), Cheltenham's raison d'être rapidly became the production of army officers and government officials for the Empire. This lofty ambition reinforced concern among the school staff to manufacture gentlemen with 'moral stamina', but a considerable obstacle to this puritanical ideal emerged with the foundation of the neighbouring Cheltenham Ladies College in 1853. Contact between the boys and girls of the two schools was completely forbidden and as late as the 1950s the girls were given maps with red lines indicating the areas which were out of bounds. 'The red lines grow thicker and more numerous the closer they come to the boys' school until, as they reach it, they become completely solid, and the school leaps out at you, a flaming red ball . . .'[1]

On one occasion a Cheltonian boy was observed kissing one of the college girls in the town. Miss Beale, the Principal of the Ladies College, immediately asked Revd Kynaston (headmaster of the Boys' College 1874–88), to expel the culprit. Kynaston's reaction – 'It takes two to make a kiss' – came as a shock for Miss Beale and it appears to have been the start of a cold war between the two colleges. It was not until 1930 that the first joint dance was organized and even this was abandoned after just five years and not revived again until the Sixties.[2]

The only alternative for the boys was friendships, whether platonic, roman-tic or physical, with other young male Cheltonians. The writer Sir Maurice Bowra recalled:

I even made a friend. His name was H.N. Crooke and like me he was thought an oddity and not much liked. He was rich in witticisms and, being the son of an Indian civil servant, had a background not unlike mine. I went everywhere with him and a sarcastic master compared us to a pair of turtle doves. We did not mind, but did not think it very funny.[3]

Contributions

REAR-ADMIRAL DAVID WILLIAMS. At Cheltenham in the 1920s.

My first term at Cheltenham we were given an individual talk by the house-master, a bachelor with an MC from the First World War. He opened the bowling by asking if I knew the difference between a boy and a girl. I said yes as I had a sister eighteen months younger than me. He then went on to talk about self-abuse and abuse of others but I really had no idea what he was talking about and was glad to escape.

SIR FREDERICK CORFIELD. Conservative MP for South Gloucester, 1955–74. At Cheltenham in the late 1920s/early 1930s.

While I was myself at College I was a house prefect for over two years and senior prefect or 'head of house' throughout my last year (1932/33). In those days prefects had considerable authority with the heads of houses in regular and frequent consultation with their housemasters and, although less frequently, with the headmaster. In my case my housemaster treated me very much as an equal and although all matters of discipline within the house (comprising sixty boys from the age of about thirteen to eighteen) were frankly discussed, I can recall only one case in which any matter of a remotely homosexual character arose. And that was no more than an apparent affection of an older boy for a younger on which I was asked to keep an eye. This I and my junior prefects accordingly did but nothing at all untoward transpired and although the older boy appeared to have an over-solicitous regard for the younger there was never any evidence of physical contact. I of course kept my housemaster in constant touch and although I cannot now remember whether he spoke to the boys concerned, I think he probably did.

JOHN CAMPBELL. Consul-General at Naples, 1977–1981. At Cheltenham in the 1930s.

I was of course aware of the existence of homosexuality – whether I knew it by name or not is something I cannot now remember. We were, in my house at Cheltenham (I do not know whether or not all houses were the same), made conscious of its existence by the fact that there were no doors on the lavatories.

This was such a strange thing that one had to ask why; I do recall being very shocked when I was told!

LINDSAY ANDERSON. Film and theatre director. At Cheltenham in the 1930s. In 1968 Anderson chose Cheltenham as the backdrop for his film If.

Prefects would sometimes linger at the bedside of a particularly good looking or pretty boy in the dormitory when superintending the bedtime ritual. I do remember looking through a crack in the partition of my cubicle, to see one older boy chastely kissing my next-door neighbour on the forehead.

CHRIST'S HOSPITAL

'Preserve us, O merciful God, from all evil dreams, from all affrighting and distracting fancies, from the horror of the night, and the works of darkness.'[1]

This was part of a grim and solemn prayer, written by Henry Compton (Bishop of London 1675–1713), which Christ's Hospital boys were still repeating nightly before bed in the late nineteenth century.

Over three hundred years earlier in the mid-sixteenth century another Bishop of London, Nicholas Ridley, had so moved the young Edward VI during a sermon that the king had decided to found a school, since known as Christ's Hospital, for the education of the poor.[2] Originally sited in the City of London the school moved to Horsham, Sussex, in 1902.

Until the late nineteenth century the boys' leisure time was unsupervised and chaotic. One Old Boy described the school as 'a kind of noisy, multitudinous, ill-regulated city'.[3] But gradually more and more time was taken up with compulsory games, the Cadet Force, PT, choir practice, band practice, assemblies before daily chapel and assemblies before meals. 'The school marches to chapel and to meals, because that is the quickest and most orderly way to get 834 boys to the right place at the right time,'[4] the headmaster, H.L.O. Flecker, explained to the *Sussex County Magazine*.

Discipline and architecture were allied forces. At Horsham the drab uniformity of the boarding houses and the constant drilling on the vast central quadrangle deprived boys of those enchanting evening ambulations that had been the custom amid the cloisters of the old school in Newgate Street. There the relatively lax control of a boy's free time and the intimacy of the architecture had combined to produce an optimum environment for the making of friends. One of the most eloquent testimonials to such friendships came from the Old Boy and renowned Romantic poet Leigh Hunt (1784–1859):

> If ever I tasted a disembodied transport on earth, it was in those friendships which I entertained at school, before I dreamt of any maturer feeling . . . I loved my friend for his gentleness, his candour, his truth, his good repute, his freedom even from my own livelier manner, his calm and reasonable kindness . . . With the other boys I played antics, and rioted in fantastic jests; but in his society, or whenever I thought of him, I fell into a kind of Sabbath state of bliss; and I am sure I could have died for him.[5]

But for another man Christ's Hospital was to prove the undoing of an otherwise distinguished career. One night in 1815 Lieutenant-General Sir Eyre Coote, MP, was discovered quite literally with his trousers down:

> I . . . saw a gentleman uncovered as low as his knees from his breeches, was closing his trousers. I asked him what he was doing there . . . 'I am doing no harm, upon my honour. I was only flogging those boys . . . do let me go, you don't know who I am, nor what I am.' I said who you are I do not care, but what you are I plainly see . . .[6]

Mr Corp, the President and Chief Clerk of Christ's Hospital, tried to cover up the matter and said that by paying the boys to flog and be flogged by him, 'nothing could be traced beyond an act of unguarded folly.' However rumours began to circulate and before long the case came up before a civil court. Many felt that the years of military service had deranged his mind and the MP was acquitted, but his reputation had been permanently tarnished and the Prince Regent stripped him of his military rank.[7]

Anonymous contribution from an Old Boy at Christ's Hospital in the 1920s.

I remember as a senior boy I had romantic feelings towards a boy of nine or ten but I never touched him in any way. I think most of us had these feelings but did nothing active.

On the dark side a housemaster came to our ward after lights out and put his hand under the bed clothes and handled my private parts. He then told me to come down to his study where he rambled on in a way I did not understand

and I thought he was letting me off. He did not touch me again . . . The incid\-
dent must have impressed itself very strongly as I still remember it.

CHURCHER'S COLLEGE

In the late nineteenth century Churcherians had the unusual luxury of a daily
bath. Time pressure meant that this had to be done two to a tub and to prevent
the obvious dangers a monitor was assigned to oversee each pair. A more tor\-
tuous daily ritual was the morning cold wash under the common pump, for
which, even in winter, boys had to stand shivering in line along a long
draughty corridor.[1]

Anonymous Contribution

In 1951 my father's army career took me to Egypt. After a year of nomadic
existence moving from school to school, he arranged for me to sit a scholarship
for the English school in Cairo. But no sooner had I won my place than anti\-
British riots swept through the city. My anxious mother wanted me to return
to Britain. Fortunately I was able to sit another scholarship almost immediately
for Churcher's College in Hampshire, and as soon as the news of my success
arrived, I was whisked off to the airport.

For a few hours I was engrossed by the excitement of flying but once the
Avro York had touched down at Blackbush I felt uneasy. As I was arriving a
month late I would be the only true new boy in the whole school.

I was not encouraged by the solemn view through the misty windscreen of
my aunt's car on a cold and drizzly October morning. The college still
retained its original nineteenth century stone structure which had become
badly blackened with age. Never before or since has my heart sank lower than
that moment when I first glimpsed those bleak buildings.

Churcher's College was a school for both boarders and day boys or 'day
bugs' as we called them. It was split into a junior school and a senior school,
straddled either side of the A3. Being only twelve I was assigned a dormitory
in the junior school with six other boys. We were overseen by a dormitory
captain who was about fourteen, the age of the oldest boys in the Junior School.

There was one older boy, I'll call him Stanley (a false name), who I fancied
madly from day one. Much to my delight he seduced me one evening after

supper in the shoe corridor. He was chasing me with a shoe brush and I ran for the small toilet at the end of the corridor, hoping to lock myself out of danger. However, Stanley caught up with me just as I thought I had reached a safe refuge and, either by accident or design, fell on top of me, forgetting altogether to deliver the painful blow I had expected. Instead his hands found a more pleasing objective and as his willing victim I enjoyed the first of many humping sessions which either good luck or reputation brought my way.

It was my first real introduction to sex but by the start of the second year, when our bald ineffectual headmaster summoned us to the science laboratory for a lecture on reproduction, I and most of my friends were already cognoscenti and we were scornful of his pitiful attempts to skirt a subject our seniors had already explained to us in lurid detail.

The poor old head can have had no idea of the sort of sexual mischief we regularly got up to in the Junior School. I remember one night in particular when our housemaster had to go out for some reason and the dormitory captains, instead of keeping order, ran wildly from one dorm to another getting their way with their preferred juniors.

When I finally graduated to the senior school I joined the army wing of the school cadet force and this turned out to be a virtual Sodom and Gomorrah. Needless to say, I loved every minute of it. I enrolled as a drum player in the band and we paraded every Tuesday, which required a lot of practice on weekday evenings.

Corps practice took place at the appropriately named corps hut located at least a hundred yards from the cricket pavilion at the remotest and darkest end of the games fields. Within the hut there were three lockable cubicles for the army, navy and airforce sections, each of which required a separate key. Fortunately the keys were allocated to boys in such a way that each boy had access only to his particular section. This provided a wonderful opportunity for relatively safe sexual promiscuity and on some nights all three cubicles were used at a rate that would have amazed even a bordello proprietor. I was always horny and all I needed to say to one of my friends would be, 'Are you coming up to the Corps hut?' It was so easy. All the boys regarded fucking and mutual masturbation as quite natural. It was only sucking, or 'gamming' as we called it, that we thought of as being in any way dirty. Anyway, there was no problem finding a willing partner for the first two methods and at the agreed time, which was almost always during the evening, we would saunter up to the hut, open up one of the cubicles, lay out our field overcoats on the floor and have rampant sex. It was absolutely wonderful.

One of the other popular locations for sexual trysts was the music school. There was a little annexe which contained the various practice rooms and I had a handsome red-headed friend with whom I used to practise my piano playing. When we grew bored of our task one of us would initiate proceedings and we would retire to the tiny music school toilet. It may sound odd, but a lot of sex in my schooldays took place in toilets. I suppose being lockable they were a relatively safe location.

Sex, however, was not always safe and several boys received what we called 'six for sex'. I must have been very lucky to avoid getting caned as I was a terrible slut. I even remember having a mutual wank with a boy during a lesson which was held in the library. Since the book shelves acted to prevent the teacher from surveying all the boys from one spot, he walked up and down the room and whenever his back was turned, my companion and I quickly unbuttoned our trousers. It was totally reckless as the library had flat-top tables, not desks, and had the teacher suddenly turned round we would have been caught in flagrante delicto.

However, I was never as anxious then as I was one evening when boredom had driven me into bed with an unattractive but very persistent boy who shared my dormitory. Little did I realize that he had planned the whole episode in order to frighten me and while we were in bed, one of his friends opened the door ajar and grunted with disgust in an exact imitation of our housemaster. I heard the grunt and when I saw that the door had been opened I was convinced that we had been seen and until that next afternoon, when my friend confessed it was all a joke, I was terrified that I might be expelled.

Unfortunately my time at school was eventually cut short when at the age of sixteen, my parents decided that they could no longer afford the cost as the scholarship was paying for only part of the termly fees. So I left and obtained a job at the London office of the Bank of West Africa, subsequently taken over by Standard Chartered, for whom I worked for the next thirty-five years.

Amazingly, I didn't come to think of myself as gay until the age of thirty-six. The years between leaving school and then were very barren years. One of my few sexual experiences outside school was with the uncle of one of my school friends who had been a regular visitor to Churcher's every founders day. He used to invite me to a room he used to take at one of the local pubs. I knew he was interested in me but I never let him do anything as he was forty or fifty and I didn't find him at all attractive.

However, after leaving school there were no more opportunities for sex and desperate times required desperate measures. I lived in Norwood and I still had this man's Clapham address, so I rang him and he seemed very eager to invite me over. I was sexually frustrated and, feeling very horny, I gladly accepted the invitation. Predictably we ended up in bed that night but the next morning he became intensely depressed. He told me how he should have been a girl and then sat at the piano and played a Noel Coward tune, *There are Bad Times Just Around the Corner*, the tears rolling down his face. It was enough to make anyone feel suicidal and I left his Clapham home feeling more dispirited than ever. It sounds very cheap-grade B movie stuff but it was really very sad. This guy was gay and yet clearly he couldn't accept it.

Anyway, I suppose I can't be judgemental as once back in Norwood I crept back into the closet where I remained for many years. I thought it was all just a phase, if a somewhat prolonged one, and I tried to sublimate my sexual urges by immersing myself in work. Finally, in 1976, my salvation came when I decided to write to the Agony Aunt of the *Luton Evening Post*. She wrote back a sympathetic and helpful letter enclosing the address of the Campaign for Homosexual Equality (CHE). I joined the local group and it must have been the great turning point of my life as I am now a very happy and confident gay man.

CLIFTON

Founded at Bristol in 1862, Clifton's first headmaster, the Revd John Percival, had a strong Cumberland accent and used to threaten boys with 'a tooch of the barch'.[1]

Famous Old Cliftonians include Sir David Wolfson, chairman of Next, and the actors Sir Michael Redgrave, Trevor Howard and John Cleese. Redgrave recounted in his autobiography how he had to hide in a toilet as two prefects fought over him. It started when he was first accosted by McOstrich, the humorist of the house: 'Ah! The very chap I was looking for! You're Redgrave, aren't you? A little bird tells me that we have here the rival of the divine Sarah. Are you she? Myself I am but a lowly stage-manager.'[2] Redgrave was encouraged to come to McOstrich's study at seven every morning to complete his early prep and discuss literature, theatre and other similarly pressing issues. Then on the last evening of the second term, McOstrich informed Redgrave that there was to be a party in the senior dormitory but that sadly it would be too risky for his younger friend to attend. 'It was impossible to go to sleep that night with so much conspiracy seething in the darkness'[3] remembered Redgrave, who eventually fell to sleep, but not for long:

I was woken by someone sitting on my bed. 'Hello, McOstrich', I whispered. 'Its not McOstrich, you silly little fool.' It was Simpson, the butt of the house. He leant over me and said, 'Bloody good party.' His breath smelt absolutely foul. 'Yes,' I said feebly; 'Was it?' His voice went on mumbling. 'Look here, I'm getting cold. Let me get into bed.'[4]

That was the moment Redgrave decided to make a dash for the 'rears'; but, as soon as he had locked himself inside, Simpson began to petition Redgrave loudly to come out. Then McOstrich arrived, hideously drunk. Redgrave heard the words, 'Bugger off, Simpson.' A fight ensued. McOstrich collapsed noisily to the floor and Simpson fled the scene of the crime.

Contributions

PROFESSOR JOHN BLANDY. A Consultant Surgeon at the Royal London Hospital since 1964. At Clifton in the 1940s.

. . . It was not uncommon for it to be said that so-and-so had a pash for such-and-such. There was some sniggering but it was accepted in a good-humoured way as being something that was normal and not very serious. From time to time I suffered from having this kind of odd remark thrown in my direction; if the source was smaller than me I would hit him, if larger – I had to contain my embarrassment but nobody took it seriously . . .

We knew very little about sex or sexuality. One or two boys claimed to have read Havellock Ellis, largely as an excuse to boast about their Latin . . .

As for homosexual masters, in retrospect I think I can identify three: all long dead, all bachelors and all remarkably artistic and interesting people. They threw themselves into their teaching (all were outstandingly good at it) and organizing plays, concerts and visits to the theatre out of school. It was at their inspiration that I saw Wolfit's *Lear*, with Guiness as the Fool. They seemed to be able to keep a clear distinction between their interest in boys and anything physical and I think they kindled an interest in the arts that otherwise we might have missed. In retrospect I believe they were able to contribute something of great value to our education and I salute their memory.

DR DUNCAN EGDELL. A Consultant in Public Health Medicine. At Clifton in the 1950s.

We were intensely conscious of homosexuality and fearful of being thought to be that way inclined. We felt that there were eyes watching us the whole time.

This militated strongly against normal socialisation – the making of friends. Looking back, I realize what a disastrous effect it had upon my own social development.

I started off with the disadvantage of being an only child with a snobbish mother who forbade my playing with the local children. I was lonely and shy, and I had (and still do have) a preference for genuine, close friendships rather than conviviality in a crowd. My only hope was to have made friends at school, but at Clifton that objective was doomed. One dared not actively 'make' friends lest an observer should get the wrong idea. Friendships had to 'happen', and even then they must not appear to be at all close. Thus one's 'friends' were people whom one did not necessarily like very much, and the people one wanted to make friends with remained, perforce, frustratingly out of reach.

CRISP'S SCHOOLDAYS

Quentin Crisp provided this incisive and witty recollection of romance at his school.

Contribution

'What are you writing?' the master asked of a boy sitting in the front row of desks.

'Nothing, sir,' said the accused.

The master snatched up the piece of paper on which the boy was writing.

'What are these names?' he asked more emphatically.

'Just names,' said the boy with insolent calmness.

'Why are they bracketed together?'

'No reason,' said the boy. The air was electric as though before a thunderstorm. Those of us who were near enough to hear this dialogue sat very still but kept our eyes firmly focused on our lesson books. To our relief and disappointment the crisis passed. The master handed the piece of paper back to the boy. The storm did not break. The lesson resumed.

The boy in question was known to us as a carrier of letters from prefects to 'ordinary' boys (to whom they were forbidden to speak) bearing messages arranging assignations of a romantic nature.

I use the word 'romantic' advisedly in preference to the word 'sexual'. I am fairly sure that neither oral nor anal intercourse ever took place. That would have been too definite, too dangerous, too disgusting.

I have expressed this opinion to many ex public school boys in England and they have emphatically denied that such a situation ever existed. That does not prove that I remember my teenage years imperfectly because the English are great denyers. Of what Mr Coward called Mr Kinsey's 'deafening report', an Englishman said, 'well they may carry on like that in the state of Indiana but they certainly don't anywhere else.'

In my opinion, adolescent boys have emotional needs just as urgent as their physical urges. When I was at school, I constantly heard such emotionally-charged remarks as, 'I saw you going down the drive with Smith Minor. I thought you were *my* friend.'

The need to be cruel was also just as pressing as the desire to be amorous. This to my mind was the worst aspect of public school life. The victim could not get away from the bully and the other boys enjoyed the spectacle of repeated sadism. Furthermore, to legalize, as it were, this practice, the prefects were empowered to administer punishment to the 'ordinary' boys. Whoever invented or even subscribed to such a system?

I escaped this part of public school life miraculously because I was easily the most unpopular boy out of two hundred and fifty – just as I escaped being arrested until I was thirty-four, though I was the most conspicuous boy in the West End of London.

In spite of the horrors of public school life, I am glad, looking back, that I experienced its dehumanization. If I had gone straight from home into the outer world, it would have been like falling off a high cliff. In attending public school, I was treated to a doll's house version of real life.

DORMITORY PREFECT

The dormitory prefect was an invention of the Victorian era. His purpose was to maintain discipline and a quiet order in the dormitories and to ensure, above all, that boys did not experiment in physical homo-sexuality. However, by giving arbitrary powers to seniors over new boys, the school authorities often ensured the opposite result, as this former pupil recounts.

Anonymous Contribution

I well remember September 1964 as it was the first time that I had ever been away from home for any length of time. For reasons that were never explained to me my father decided that an education in a boarding school would be of benefit to me and would help me to become a man – his words.

Arriving at the school we were shown to the headmaster's study and told to wait, along with other newcomers. Each set of parents was interviewed and then we were told to say our farewells and were taken to the dormitory by a prefect.

Waiting for us there was what I now know to be the senior boy for the dormitory who allocated each boy a bed. In the room there were, as far as I can recall, sixteen beds, each with its own personal locker for our things. At the far end of the room was a smaller room which was the head boy's room. This boy was responsible for all of us and in charge to maintain discipline. I remember him introducing himself to us and explaining all the rules and customs of the school and what would be expected of us while we were there. Having shown us around and pointed out the bathrooms and showers, he told us we must all get undressed and stand by our beds. Being young and innocent I did as I was told, except that I declined to stand naked as all the other boys did since I couldn't see that being naked in front of him had any-thing to do with settling in. The senior boy, I'll call him Martin for ease of reference, who was about sixteen, then inspected each boy, paying special attention to his private parts. Reaching me he asked why I hadn't taken off my underpants and to get them off at once or suffer the consequences later. Embarrassed as I was, I did as I was told, feeling really miserable as some of the other boys started to laugh at me. At thirteen I was just beginning to grow some pubic hair and didn't know that all boys around this age would start sprouting hair in these parts, until I plucked courage and looked around me. Then I realized that I was not the only lad in the room with hair in these regions. After his inspection Martin then told one boy that he would be sleep-ing in the end room that night and that he must not tell anyone outside the dor-mitory about this arrangement, unless he wanted to be punished for disobedience.

Supper eaten, we were told to prepare for bed and lights out. This if I recall correctly was at 9.30pm although we had to be in bed by 9.00pm. As soon as the lights were out the boy that Martin had designated was called to his room and the door was closed. During the night at different times I remember hearing the sounds of the boy crying coming from the room but as some of the other lads in the dormitory were also crying I thought that perhaps it was because he, like us, was feeling homesick. At this time none of us knew what had gone on in the room that night . . .

This went on each night, Martin taking a different boy to his room and we soon saw that he was taking us in turn, always a different boy. Eventually it had to be my turn and by now we all knew what was taking place. Sex to me at that age was still something new and in some ways to me unhealthy as this was the way that I had been brought up prior to coming to this school. Like all kids of my age I had experimented at different times and listened to the older boys talking about what happens when you do different things but full sex or a full sexual experience was yet to come. I know that in some ways I felt excited about going to Martin's room that night but at the same time I was also apprehensive as to what was going to happen.

Some nights the boy in Martin's room had really been crying out as if in pain and naturally, as everyone got to know each other, some of the boys were now talking about what they had to do . . . [however] being the ages we were we didn't really believe them as we understood very little about sex, except that if you played with it sometimes you got a funny sensation and the experience was quite pleasant when it was all over. I had never had this sensation although I could obtain an erection.

When it was my turn I went to Martin's room as I had been told to. Martin was there, dressed in his swimming trunks and nothing else, waiting for me. He told me to take my night clothes off and lay down on his bed. At first I thought of refusing and then decided that this would be a waste of time since none of the previous boys had ever come out of the room before morning. Lying naked on the bed Martin started to stroke my body all over, making remarks all the time about how lovely it was to see a naked body and saying what he was going to do with it. I noticed that he was paying attention to my penis, which to my fascination was growing larger under his hands. Taking one of my hands he forced it down the front of his trunks and I could feel his erection, which to me at my age felt enormous. He encouraged me to play with it and eventually pulled his trunks off and lay down beside me on the bed. Then he started to caress me and tried to kiss me. I tried hard not to give in to his demands as I had never had sex before and never thought that two boys would try to kiss each other, yet at the same time I found that it was giving me pleasures that I had never had before and that I was getting really hard now. This foreplay went on for some time and I thought that if this was all that I had to do there was nothing to feel concerned about and in fact I was rather enjoying the experience, since the closest thing to sex that I had ever had was playing with myself in bed at night when my younger brother was asleep, which in the end never resulted in anything anyway.

'Tom's visit to Arthur after the fever'.
Tom Brown's Schooldays by Thomas
Hughes (1869 edition)

'Oh, the pathos of that recumbent
figure!' *The Hero of Crampton School*
by G.Forsyth Grant (1895)

'Jack and Ralph in the tree'.
Jack's Heroism by Edith Kenyon
(1883)

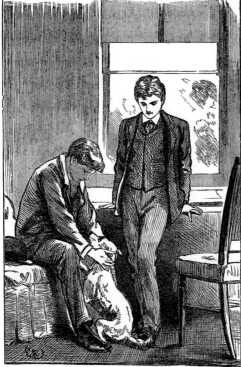

'You must come' said Jack 'it'll be
grand fun'. *The School's Honour*
by Harold Avery (1895)

'Oh, Herc, Herc! What do you think? I'm to play in the Rotherby match!'
The Hero of Crampton School by G.Forsyth Grant (1895)

The Paperchase
Jack's Heroism by Edith Kenyon
(1883)

Illustration from Talbot Baines Reed
*Parkhurst Sketches and Other Stories of
School Life* (1899)

"I don't care what Parliament decided on Monday night, Watson. A little black number would be more suitable for this school!"

JAK cartoon, 23 February 1994

The Eton Wall Game 1939

A Christ's Hospital dormitory – the late nineteenth century

A Christ's Hospital dormitory in the fifties.
Little has changed except that the gap between the beds is noticeably wider

The morning call at Ampleforth

A good cause to smile. A housemaster at Ampleforth pays out pocket money

A gymnastics class at Sherborne

The swimming pool at Sherborne

Alan Ayckbourn, aged fifteen

Quentin Crisp

George Melly

Eventually I drifted off to sleep in Martin's arms for a while. Then I recall being awakened by Martin turning me over on my stomach. He was gently stroking my buttocks and probing with a finger, which didn't feel very comfortable. Then I felt him rubbing something around my anus and he put his finger in, slowly at first and then quicker. I tried to stop him but he still carried on and gradually I became used to the sensation. Then he told me to lay on my back and raise my legs onto his shoulders as he leant forward, pinning my shoulders to the bed. I felt him thrust something into me and I shouted out with the pain. He covered my mouth with one of his hands and told me to be quiet or he would cover my face with the pillow and then I would be in trouble. Eventually when it was all over he said that I was the best he had ever had and that this was going to become a regular thing. I was still uncertain as to whether I should complain to the housemaster and yet I had to admit that I had enjoyed being what I now know to be raped. I don't think that even then I had ever reached a climax.

After the first month I think every boy in the dormitory was sleeping with a different boy each night, some of the boys could reach a climax and others couldn't. I knew I was one of those that couldn't and it used to worry me as I thought something was wrong . . .

Another incident that I recall . . . was a boy being tied to a tree naked for failing to acknowledge a senior boy. He was taken from his bed and stripped naked and tied to a tree on the edge of the football field and left in the pouring rain for most of the night. In fact this was a fairly common punishment and as far as I know no boy ever reported it to the teachers and up until the day I left this kind of bullying was still going on . . .

If I had never gone to boarding school I don't know if I would have been gay or whether the school was the reason for me being gay. It might have been the bullying and the sexual nature of it . . . I expect that the same things happen in some of our day schools, although of course they do get more home life and mix with girls of their own age, a thing that was denied to us by virtue of the conditions that we were living under. My years at that school probably had a bearing on my later life. The bullying perhaps in the end gave me strength of character and taught me to stand my ground. Whether my circumstances would have been different had I gone to a state school I suppose I will never know. I left the school at seventeen and have never been back there to visit since then. Sometimes I feel that I would like to revisit the place that played such an important part in deciding my future, but at the moment I have no intention of doing so, mainly because of business commitments.

DOWNSIDE

Downside was founded in France, as a Catholic school, in 1606. It moved to England during the early stages of the French Revolution, first to Shrewsbury and in 1814 to Downside, near Bath. *The Independent Schools Yearbook* comments, 'All the houses are under one roof in different parts of the school, and thus the social life of a boy is not confined exclusively to members of his own house.'

The tradition of the annual school play dates back several hundred years. Meticulous records have been kept since 1823. Until recently not only were females excluded from any role in a play's production, but even any reference to women was censored with interesting transformations of original text, such as, 'Frailty, thy name is man!'[1]

Female domestic staff of whatever age were known as 'hags' and anything feminine was 'haggish'. For example, it was 'haggish' to comb one's hair in a certain way and, 'It was haggish, and incidentally as much as one's life was worth, to treat one's chilblains with cold cream.'[2]

Contributions

ROBERT WALKER. *Barrister. At Downside in the 1950s.*

You use the word 'homosexual' frequently in your letter but at a boys' boarding school (at least then) there was only one sort of sex [possible], regardless of later sexual orientation . . .

There were lots of romantic friendships, usually a gap of one to two years between the pair, no doubt sexual underneath but, I would guess, pure and unrequited. There was a certain amount of experimentation between pairs of boys but (again I would guess) very much less than the schoolboy gossip, which was relentless but fairly good-humoured, supposed. John Rae said much the same in an article in the *Observer* in about 1953 which was read and discussed with interest at school . . .

I think even then (it was the Wolfenden Report era) most boys knew in general about male homosexuality and also knew that what happened at school was a passing phase for most. I specialized in the classics, and we had quite a hot-house atmosphere (intellectually) – if you are reading Plato and Aristophanes at fourteen, you know a lot, in theory.

RUPERT ALLASON, MP. Writes as Nigel West on espionage. At Downside in the 1960s.

The only story I recall, and it is probably apocryphal, is that the headmaster in mid-afternoon, while showing some prospective parents around, threw open the doors to the senior dormitory in the recently opened new building and announced: 'And this is a sight I'm particularly proud of.' There, on one of the beds, was the head of house buggering a fag.

EASTBOURNE COLLEGE

Founded in 1867 in a residential part of Eastbourne, the school has accepted girls into the sixth form since 1969. Old boys include weatherman Michael Fish and Labour politician Woodrow Wyatt who in his autobiography *Confessions of an Optimist*, described how in the holidays he walked miles to visit a fair-haired boy whom he had befriended in term-time. Again and again Wyatt attempted to seduce him without effect, but then one day at school it all happened:

> We went secretly in the early morning to an attic room at the top of the main block. He quickly undressed, revealing the physique of an ancient, but boy, Greek about to take part in an athletic contest. Quivering with excitement I held his balls and gently stroked him, stopping short of a conclusion. He showed no interest in my private parts and that was all there was to it. After several of these dangerous meetings which, if discovered, would have got us expelled, we gave it up. He was bored, and the satisfying of my curiosity as to how other boys reacted damped down my fires.[1]

Contribution

HAROLD SNOAD. Produced and directed many comedy series including The Dick Emery Show and Keeping Up Appearances. At Eastbourne in the late 1940s/early 1950s.

The only real experience I had was in one particular class where I shared a double desk with a fellow student who made it clear in the first lesson that he was that way inclined. Although I rejected his advances he persisted and it became very difficult to concentrate on the subject of the lesson and especially to make notes when the hand I needed to hold the pen had to be under the desk protecting my ancillary equipment.

Even if I had wanted to complain to the teacher (which would probably have been regarded as 'sneaking') I doubt if it would have done much good as this particular teacher was of a similar persuasion.

I did eventually confide in another boy and the two of us bought the lad with the wandering hands a present which we wrapped up carefully. It was a copy of *Health and Efficiency* (the only 'naughty' magazine you could buy in those days) and we cut out all the nude males leaving only the females. In retrospect I might have been more successful in stopping him had I invested in a mousetrap.

ETON

Founded in 1440, a great scandal shook the school in the early sixteenth century. Nicholas Udall (headmaster 1534–43) had a formidable reputation for his frequent and savage beatings of pupils. He was also dangerously open about his sexual predilections for boys. When in 1543 two pupils stole some silverware they threatened to reveal all unless the head overlooked their offence. Udall, however, did not relent and accusations flew. Before long the Master of Eton was up before the Privy Council. He was found guilty, but the death sentence was commuted to imprisonment. Ironically, it did not do his career too much harm in the long run, since soon after his release he was appointed headmaster of Westminster.[1]

Today, there are over 1,200 fee-paying 'Oppidans' accommodated in twenty-four boarding houses. Because of its size, it is difficult to make any generalizations. Most boys know little about the goings-on of those in other houses. However, it seems likely that, as in other public schools, homosexual feelings must have been a predominant force in many Etonian lives; for despite its almost metropolitan location close to the outskirts of London, Eton used to have a distinctly monastic atmosphere as the MP Christopher Hollis recalled:

From the beginning of term, or half, to the end the boy for all intents and purposes never set eyes on any woman except the matron and perhaps the housemaster's wife. Immorality, such as it was, was exclusively homosexual. I remember hearing of a boy in . . . (one) house who, it was said, was caught in bed with some woman up in Windsor. He was indeed expelled, but the general reaction was that he had been caught doing some thing quite extraordinary and almost unnatural.[2]

Up until the mid-nineteenth century even the staff at Eton seemed fairly indifferent to the homosexual affairs of the boys. The wife of one Eton master was astounded at the outcry created by one such uncovered incident. 'It's the traditional, ancient, aristocratic vice of Eton,' she declared, 'What do they know of it in those modern, sanitary, linoleum schools?'[3]

But in the latter part of the nineteenth century staff attitudes hardened. Two prominent Eton masters, William Johnson and Oscar Browning, notorious for their close friendships with certain boys, were forced out of the school. There was no evidence of any sexual impropriety but their easy ways with boys horrified their colleagues, most of whom liked to keep a cool and dignified social distance between themselves and their pupils.

But life at Eton continued to remain less regimented than at other schools. Boys could always retire at will to the privacy of their own study bedrooms, where tradition held that masters were required to knock before entering, an unheard of luxury in most schools. And while the staff were terrified about the possibility of a sex scandal, the boys themselves were disarmingly frank and jocular when discussing the latest school affairs between themselves. Derek Malcolm, the *Guardian* film critic, recalled:

Homosexuality was a very prominent thing in my day (the 1940s). Just to show how prominent it was, when I was about fifteen I came back from holiday, and we grouped in a room together, about five or six of us, and I said, 'Well, I don't know, I think women are really quite interesting, and I'm not so sure about little boys . . . perhaps one should forget about all this.' And everyone in the room turned on me and said (I will never forget it), 'You bloody pervert!' They were saying it in a half-mocking tone, but by God I think they meant it.[4]

But sometimes for a new boy the sexually charged atmosphere could prove almost unbearable. The intrepid explorer Sir Ranulph Fiennes explained in his autobiography, *Living Dangerously*, the distress which could be afflicted on an attractive junior:

Quite when and how the horror started is now lost to me since the mind does its best to heal the deepest sores . . . I was daily troubled by new faces to which I could put no name, boys who pinched my bottom in the crush outside morning chapel, who pursed their lips into a kiss while nudging their companions as they passed in the street, the wolf-whistles and 'coo-ees' from the windows of houses all about us as I passed below.[5]

Fiennes contemplated suicide, but a desperate plea made by his mother to the school authorities for permission for her son to wear tailcoats, like the bigger boys, was successful and gradually the teasing diminished, with the help of a permanent scowl that the young Fiennes created as his only other means of self-defence.[6]

Contributions

LORD GLENDEVON. *Conservative MP, 1945–64. Minister of Works, 1959–1962. At Eton in the 1920s.*

There is one delightful story of about 1900 when Warre was headmaster. Evidently there was some homosexual trouble afoot and Warre touched upon it in Chapel with the words 'a most undesirable element has reared its head among us.' The boys thought he had said 'elephant', which rather lessened the impact of his warning.

LORD CAMPBELL OF ESKAN. *Chairman of the New Statesman, 1964–77. Director, London Weekend Television, 1967–74. At Eton in the 1920s.*

I was minorly assaulted by a boy in my first half at Eton, and reported him to the housemaster. The next time I saw him (about forty years later) was when I was invited to lunch with the board of one of the clearing banks and I found myself sitting next to him. We did not remind each other.

PROFESSOR JOHN WATERLOW. *Professor of Human Nutrition at the London School of Hygiene and Tropical Medicine, 1970–82. At Eton in the 1930s.*

When I was captain of the school the master in College drew my attention from time to time to the problem of sexual affairs between boys and asked me to do something about it. What could one do? I remember that I had been reading Havelock Ellis and tried to explain things to these boys and reason with them, but neither that nor a beating (which I only resorted to once) was any use.

LORD HOLDERNESS. Conservative MP for Bridlington, 1950–79. Minister of Agriculture, 1954–55. At Eton in the 1930s.

I think most of my friends accepted homosexuality as the natural result of living for much of five years in a closed (male) society; and, in the vast majority of cases transferred to heterosexual relationships as soon as they moved into a 'wider' society.

PROFESSOR CHARLES SHUTE. Professor of Histology at Cambridge University, 1969–1984. At Eton in the 1930s.

I am afraid I cannot help you a lot in your pursuit of homosexuality at Eton. It was certainly practised, since on my first day there I was warned by an older boy not to go near the railway arches on Sunday afternoon, because that was where boys 'went to be immoral'. I do not think, though, that it was rife. Contrary to what might have been expected, I attribute this in part to each boy having a room of his own. Privacy engendered a certain modesty, whereas single-sex dormitories, according to what my friends told me at university, seemed to break down all sense of shame.

As opposed to overt sex, 'crushes' were common and even fashionable. I was small and considered quite good looking, and so was occasionally the recipient. I was not particularly interested myself, and no boy ever touched me or tried to pressurise me into sexual activity at school. I think the general attitude of boys was fairly relaxed. Not so the headmaster, who would not allow 'pretty' boys to take female parts in Shakespeare plays. Since assistant masters undoubtedly had homosexual inclinations, expressed in various ways but maybe not physically. I learnt to deal with unwelcome approaches by opening my eyes wide and pretending not to understand, as a result of which, as my reports at the end of half testified, I was considered to be more innocent than perhaps I was. My personal philosophy was that masturbation was likely to be less troublesome than any alternative available at the time.

MAJOR COLIN MACKENZIE. Vice Lord-Lieutenant of Inverness since 1986. At Eton in the 1930s.

Romantic friendships – yes. Never knew of buggery. Some masters certainly liked some of the boys too much. Boys talked about sex. Most knew little about it. One joke I remember was when the housemaster on his late rounds said to a boy, 'How often do you do this?' The answer was, 'Once a week'. He was shaving. It was overheard and everyone thought he had been caught masturbating, which did happen.

Anonymous Contribution. At Eton in the 1930s.

What a perfectly repulsive little book you have in mind . . .

I assume that your concern with homosexuality arises from your being yourself of that persuasion, and that you have got hold of the story which used to be current among people of the ignorant and vulgar sort, that Eton was a hotbed of buggery. I owe it to my old school, and to my contemporaries there, to tell you that this is, and always was, a lie. Beyond that you will get no help from me, and I hope none from anyone else to whom you address your impertinent letter.

LORD MOSTYN. *At Eton in the 1930s.*

I went to Eton in 1933 and left in 1938, so I am both old and old-fashioned. Homosexuality in those days was rampant in some but not all houses and it seemed to stick in those houses and not move around. A boy could get beaten, birched, expelled, have all leave stopped or have to write out thousands of Latin or Greek lines of verse.

Most young boys were bullied into it but a small proportion went into it like a female prostitute; i.e. to make money and enjoy popularity. Masters seemed to try to hush it up . . .

The Officer Training Corps camp always had a lot of tents heaving on the job . . . One young and very popular [boy] charged £3 a go [though] when he left he took to the girls in a big way. Later he was killed in the war.

DR NIGEL DAVIES. *Author of several books on Aztec Mexico. At Eton in the 1930s.*

. . . More notable than the presence of homosexual gossip was, as far as I can recall, an almost total lack of heterosexual talk. I can remember no mention of movie stars or of holiday girlfriends at all. We had separate bedrooms, but I recall no pinup photos!

LORD GAINFORD. UK delegate to the United Nations in 1973. At Eton in the 1930s.

My Eton career was short. I was at Tatham's . . . from May 1935 to December 1937. I was not sacked or 'supered'. My parents were worried that Eton and I weren't doing each other much good. I went home for Christmas 1937 to receive the bombshell news that I was not going back. They had heard of a new school in the north of Scotland which might help me. So I became one of the earliest pupils at Gordonstoun, where, I am happy to say, I flourished . . .

But there was one incident during the summer half of 1936. Gus Tatham summoned the entire house demanding to know who had entered a boy's room and cut off the fly buttons of all his trousers. There were two further summons by M'Tutor [our housemaster] and we were each quizzed individually by the house captain, but who the culprit was I never heard. Gus seemed oblivious to the fact that the culprit might have been a member of another house. The boy concerned was about six months older than myself.

OLIVER CLAUSON. Underwriting member of Lloyds since 1956. At Eton in the 1940s.

There were certainly those among the seniors, and among contemporaries as we became senior, who had a reputation . . . [and] among the juniors there were those known to be compliant, but . . . thought to do so for gain rather than that they enjoyed the experience. One in particular I can recall who was the library fag of one particular house, which meant that he was relieved of the other more tedious duties [and] was said to be passed round the members of the library for cuddling.

THE HON. PETER DICKINSON. Author and Assistant Editor, Punch, 1952–1969. At Eton in the 1940s.

I think you are going to need to distinguish between true homosexuality . . . and . . . the use of pretty junior boys by seniors who would, given the chance, have wanted girls. This was what the gossip tended to be about. I remember being asked by one boy not in my house who our tart was. Not to show my ignorance I made a guess (I still don't think we had one) and he laughed. I also remember being sent round after lock-up to get something from that boy (a rare event), knocking on his door, and finding about five boys standing around looking a bit embarrassed. I got what I wanted and then my friends said, 'Push off, will you? Can't you see he was just about to take his trousers down?' I think this is as close as I got to anything of the sort.

There was one boy . . . from a wealthy background, with a several times divorced mother who one birthday gave him an illustrated manual on hermaphrodites, which he brought back to school. His housemaster confiscated it, describing the mother, with some relish as 'the modern Messalina'.

This boy had a very pretty younger brother in another house. Shortly after I left both brothers and several senior boys were expelled, because the older brother had been pimping for the younger and charging a fee for the use of his own room. I was told this by another housemaster . . . who was very scornful of [the older boy's] housemaster for not having known what was going on.

SIR HENRY HOLDER. Production Director and Head Brewer at Elgood and Sons, 1975–93. At Eton in the 1940s.

Boys in those days were probably more naive than now, and I was about sixteen before I realized that the penis had any other use than for urinating. I do remember in 1944, in the midst of the doodlebug attacks, that Nigel Wykes, M'Tutor [housemaster], did institute an investigation into buggery in the house, but I can't remember anyone being sacked as a result . . .

As we were in the middle of a fairly serious world war at the time, the accent was on war work, and in the evenings, after prep, I would go to the School of Mechanics and work a capstan lathe, producing parts for the war effort. Others would go to Slough railway station to clean locomotives. I don't think there was much time for unnatural relationships.

A Distinguished Author. At Eton in the late 1940s/early 1950s.

I'm sorry to say that no one made a pass at me at Eton and though no doubt much must have been going on, I was too innocent to notice it.

MICHAEL HOLROYD. Biographer of Lytton Strachey, Augustus John and Bernard Shaw. At Eton in the late 1940s/early 1950s.

My memory is that romantic friendships between boys at Eton were fairly widespread and considered quite natural by the boys themselves. The

Eton schoolboy's clothes – special glamorously coloured scarves and caps and waistcoats were worn by those who were successful socially, intellectually and, above all else, at games – were designed to dazzle and provoke hero worship among younger boys. Most schoolboy crushes were sentimental and not physical . . . though inevitably there was some sexual experimentation.

The attitude of the housemasters on this subject was forbidding, inexplicably so to most boys themselves. They couldn't understand what was wrong about this natural process of sex education, what business it was of the masters, and why private relationships were considered a matter for expulsion. There were very few expulsions, as I recall, but rather more late-night round-ups of boys suspected of homosexual romances and warning reports dispatched to parents. These actions left the boys themselves rather frightened and bewildered, and spread faint ripples of speculation round the school. From this arose a strange atmosphere of excitement and intrigue based more, I suspect, on rumour than on facts.

THE MARQUESS OF LONDONDERRY. *At Eton in the 1950s.*

I have received some strange letters in my time but none so strange as this. I am not sure if I can really help you, as I have no wealth of pubescent homosexual anecdotes wherefrom to draw . . . Whatever homosexual practices occurred during my time at Eton happened *faute de mieux*. Ignorance . . . was the norm, parents and preparatory schools having signally and comically failed to inculcate the principles [of sexual theory and practise].

The vast majority of apparent homosexuals at Eton discarded [such inclinations] as soon as they left school or during the holidays. I occasionally come across Etonian contemporaries who were active homosexuals then but are quite the contrary now. In fact I can recall only one of them who remained 'out of the closet' after leaving school. These days I would imagine the incidence of homosexuality at schools is much reduced, given the atmosphere of far greater sexual awareness, not to mention opportunities for heterosexual encounters.

VISCOUNT GLENAPP. *Director, Macneill & Co. At Eton in the late 1950s.*

I can recall the remark of one boy who went on to be captain of the house . . . He said that he had read that one person in twenty five (males) was a homosexual. That meant there were two in our house, or M'Tutors as it was called, and who were they? This of course caused a great laugh, and we all thought about it, but could not decide who they were.

FETTES COLLEGE

Built on the edge of Edinburgh in 1870 and surrounded by eighty-five acres of parkland and playing fields, Fettes was once famed for its barbarous discipline, its unrelenting emphasis on the classics and the intrusive puritanical dogmatism of its staff.

In 1907 the school authorities demonstrated an untypical leniency in allowing the performance of a pantomime by the boys but when the Fettesian playing the principal girl executed a skirt dance it proved too much for the head who called an immediate halt to the proceedings.[1]

One Old Boy, Cecil Reddie, who later founded Abbotsholme, blamed Fettes' backward-looking ethos for his own youthful sexual confusions:

> Listen to the four maxims . . . perpetually dinned into the boy's ears. Be industrious; that is, try and get above your comrades. Be self-restrained; cork up your feelings and be cold, formal, and 'moral'. Be modest; that is, be prudish and affected, be 'gentlemanly' instead of natural and healthy. Be pure; that is, conquer and kill [sexual] lust . . . but never a word against lust of money, lust of power, lust of comfort. These are the 'moral' maxims of an immense school.[2]

While Abbotsholme was soon pioneering sex education for its students, Fettes, like many other public schools, continued its vigilant repression of the slightest sign of homosexual activity. One Fettessian, who became a life-long friend of the great 1930s rock climber John Menlowe Edwards, recalled the latter's futile protests of innocence, when disciplined for having wandered from his bed: 'One incident I remember . . . is of Menlowe being found out of bed by his housemaster and being beaten then and there with a slipper, and how he argued vigorously and at length about the injustice of it all, as he considered he had a legitimate excuse.'[3]

Contributions

DONALD CRICHTON-MILLER. A pupil at Fettes just after the First World War. Headmaster of Taunton (1936–45), Fettes (1945–58) and Stowe (1958–63).

I find it difficult to answer your letter, not knowing how much of this complicated disorder you fully understand; very few people do, including doctors . . . . I first learnt of the subject in 1920, when at boarding school, and I witnessed half a dozen 'sackings' that occurred before 1925, and discussed it with my contemporaries.

The worst period in boarding schools was during and after the First World War. This I attribute to the slackening of moral discipline through the influence of the Church . . .

Generally I found that it was at the age of fourteen to seventeen that most boys were potentially ambivalent and therefore vulnerable to circumstance and suggestion. But during the mass evacuations of the Second World War it was found that a high proportion of much younger boys, who had never been at boarding schools, were set on jumping into each other's beds 'to explore'!

Anonymous Contribution from a Fettesian who was at the school in the 1930s.

Fettes stood in its own grounds and was isolated from the outside world by ten foot high cast-iron railings, which survived the war-time drive to collect scrap iron. In those days there were about 250 pupils, and everyone had to pull his weight to man the school choir, the orchestra, and the various societies.

The school was almost free of feminine presence. The headmaster and some of the masters were married, but we seldom saw their wives. Each house had a matron, by definition a mother figure, and the female domestics were with some justice called 'the hags' . . . Before Fettesiennes arrived some forty years later, female parts in the plays put on by the school dramatic society were taken with various degrees of gaucherie by men . . .

Except when a school match was being played, when of course everyone turned out to support, one's house was one's world. We played rugger for it in 'house-belows', cricket in house-matches, and Corps in guard-mounting competitions. Pressures to conform were immense. One new man who demanded exemption from Corps as a pacifist was regarded with horror. We associated mostly with our house contemporaries, but relations were fairly impersonal. We were all 'men', and addressed each other by our surnames. If one had a younger brother, he was one's 'minor'.

Organized activity was practically continuous, and there was very little privacy. The day started with a cold shower, followed by early school at 7.30am, except in the Easter term, and we seldom had more than about half an hour spare at any time of the day.

There was always a certain amount of talk about homosexuality, of which I was most aware in my middle years. This was probably mainly due to the stage of development I had reached. Due to the lack of privacy there was very little scope to experiment, supposing anyone wanted to. As for school terminology, the nearest equivalent word to 'homosexual' was 'cherub' and the verb was 'cherubing'.

I remember once a man was caught attempting to climb into a window of another house at night. This was in itself a punishable offence, since it was illegal to be outside one's own cubicle, far less one's house, after lights out, and he was very properly caned for it.

I also remember the headmaster, who took the Classical Upper Sixth personally, giving the members of that form, which included myself, an impassioned address on 'pederasty, that cancer at the heart of ancient Greek society.'

HUGH M. BARCLAY. *Clerk of Public Bills, House of Commons, 1988–91. At Fettes in the 1940s.*

I remember that when I was made a prefect my housemaster asked me to do what I could to keep an eye on a particular boy whom he believed to be promiscuous. My housemaster said that he had been anxious about the boy and had gone so far as to arrange for his younger brother to be admitted to the school somewhat below the usual age in the hope of putting a calming influence on the elder brother. But my housemaster said sadly that he did not believe that there had been any reduction in the boy's activities. It was all news to me and serves to reinforce my recollection that any activity was extremely discreet.

GRESHAM'S

Gresham's, located in an isolated part of North Norfolk, has always had a strict regime. 'This is not the kind of school where, if a boy is not good at arithmetic, he is allowed to keep rabbits instead,' declared one former headmaster.[1]

On the subject of discipline the Harpers and Queen *Good Schools Guide* remarks, 'Hot on this'. Old Greshamian W.H. Auden was even more outspoken, calling it 'fascist':

> ... Every new boy was interviewed separately by his housemaster and the headmaster ... and was asked ... to promise on his honour three things. 1. Not to swear. 2. Not to smoke. 3. Not to say or do anything indecent. Having done so, two consequences followed. 1. If you broke any of these promises you should report the breakage to your housemaster. 2. If you saw anyone else break them, you should endeavour to persuade him to report and if he refused you should report him yourself.[2]

One ex-Gresham's schoolmaster was angry at such ill-informed criticism. He explained that the system was more subtle and provided more time for a boy to reflect on the correct course of action than suggested by Auden:

> If you heard or saw anything wrong, and knew definitely that a boy had broken his promise, you reminded the offender that he ought to report himself; after an interval, if nothing happened, and he still positively refused to do so, you reported the matter yourself to the head of the house; the latter then used his influence to try to persuade the offender to confess; and only if he too was unsuccessful, was the matter taken to the housemaster.[3]

The then headmaster also defended the system, claiming that 'The moral problem, which is such a disturbing one to many schoolmasters ... can be dealt with very effectively on these lines.'[4] Nevertheless, presumably as an additional precautionary measure, all boys had their trouser-pockets sewn up.[5] The regime nurtured dissidence and among the roll of famous Old Boys are Stephen Spender, Benjamin Britten and Donald Maclean.

Contributions

BILL MASON. *Founded Bill Mason Films in 1970. At Gresham's in the late 1920s/early 1930s.*

Boys were told to 'Never, never fiddle with your private parts.' ... When I was a house captain, i.e. God, I found a boy in tears; he was worried sick because he masturbated. In ... indignation I went along to our housemaster, a really sweet man, and told him I thought he was being irresponsible putting such fear into boys. He said he had never really thought about it but that I had a good point.

JOHN H. ROWLEY. Teacher of mathematics at Gresham's since 1975. A pupil at Gresham's in the 1940s.

I feel it is likely that, if we had been told that a certain boy was homosexual, the reaction would have been bland indifference. I cannot see that we would have been interested: condemnation or acceptance would have had no place, I think . . . I do not believe that any of the boys had any clear idea of what homosexuality was. No doubt we would have been able to define it, but we [myself and others to whom I have shown this letter] cannot recall it ever having been given a thought – much less a name . . . We cannot recall any hero worship, crushes or romantic friendships at all – and if there was any homosexual relationship or experimentation then none of us knew of its existence at Gresham's.

As far as prep school was concerned, I was totally sexually naive. This in spite of having sisters, and indeed, having always been bathed with the youngest until the age of around eleven. The consensus at school, at the age of twelve, was that babies were produced 'from the bum'. There was a 'pretty' boy who volunteered (or perhaps he 'was volunteered' – though I do not believe there was any element of force and the 'experiments' were always by mutual consent) to offer his 'bum' after lights out in the dormitory. I was one of two or three who tried it once or twice over a period, I suppose of two or three weeks. I remember coming to the conclusion that it was impossible – and so gave it up, reckoning that I must have got something wrong! I remember, on the only occasion I tried it, being very nearly caught, by the headmaster, with this boy in my bed. Perhaps that had something to do with the fact that it wasn't worth another try! But the boy was never popular with anyone because he was, as we felt, absurdly naughty; he was just a 'pest'.

HAILEYBURY

Founded in 1862, the school lies twenty miles north of London. Its fine Victorian chapel, with a green Romanesque cupola, overlooks the largest academic quadrangle in England. In 1936 the Revd Canon Edward Bonhote, headmaster, spent £15,000 on rotating the chapel pews so that the senior boys could not gaze covetously at their juniors opposite them,[1] and in an attempt to eradicate the evil influence of hero worship he abolished individual prizes for athletics.[2]

Fifty years earlier, in 1884, another headmaster, the Revd James Robertson had been equally concerned about the prevalence of homosexuality and wrote to all parents urging them to warn their children against 'talk, example, or impure solicitations' to which they might be exposed.[3] But measures did not stop there and in 1886 the revised school rules contained instructions that 'At pastimes, the impersonation of females is, with certain rare and unobjection-able exceptions, to be avoided'[4] and that 'bare legs are not to be exposed at all either in athletic competitions or in ordinary games.'[5] At about the same time the housemaster of Melvill decided that the pink stripes worn on his boys' caps were demeaning and they were recoloured Empire scarlet.[6]

Ironically, one typical Victorian reform was late in coming. Until recently all the boys of all ages in each house continued to sleep in one big dormitory. Only a limited degree of privacy was allowed by a three foot 'compart' or enclosure around each bed.[7] However, by 1990 three of the ten houses had been 'modernized' creating smaller dorms and bedsitters.

Contributions

SIR BENEDICT HOSKYNS. In general practice from 1958. At Haileybury in the 1940s.

My housemaster did warn me not to accept invitation to tea from an older boy in his study but he did not explain why.

ALAN AYCKBOURN. Playwright. At Haileybury in the 1950s.

My experience of homosexuality whilst at Haileybury chiefly involved me hiring out my services to write scurrilous poetry for the object of other people's desires. A sort of Cyrano figure, I suppose.

I think I was probably seen as the plain friend and my somewhat ironic outlook on life caused people to steer clear of me.

ADAM RUCK. Travel writer. At Haileybury in the 1960s.

At Haileybury, DPs (dormitory prefects, as we called house prefects) had fags; this was before the word had any homosexual connotation. The fag made the fag master's bed, cleaned his shoes and (if unlucky) had to press, blanco and polish any corps uniforms. I forget how fags were chosen, probably the most senior DP had first choice from the available pool of faggable boys.

There was plenty of hero worship and crushes between the most junior and most senior, in both directions. I would say this was almost the norm, but the odd thing is, it was strictly limited to one's first and last year at the school. The rest neither participated nor took any interest.

Juniors argued incessantly about which cool man was the coolest of the cool men. The cool men were usually the best cricketers or rugger players, who ponced around in self-conscious dandyish fashion just as you would expect of seventeen-year-olds who are encouraged to consider themselves important. MPs in the making.

DPs talked about pretty juniors, joked about having crushes on each other's fags and played tricks on each other. One might for example get one's fag to go to one's friend who had a crush on him and have him say 'my fag master says you have a favour to ask me' and then watch one's friend go red.

I can't remember any example of crushes or hero worship becoming friend-ships, let alone going sexual. There was rarely any communication at all, beyond a pretty blush. It certainly wasn't done to tell a junior that so and so had a crush on him. As a junior I wasn't aware of anyone having a crush on me, and as a senior I wasn't aware of anyone hero-worshipping me. But then, I was only a DP for about half a term.

There was very little friendship or contact between non-contemporaries; conversations between fags and fag masters were, in my experience, brief and formal, along the lines of, 'Why the hell are my shoes covered in talc, you creep?' Fag masters were always keen on talc and usually failed to click the revolving top shut.

Among the ranks all the talk about sex was about wanking, which I assumed people did on their own, and girls – who had done what during the holidays, plans for the school dance with Queenswood etc. Alas, I had nothing to contribute to these conversations but I listened with interest and, to be frank, some scepticism. That all went on at DP level too, and there was no conflict between talk about in-house crushes and talk about giving the girls 'a bit of finger' (most unsavoury) at the Thurlestone tennis tournament dance.

HARROW

Christopher Hollis, the biographer and MP, remembered one boy informing him at Eton, 'There is more immorality here than at any school except

Harrow.' Hollis' comment is telling: 'I do not know on what precise evidence he based his accusation against Harrow, though certainly at that date [during the First World War] Harrow's general reputation was not very high.'[1]

Lord Rothschild arriving at the school in the 1920s recalled that eleven boys were expelled from his house for homosexuality during the first term.[2] Harrow masters showed no tolerance of the slightest sign of homoeroticism and they remained vigilant, placing little reliance on the willingness of boys to keep them informed of in-house affairs. When the future writer George Hayim, who was at Harrow in the 1930s, was seen staring towards another boy's door, his housemaster was immediately suspicious. What was he staring at? Stupidly, Hayim confessed to a platonic fondness for the unseen occupant and was immediately summoned to the housemaster's study:

> Would he put his arms around me and call me 'silly sausage'? He might say, 'Today it's Bennett, tomorrow it's Gibson. Little boys are always getting crushes on bigger boys. Off to bed with you now. Good night.' Instead, he narrowed his eyes, and he spat. Words came out with hate and venom: perverted, twisted, filthy, depraved . . . How could I be allowed to sleep under the same roof as his respectable wife?[3]

Hayim decided he had had enough of Harrow and voluntarily took a one-way ticket to London.

While the staff at Harrow tried to instill puritanical morals through pep talks and cold baths, the boys themselves, though they may have disapproved of blatant sexual bullying, were fully supportive of individuals who were open about their affections. So much so, indeed, that a foppish demeanour and a licentious tongue became rather fashionable, and the future actor Terence Rattigan was only one of several Harrovians who could be regularly found standing by the entrance of his house, pointing out to his friends those whom he considered to be the prettiest of the juniors.[4]

Contributions

THE MOST REVD ROBERT TAYLOR. Archbishop of Cape Town, 1964–74. At Harrow in the 1920s.

I was at a boarding school from the age of eight. I remember I had a 'crush' on a boy at my prep school. I can't even remember his name or anything about him. There was of course no physical relationship, but even at that stage I think I realized there was something unhealthy in the relationship.

At Harrow, I don't think I knew what homosexuality was all about. I cer-tainly can't remember it ever having been discussed, though I did hear rumours that some of my contemporaries were romantically linked. At the time I had no idea what activities they were engaged in. My only personal memory was an occasion when I was engaged in some horse-play on the floor with one of my friends. He got hold of me in a way to which I objected. And that was the end of the session. When I left Harrow, I think, I was still in a state of compar-ative innocence.

THE MARQUESS OF ABERDEEN AND TEMAIR. At Harrow in the 1930s.

First, I will declare my own colour, which is totally heterosexual . . . [however] I had friends who later turned out to be homosexual: they were all tough games players! In my last two years, from seventeen to nineteen, the 'homos' and 'heteros' became apparent to each other and left each other to get on with their preferences. The only direct evidence of homosexuality I encountered was seeing surreptitious caresses, usually of the bottom, and once I walked late at night into one boy's room and another was getting into bed with him. I felt no disgust at these overt acts, only *laissez-faire* . . .

Ducker, the vast open air swimming pool at Harrow, was surrounded by shrubberies and a high fence and all swimming was naked. One summer a plump bald man with a prissy mouth started coming there and made friends with the prettier boys. After several of these visits, when he had been coming for a week, the whole school, by some form of mutual telepathy, began splash-ing him as he left after he had got dressed. By the time he reached the exit he was soaked. He never came back. He was out of order anyway as only Old Harrovians were allowed in with the boys.

THE REVD CANON REGINALD ASKEW. Canon Emeritus of Salisbury Cathedral since 1988. At Harrow in the 1940s.

It is difficult to do justice to your enquiry. Schooldays are now a long time ago . . . I was a child, not a very good witness. But two things are clear to me.

1. . . . (that) neither self-conscious decisions about sexual orientation nor pressures to admit or discover sexual identity were evident. Rather, there was a shared, unexamined assumption, among children of the same sex, of peer sympathy, friendship and bonding in loyalty. For the most part this was at an agreeable and cheerfully comfortable boyish level, but it was also capable of

greater emotional strength, of tenderness, of fiercer loyalty, which might issue in acts of bravery or generosity that could be difficult to explain dispassionately; and sometimes amounting to love, and to sacrificial love. It is well known that life-long friends can emerge from such amiable encounters in schooldays. Old Harrovians are quite good at recognizing this . . .

2. That there should be an erotic expression of such intimacy is not in the least astonishing. It could be sentimental; it could be clumsy. For some boys to take Shakespeare's women's parts (as he intended) and to be shown to be strikingly beautiful, and at least as beautiful as their sisters, was part of the extraordinary magic of the Harrow play. 'Lord, what fools these mortals be,' says Shakespeare. For the discovery of such boys in women's parts was both funny and blush-making, and sexually exciting, at the same time . . .

VISCOUNT WOODSTOCK. Better known as the actor Timothy Bentinck. At Harrow in the 1960s.

It really wasn't thought of as homosexuality. When seven hundred boys are all locked up together with no women, just at the time when their sexuality is awakening, heterosexual boys will be attracted by anything that vaguely resembles a girl. The 'Whizz Kids' were fancied because they looked like girls, not because of any acknowledgement of homosexuality, and therefore the banter was quite open. Doing it however was something else entirely, and was socially totally unacceptable. The Whizz Kids were teased but not bullied, almost as if there was a girl in the class, but they would be treated quite gently on the rugger pitch or in other contact sports.

KING'S SCHOOL, CANTERBURY

Founded in 597, it claims to be England's oldest public school. Originally part of the sixth-century Benedictine monastery and set in the precincts below Canterbury Cathedral, the school long retained a cloistral character. Boys had barely a monk's chance of meeting another girl in term time. 'Monastically separated from girls as we were, a good deal of this kind of thing [homosexuality] went on, and my first serious love affair was with a younger boy. We did nothing about it physically except hold hands, and as soon as I could escape from school I sought the company of girls.'[1] The only other alternative was the equally unrequited crushes boys developed on teachers and even, in the case of Somerset Maugham, on the headmaster, the Revd Thomas Field.[2]

At other times it was headmasters who seemed overly fond of the boys. One Old Boy commented on the Revd Frederick Shirley (headmaster 1935–62): 'It occurs to me that he may have been a lonely man . . . Perhaps he met this need to some extent by talking to his boys. If there was any homosexual element in this relationship it was completely under control and we were not embarrassed by it.'[3] Unfortunately Shirley also appears to have harboured a sadistic streak, producing his cane from inside the wings of his gown with a triumphant smile, and sometimes doling out as many as thirty-seven strokes on a boy at a time.[4]

Contributions

DAVID MOREAU. Entrepreneur and author. At King's in the 1940s.

Predictably, angel-faced blond boys were most at risk from attempts at seduction, usually from about fourteen on. Fancying such a boy was usually described in school slang as 'getting a hack out of him.' This was not regarded as particularly disreputable . . .

Anonymous Contribution. At King's in the late 1940s/early 1950s.

I was at King's Junior from the age of nine to fourteen before going up to King's Senior for just one year.

I was very happy by and large. Of course there was some bullying and I hated the food, especially the bacon which I used to hide in my top pocket. I remember matron once waving the remains of the evidence before me: 'This has been returned from the dry cleaner's.' But, unlike some other boys, I never suffered from homesickness. My mother kept the first letter I wrote to her. It began, 'I hope you're not missing me because I'm certainly not missing you.'

Before the final decision to send me to King's, my parents had considered other schools, including Millfield and two Quaker schools. However, my father, although from a Nonconformist background himself, wanted me to be an Anglican and so determined on King's.

We lived near Manchester and I had not had any opportunity to see the school before I started my first term there. However, I remember that on the day the brochure for the school arrived I was immediately lured by the frisson of history, which had not been part of my environment at home. The idea that one would be living and working in such a historical location excited me.

Although the Junior School was in Sturry, about two miles outside of Canterbury and surrounded by countryside, every month we were able to go into Canterbury for cathedral matins with the Senior School. These occasions greatly impressed me as my first experience ever of a cathedral.

My earliest sexual awakenings occurred by the riverside. The school rowing for both the Junior and Senior Schools took place just downstream from Sturry and it was one of the few occasions, along with cathedral matins, when the boys from both schools could actually mix. It was there, gazing at the seniors heaving at the oars, that I first began to look forward impatiently to the moment when I too would be an older boy and part of all that excitement. It was also there that I sensed for the first time a certain attraction to their conspicuous masculinity.

At Junior School sex was on the agenda from the very beginning. It had never been mentioned in any way at home. I remember asking the matron how reproduction took place and unwisely she advised me to ask my parents first. So one evening at tea I broke into the casual table talk with, 'How does a man get his sperm in a woman?' and there was just a shocked silence. In the school dormitory by contrast sex was the focus of many, if not most, of our conversations.

Nevertheless, my first sexual experience came as a complete surprise to me. I was about eleven. We used to have regular walks crocodile fashion on Sunday afternoons and this particular one was across a golf course which was covered with numerous gorse bushes. I remember that a group of us were straggling. Suddenly the other two or three boys jumped me and I fell backwards into a bush. In seconds my shorts had been yanked off and they began to masturbate me. I didn't ejaculate but I was left feeling both confused and excited. The leader of this group, X, who was older and larger than me, continued to seduce me into various acts of sexual initiation during the following months. There was no tenderness or affection on either side. They were purely physical liaisons and his superior strength sometimes played a part. He rarely did things to me but rather he would get me to masturbate him or fellate him, and he would also make me grovel at his feet. I felt very ambivalent about it. It excited me but I also felt guilty and wanted to break free from the relationship. I think I even considered confessing my 'crimes' to one of the masters though I never did.

Anyway I had started to have sexual relationships with boys of my own age. A lot of this involved fooling around in the dormitory. Sometimes for example a boy would be forcibly debagged, ostensibly to discover whether he had pubic hair. Those who were normally the victims were boys who we considered to be too discreet about their sexual activities. Boys who had a tendency towards exhibitionism were usually left alone.

I remember I was particularly attracted by a tall, dark-haired boy, Y, in my dormitory. He was only thirteen years old but very well endowed. One day I managed to lure him to a dark airing cupboard next to the school changing rooms. I then persuaded him to get his penis out and started to wank him. A few seconds later he came bucketfulls. It was the first time he had ever ejaculated and he was convinced he was bleeding to death. He and I both panicked. He begged me to let him go to see the matron and I tried desperately to persuade him that this was unnecessary. Fortunately I found the light switch and he was able to see that it wasn't blood that had shot out of his penis.

Sometimes I did feel guilty. I remember once standing in the school toilets and trying to stop myself masturbating by imagining what my parents would say if they could see me. Fortunately common sense eventually prevailed.

Senior School took little getting used to. At Junior School we had sometimes mixed with boys from the Senior School and many of my classmates entered the Senior School at the same time as I did. Senior School was however run on a house basis and friendships rarely sprang up between boys in different houses. Fortunately most boys from the Junior School went to just one or two of the better Houses. The one I went to was Meister Omers which several centuries earlier had been an Elizabethan dining hall.

The prefect system consisted of a head boy, school prefects who wore purple gowns and who had authority over other boys anywhere in the school and house monitors whose powers could only be exercised within their own particular house.

When we first arrived we were all 'common fags', which meant that we could be called upon by any of the prefects to do various chores. However, in addition to the 'common fagging' there was the private fagging which went on within each house. In private fagging, a fag served only one senior boy and looked after him on a long-term basis – cleaning his room, cooking his food and fetching anything for him. In return the senior boy would always pay his private fag ten shillings termly, take him out for tea at least once a term and ensure that the junior was adjusting well to life at the Senior School.

In all other circumstances it was very difficult for boys of different age to mix. I remember one boy who was two or three years my senior taking an interest in me and he got very rough treatment from other boys in his year who were either scandalized by the relationship or simply jealous. He was an excellent pen and ink drawer and one day when he was sketching the cathedral I had demonstrated an interest. So he started to give me his drawings and he would come into the junior common room and invite me out on walks, but I can't remember any incident that verged on the sexual. Anyway, after he was beaten up by his classmates he had to drop his interest in me.

I think that it was through this relationship that I acquired some sort of a reputation and soon afterwards I was invited by a senior to go with him to Sturry woods. The woods were infamous and I knew what went on there and to my great regret I declined the invitation.

Perhaps one of the reasons for my refusal was the religious phase that I was going through. This had begun while I was still at the Junior School, but it was at the Senior School that religion rapidly became much more important to me. I remember vividly the tiny chapel near the Norman gateway. Inside, just next to the altar, was a beautiful sculpture of a naked Christ on the cross which fascinated me. The chapel was also a place where I could mix with older boys who were helping the school chaplain. One of their many tasks was to sustain the juniors, like me, in their faith. Their attentions were enthralling and clearly all this had considerable sexual connotations. However, while I may have been vaguely aware of this, I struggled to think and act like I thought a good Christian should. I read the Bible regularly and by the end of my year at Senior King's I had begun to think seriously about a vocation as a priest. This meant that I became very puritanical about sex. I even managed to give up masturbation altogether. How I ever refrained for so long I will never know.

As this was also my last year I lost any further opportunities for sexual exploration. My father could no longer afford to keep me at King's, and my next school, being a coeducational one near Manchester, did not offer the same sexual ambience. Nor did it have the religious and historical character of King's which I also greatly missed.

LANCING COLLEGE

No other public school has such an intriguing Old Boy list including Tom Driberg (Labour MP and cottaging devotee), Evelyn Waugh (whose auto-biography was banned from the school), Peter Pears (Benjamin Britten's other half), Michael Mason (of *Capital Gay*), Andrew Lumsden (the founder of *Gay News*) and Rick Ramrod (the male stripper). Michael Mason commented in a letter to the author, 'Lancing, a high Church of England School, seems to have produced commendably few admirals and cabinet ministers but plenty of 'bishops and [bohemians]'.'

The writer Michael Davidson was electrified by the sexually charged atmosphere of the school:

> Nowhere . . . I think, have I seen exchanged so many meaning glances (of
> which the glancers barely knew the meaning) as 'round the cloisters' during
> those enchanted evening ambulations of fifty years ago. It was the fashion;
> and I was alone, as far as I know, in seeing with absolute clarity before even
> my first explosion of love had blown me sky-high, that it wasn't just fashion
> for me: that here was the unchanging direction I was to follow.[1]

It was perhaps in response to such activities that the headmaster issued a decree
which, while recognizing the right of prefects to 'walk across the quadrangles
except the lower one', warned the boys that they could not 'promenade on
them'.[2]

Contributions

DESMOND FLOWER. Chairman of Cassell & Co., 1958–71.

I was at Lancing from 1921 to 1926, and then went up to King's, Cambridge
. . . Evelyn Waugh (whose last year was my first) has, I think, referred somewhere to having had an affair at the school. Tom Driberg, who was also several
years my senior, was a roaring queer on his own admission, but I only remember him carrying the cross on saints' days looking very sanctimonious . . . Peter
Pears was a good friend of mine, but I never knew he was gay until he took up
residence with Britten . . .

I myself was so green that I did not know what homosexuality was; I could
not imagine what it was that Oscar Wilde had got up to that was considered
so wrong.

MICHAEL MASON. Co-founder and Editor of Capital Gay. At Lancing in the 1960s.

I was at Sanderson's House from 1960 to 1965 when sex between boys was
enjoyed casually and often, though it is interesting to note that those most
energetically involved in sex went on to marry and lead heterosexual lives. For
three of us who knew we were gay, sex was a little more precious and important and we were more reticent when it came to 'orgies'. For me, arriving
at Lancing as a new boy, sex was nothing new; I had enjoyed the pastime

regularly at my prep school since the age of eight, though I was twelve before I knew that what I was doing was called 'sex' . . . I had a lover from my first term at Lancing and we remained 'lovers' on my side, 'sex partners' on his, until the age of twenty-one.

X was one of the most beautiful boys in the school and for an unprecedented three terms was top of the school's 'Ding List'. This roll of honour was a quasi-official list of the best looking boys in the school. It was drawn up once a term by members of the Privilege room – a common study shared by A-level students for whom there were not sufficient private studies to go round.

X left Lancing after his A-levels while I stayed on to take Oxford entrance and took up with a footballer. Y was eighteen months younger than me. It was the occasion of one of my proudest moments at school. My housemaster had a good idea of what was going on between me and Y. One day he called me in to his study to talk about nothing in particular, it seemed, but as I left he said quietly, 'Michael, I think you should find friends more your own age.' No mention of Y, just an avuncular caution. Anyway, I was then a house captain and commodore of the school sailing club and as such had keys to the room in which we stored the boats in winter. At the back of the room were two loose panels and behind the panelling a small chamber, perhaps ten feet by four feet. Y and I had fitted it out with one of the kapok mattresses used to protect the boats from the concrete floor, and a candle in a Mateus Rose bottle for atmosphere. We would often meet there during a period of free time after Evening School (prep) and before bed for a cigarette and, more often than not, a moment of intimacy. On this particular night Y did not stub out his cigarette carefully enough and when we left (separately, with our customary caution) we did not realize that the tip was smouldering on the mattress. Now, I don't know whether you know what happens to kapok when it catches light. Rather than go up in flames, it burns slowly giving off belching clouds of black smoke.

Half an hour later I went on dormitory rounds. As house captains, we used to tour the dormitories to make sure that everyone was back in house and ready for bed. After putting down the junior dormitory I returned to the 'Pitts Passage' (the corridor off which ran the senior boys' studies) to find it thick with smoke, and with the housemaster flying up and down yelling for the head of house to call the fire brigade while he secured the safety of the boys. The Pitts Passage was two floors above the sailing club room, with the school library on the floor between. It didn't take me long to guess what had happened. I ran down to the sailing club room, pulled out the mattress and doused it with water before returning to explain to the housemaster what had happened – that I had been smoking and started the fire (no mention of Y!).

Next morning the library and the classroom off it were unuseable. I was sent to the headmaster (William Gladstone, the prime minister's great grandson) who stripped me of my house-captaincy, the outward and visible sign of which was that I could no longer wear a sports jacket and shoes of my choice but had to revert to wearing the standard school jacket of grey and white herring-bone tweed. Word was out by now, how I had sacrificed high office to protect my lover so that my entrance into dining hall in plain uniform felt to me no less triumphal than that of a conquering Caesar into Rome. Less charitable souls might have calculated that it was safer to hang as a smoker than a sodomite!

LINCOLN CATHEDRAL SCHOOL

Anonymous Contribution

My parents found out I was gay one weekend when I invited my best friend from the Lincoln Cathedral Choir School home to stay. The first evening we started comparing sizes in my bathroom. His was rigid and almost elephantine and events soon attained an inevitable momentum. When early next morning my nanny opened the door she was greeted by the shocking spectacle of the two of us in the same bed. Within minutes I was summoned downstairs by my stepfather who, surveying me grimly from his desk, warned me that I might turn into a queer if I let such incidents happen again. I brashly announced that I already was.

A few days later I was deposited at a psychiatric hospital where I underwent aversion therapy. Electrodes were attached to either side of my head and straps were placed round my arms and legs. Then I was shown images of male and female bodies and whenever a nude man came up I would get aroused and immediately punished by a painful pulse of electricity. This treatment went on once a day for two weeks and on leaving I was given tablets. Until I threw these away six months later I had hardly any sexual feelings whatsoever and for the only time in my life I remember being confused as to whether I was homosexual, heterosexual or asexual.

I think I knew I was gay by the time I had reached the final year of my prep school, St James's at Grimsby. For other boys homosexual activities were just another pleasurable pastime, along with smoking and fighting, but for me sex with boys, and particularly older boys and men, was an obsession. I remember sneaking into town and going into shop after shop looking for good looking young men. After some searching I found the perfect specimen, a seventeen-year-old who ran a small corner shop. I stood looking at all the various shelves of merchandise until he asked me if I needed any help. I said I was bored and didn't know what to do. He suggested we went for a coffee and an hour or two later we ended up having sex in a dark and deserted air-raid shelter in a railway goods yard. Of course I was very late back to school and missed most of the afternoon lessons but by some miracle the staff believed my pathetic excuse. 'I'm sorry sir, I got lost.'

When I graduated to Lincoln Cathedral School, the young proprietor of the Grimsby shop, I'll call him David (a false name), continued to visit me, but we had to meet outside the cathedral precincts as otherwise questions would certainly have been raised. One Saturday, while I was waiting in a hotel lounge for David, I spotted this handsome well-built man and as it was seeming increasingly likely that David was not going to turn up, I thought no harm could come from staring at him. He noticed this and came over to me. We chatted for a while and then he invited me for a ride in his Triumph Herald. As we drove along he put his hand on my leg and I made obvious movements to indicate that I wanted him to explore further.

We met again for sex on several subsequent occasions. Then one Sunday while I was progressing up the central aisle in my choir robes I spotted him in his police officer's uniform standing near the front of the congregation. I was petrified as on seeing me he would immediately know I was at the Choir School. I decided not to go to our next rendezvous. Soon afterwards, however, I met him again in the town centre and he seemed surprised at the suggestion that he might be intent on divulging our secret to the school authorities.

I know the term 'our secret' carries more than a hint of sordidness and of child abuse, but my relationships with men during my schooldays were nothing of the sort. I always initiated them and I never regretted having them. In fact I continued to see some of these men long after I left school. When I last saw David a few weeks ago he told me he wished he had had the courage to come out to his family when he had been young. His life would certainly have taken a very different course, but at least his wife accepts that there is something special between us.

MARLBOROUGH

During the headmastership of John Dancy (1961–72), Marlborough was one of the first traditional public schools to become coeducational. James

McConnell in his *English Public Schools* commented, 'The girls are . . . credited with having had a "civilizing" effect on what was previously a very communal society.'[1]

A cynic might be excused for thinking that the new liberality post1968 had more to do with the need to boost numbers of pupils and a desire to dispel parental concerns about the possibility their children might be involved in any homosexual scandal. All previous attempts to suppress homosexuality within the school had failed miserably.

During the First World War one housemaster was so determined to root out 'immorality' that he regularly crept along the dormitory corridors in carpet slippers though this only enhanced his unpopularity (see chapter one). Toilets remained doorless until 1928[2] and the regime of the cold bath continued for years after. The Nobel Prize winner Sir Peter Medawar recalled that his housemaster's interest in such strategies was motivated by somewhat divided desires:

> It was his [Mr Warwick's] duty to set me a good example and I looked on with repugnance as he stepped carefully into a deep cold bath and clasping either side with his hand, very slowly and deliberately lowered himself into it. I watched the water close over his chest until it came up to his neck, even wetting his hair. I marvelled at his fortitude until quite suddenly with a flash of insight I realized he was hugely enjoying it.[3]

And not all the staff confined their sexual interests to quiet masochism. The writer Beverley Nichols was puzzled about the procedure when he went to the head's study to read an essay on impressionism:

> He placed me by the fireplace and came to stand by my side. He then proceeded casually to slide his hand down the back of my trousers and pinch me gently on the behind throughout the entire reading. This struck me as rather peculiar behaviour from the headmaster: it was more what one had come to expect from the senior prefects.[4]

Contributions

THE REVD FREDERICK COPLESTON. *Professor of the History of Philosophy, Heythrop College, Oxford, 1939–70. At Marlborough in the 1920s.*

When I was a boy at Marlborough College, there were, indeed, plenty of romantic 'crushes' of older boys on attractive younger boys. But I am sure that

Sir John Betjeman was quite justified in saying (if my memory is correct) in his famous poem, *Summoned by Bells*, that these crushes tended to last a long time precisely because they hardly ever found a sexual expression.

In a large boarding school (some 640 boys at the time) there must have been some 'homosexual' experimentation of a tentative and fumbling sort. But there was not much privacy in Marlborough life, and I suppose such experimentation as there was tended to take place in secluded places in the countryside . . .

Shortly after a Master of Marlborough [Dancy, headmaster 1961–72] had begun to introduce girls into the higher classes of the school, I was invited to revisit the school and give a talk. In conversation with the relevant headmaster I referred to his recent move, and he told me that he had asked a prefect if he could mention any noticeable effect of the admission of girls. 'Oh yes', replied the boy, 'talk in the dormitories is now mainly about girls, instead of about boys.'

Anonymous contribution. The names of all individuals in this story have been changed.

I was despatched to my first boarding school sometime between my fifth and sixth birthday. It was a preprep school for six to eightyearolds. Nothing since has quite matched that grim experience. I was constantly bullied. One evening I had the temerity to put up a photo of my family.

'Isn't that sweet? Duckem's Diddles wants his Mum!'
'Look, Mummy's a fatty, Daddy's a fatty. So's his Sis. They're all porkers.'

I soon learned that crying only made matters worse. 'Crybaby, crybaby, crybaby.' I was deeply unhappy and started to wet my bed, a crime for which I was severely beaten by our headmaster. He had some bizarre obsessions. He used to insist that all of us lie on our left side in bed and never face one another. To ensure this he would even go so far as to wake a child and make him turn over. Another obsession of his was silence and we were forbidden to chat during our evening and morning ablutions, and whenever he caught anyone talking he would beat them with a golf club across the back. He was equally strict in class and frequently beat me in front of the others. Sometimes it was for poor arithmetic and at other times for mistakes in Latin declension or algebra. I always struggled not to cry as I made my way back to my desk and was relieved as the pain eased and a warm comforting glow stole through me. After all such occasions came the ritual of voyeurism. 'Come on, Show us your marks!' Protests ignored, the victim would be hustled off to some quiet corner, usually the lavatories, and there made to drop trousers and underpants and bend over for public inspection. It was the only time when the teasing ceased.

By the time I graduated to Highfield Preparatory School in Hampshire, I was wiser in the ways of conforming to the demands of boarding school society and so adjusted more easily to the peculiarities, official and unofficial, of the system. But I still feared the frequent beatings and the incessant bullying. On several occasions I was forced to swing naked from the ceiling while boys flicked wet towels at me and on another occasion I found myself both humili-ated and excited when I was the victim of a debagging. Of course, I was not always the victim and readily joined in when other boys were attacked. It was a case of 'You're either with us or against us.'

By the time I arrived at Marlborough I was a veteran of the boarding school system. I was assigned to Junior House and my length of residence there was to depend on my physical development, checked periodically by the house-master during bathroom inspections. The official *raison d'être* for this system, heavily emphasized in the school prospectus, was that it provided protection from bullying.

I had one pleasant surprise on arriving at Marlborough. I recognized Reynolds among the other new boys. He was an attractive and amiable youth whom I had befriended at the Hampstead Swimming Baths during the summer holidays. We were both glad to be able to renew the friendship and were soon flirting with each other in the bathroom. But one evening a prudish prefect discovered me playfully spanking Reynold's bottom and reported the matter to Thursfold, our housemaster, who decided it was best to keep a watchful eye.

So Reynolds and I opted to pursue our interests in the relative seclusion of the surrounding countryside. My aim was to debag him and his role was to offer mock resistance. Unfortunately on one occasion the puppy-like scuffle caused his nose to bleed and the discovery of bloodstains on his pants the fol-lowing day led to an investigation by Thursfold. Though he was unable to prove anything, the discrepancies in our stories made him suspicious. He forbade the continuance of our friendship and wrote to Reynold's father warning him that I was an undesirable influence.

However I soon struck up a new friendship with my bathmate Lupton. I invented a spanking game which we both greatly enjoyed, but bathnights being only a weekly event, our impatience to savour this new pleasure outgrew our caution. So one evening we slipped away to the Barn, an empty outhouse which served as a store for sports gear. Armed with a bat Lupton executed several loud swipes but then the game came to an abrupt halt. Someone had suddenly switched on the light and as I looked up I saw Thursfold standing on the upper level.

In Thursfold's study I was faced with the gravity of the situation. I was entirely responsible as I was a house librarian and senior to Lupton. I was moreover a thoroughly bad influence and a disgrace to the house. Lupton would be let off with a warning but my own inexcusable behaviour would be reported to the Master. That meant expulsion! But after much pleading Thursfold relented a little. He would not act immediately and he said he would think over my fate. For three days I fretted. I could not bear the prospect of facing my father. I remembered how he had once exploded 'Nancy Boys! Perverts! All of them should have "B for bugger" branded on their foreheads.' Finally, I received a summons to Thursfold's study. I felt a huge relief on hearing that I had escaped expulsion, only temporarily subdued by the vicious beating he gave me.

When I passed into Upper School and moved into a new house, it was the house prefects who became my new fear. At the close of evening prayers, held in the ground floor dining-room, the prefects left first to take up station on the landing where they waited, armed with canes. Each prefect had a list of all the day's offenders and as we filed past on our way to bed those boys unfortunate enough to be included were detained. The other boys continuing up the stairs sometimes paused for a grandstand view as the victim was bent over the landing rail to receive two, four or six strokes. It was an amazing charade which went on night after night.

One morning I rose early to complete some prep and decided to take a shower. I entered the shower room to be confronted by Newman, face down on the floor, flapping helplessly like a stranded whale. He had got his penis trapped between the duckboards and was struggling desperately to extract himself. 'Jerk your bum up and down,' I suggested briskly. 'What the hell do you think I've been doing,' he snarled. Somehow I managed to lift him along with the duckboard, step by painful step, to a shower where the cold tap did the rest.

On another occasion Newman got himself stuck again while experimenting unwisely with a milk bottle. In the middle of the experiment, the five minute chapel bell rang and seized by panic, his tugging only made matters worse. Worried that he might be found absent, he buttoned himself up bottle and all, and ran for the chapel. He just managed to squeeze through the doors but as he slid along an empty nave the bottle slipped and shattered on the tile floor. Fortunately the chapel organ had swelled up just as his had gone down and only a few boys noticed.

Soon afterwards I too experimented with a milk bottle and for some days was anxious in case I might go blind. But my mind was soon distracted. A rather desirable boy called Andrew Rayborn had arrived in our house. Unfortunately his dark good looks soon won him the somewhat dubious accolade of house tart and my petitions were ignored. This of course merely fanned my lust and I was soon besotted with him.

Although many lusted after Andrew, Osmand was the most resolute of my rivals and as he was my senior by a year he had the edge on me. But I was determined, and while no one else was prepared to carry the stigma of sharing a study with the house tart, I welcomed any opportunity to get closer to Andrew. Gradually my reckless persistence won over his affections and then one day, cycling through Savernake Forest, we found an isolated spot by a river and flung off our clothes to swim and sunbathe. After an hour or two swimming and wrestling, I chased him out of the water until he stumbled and I fell on top. First, I smacked him playfully and then I began to caress him but as Donald, a junior boy who had accompanied us, was looking on, the fulfilment of our desires had to be postponed.

A night or two later Andrew persuaded me to slip out of school to a hayrick. The night was sultry. Our kissing and caressing was inexpert but magical. It was a moment I would often look back on wistfully.

Andrew had a passion to fly – our study had been festooned with photos of aircraft – and he had set his heart upon becoming a fighter pilot. I decided I would have to be one too. That way we might be together again, even in the same squadron. So I joined the R.A.F. Ironically it was I, not Andrew, who became a fighter pilot. By the time he joined up, they needed bomber pilots. Once I managed to contrive a brief meeting when I obtained permission to fly over to his base. None of the magic had gone and after a night together, I left the following morning. I never saw him again.

A year later I was in India. The first letter from my mother had just arrived. 'Darling James,' she wrote in her elegant script, 'You will be distressed, I know, to hear that Andrew Rayborn and all his crew were killed a month ago today when their aircraft struck a hill on a training exercise.'

REAR-ADMIRAL JOHN HERVEY. At Marlborough in the 1940s.

I went to a preparatory school, which has long since disappeared, and to one of the well known public schools, which then was organized so that one spent a year in a junior house, then about three years in a senior house. Both schools were entirely single sex and the Second World War was on, more or less throughout my schooling. This ensured that I saw very little of my father. And my mother collapsed, first with tuberculosis of the glands, then mentally, when I was about fifteen. As I was an only child, these facts combined to ensure that school was almost my only contact with people of my own age, and none were girls.

Preparatory School

It was against all the odds, therefore, that my first sexual experience, when it came, should have been heterosexual. But with the school evacuated to Devon, I was one day taken into the local town by [a member of staff] and his wife, who was a pretty woman in her thirties. She was wearing a thin summer dress and, as there were so many of us to travel in the car, she had to sit on my lap. Instantly, I got a very strong erection, of which she could not possibly have remained ignorant. But she was a dear and never said a word. Then, not long afterwards, her husband, presumably working on information received that I was now an active volcano, gave me a talk. Since I was just about to go to public school, he felt it important to concentrate on the unwisdom of accept‑ing any offers of friendship too readily, when they came from boys much older than myself. He did not say why this would be inadvisable, but I assumed that it was for sexual reasons.

Sexual contact of a sort did anyway occur between boys at the prep school. But it was mostly restricted to ribald comments on whether one was a Cavalier (uncircumcised) or a Roundhead (circumcised), when we showered after games. I remember being very indignant, when a boy slightly older than me suggested that I could join their gang if I took the necessary steps to change my status during the summer holidays, an option all too evidently not open to him!

My father too, on one of the rare occasions that I saw him, also clearly felt that he ought to give me a few words of advice before I went to public school. This consisted of the somewhat ambiguous phrase: 'I shouldn't volunteer for the choir!' Since I have always been tone deaf, there was not much danger of my being selected for it anyway. But he clearly thought that choirmasters were more dangerous than older boys, and maybe he was right.

Public School

It was not long after I . . . [went up to] . . . public school that I became aware that [a certain] housemaster had favourites. I am fairly sure that there was no actual abuse and probably not even physical contact. But only certain boys were ever invited to the housemaster's study in the evenings for lessons in art appreciation. To be fair, they were not invited singly; it was always a group of good looking boys.

At the time, I viewed this with mixed feelings. Partly, being a fairly idle scholar, I was relieved at not having to study anything more after an already rather tiring day. But also, I did resent the fact that someone who ought to have been even-handed so obviously was not. Later in life, when I developed an interest in both marine pictures and modern art, I just came to regret that I had not had the benefit of this guidance on how to judge the works of the great masters at an age when it would have been so much easier to learn.

Much later still, in my mid-fifties, I went to call on the retired housemaster of my senior house, a happily married man, who was as straight as a die. He told me that he always knew who had received these favours in their junior [year], because they were already 'spoilt little boys' by the time they reached him; as good a reason as any for not showing favouritism, whether based on sexual or any other sort of preference.

As boys of fourteen and fifteen the sexual pressures on us were very strong. During the war, parents and sisters could visit very seldom, due to the difficulties of transport. Thus the only females we ever saw were the college maids, who were only interested in well-paid American soldiers from the local camp, and the matron, who was beyond belief as a sex object. There was no way of channelling affection into any sensible direction. Many boys masturbated two or three times a day, perhaps every time they had the privacy of a loo. And, apocryphally or not, one hero, whilst recovering from chicken-pox in the sanatorium, was alleged to have achieved a college record, seventeen ejaculations between lights out and the morning call.

The only person who seemed to show some understanding of our situation was the college doctor, N.F. Hallowes. This became clear during an athletics event, when one boy, competing in the hundred yards hurdles, mistimed his take-off at the third obstacle. At full stretch, he landed on it with one leg either side. It was enough to make anyone's eyes water, and this poor chap passed out. They carted him off to the sanny, where Niffy took one look at the swollen, blue-black damaged area, and with his customary briskness said, 'You won't be able to masturbate for six months!' Niffy may not have known what was going on in his own sanatorium after lights out, and his bedside manner would certainly not have made a fortune in Harley Street. But, unlike so many in the medical profession, he did at least know what would be most important to his patients — and got to it right away.

Despite these pressures, during my time at public school, I do not think that the feelings of one boy for another often, if ever, gave rise to actual physical relationships – not even of the arm around the shoulder or holding hands sort, and I certainly do not recall anyone having to be expelled for sexual activities. You must remember, this was an age when we all called other boys by their surnames, except possibly one's study companion.

The nearest I ever came to experiencing anything at all myself was whilst playing squash with a boy about two terms my junior. X was a good squash player, and good at team games too. Without in any way being effeminate, he was also a good looking boy. However, we started playing squash together, not because of any mutual attraction, but rather because I was a better player, and he wanted to improve his game. We were anyway both in the same house, much the same age, and the courts were just next to where we were accom-modated. Of course, squash is not a contact sport, but to play it well you have to stand very close to your opponent, especially when he is hitting a ball up and down the side wall. One day, towards the end of a very exhausting three sets, I played a good backhand shot down the left side wall. And then, as I thought I was stepping smartly out of X's way to let him play, we both went the wrong way and cannoned into each other. He fell to the floor with some force, getting a nasty bump on his head. In saying sorry, and giving the poor chap a hand to help him up, I suddenly felt an almost overwhelmingly strong wish to clasp him in my arms as well. I did not do so, but it shook me rigid to realize that so small an incident could unleash such strong protective and affectionate feel-ings. And, for the first time, I began to wonder whether I was enjoying playing these games with X for some unconscious motive, not before acknowledged to myself. I could see that he felt similarly acute embarrassment. Anyway, we fin-ished the set but we never had another game, because I told him that I had taught him all I could, and that he now needed a better partner. But I think we both knew that was not the real reason why we could never play together any more. Thus we drifted apart, and I lost one of only two good friends that I ever made at school; and from that day to this, I have never felt the slightest attraction for a member of my own sex. It was just one of those things which can happen in adolescence.

MAJOR-GENERAL RICHARD JERRAM. *At Marlborough in the 1940s.*

All I can remember from my time (1942–46) was that we had three short talks: the first when we were new boys telling us to keep clear of older boys; the second when we were late fifteen/early sixteen telling us to keep clear of little boys and the third just before we left telling us to keep away from Piccadilly Circus!

OUNDLE

Oundle resisted coeducation until September 1990. Until then boys had apparently claimed that they had plenty of time for girls in the holidays.[1]

The school was founded by a Northamptonshire grocer in the sixteenth century. As in other schools, its *raison d'être*, until recently, was the manufacture of the courteous and civilized gentleman. The ornithologist Peter Scott later looked back with virtual incredulity at some of the more ridiculous examples of such behaviour:

> I can remember quite late in my public school days having tea with a con-temporary in his study. He had been made a house prefect and I had not. As we began our tea a message was brought in to say that it was known I had not watched the match that day. As Duty Prefect it was his job to deal with the matter. 'Of course', he said, 'I've got to give you four – that's the standard thing. Shall we get it over with or wait till we've finished tea?'[2]

The Revd T.C. Fry (headmaster 1883–84) was more than willing to sacrifice boys' freedoms for the greater goal of 'building character' and he tried to elim-inate 'moral laxity' at the school by the declaration of a series of stringent house rules:

1. No study door shall on any pretence be locked.
2. No non-study boy shall visit a study; and in a house where there are junior studies, no junior study boy shall visit a senior study, except when sent for by the senior prefect of the house.
3. No boy except a prefect shall leave his study or work room during evening work without leave from a master or from the prefect in charge.
4. A boy from one house shall not be allowed to visit a boy in another house without distinct leave given on each occasion by the housemaster. Prefects may visit prefects.
5. No boy is allowed to go to any dormitory but his own on any pretence whatever, except on duty authorized by his housemaster.
6. During prayers in dormitory, after the gas is out, silence shall be observed in every dormitory: before gas is out and in the morning talking must be quiet, and general order strictly kept.

And as if these rules were not in themselves sufficiently Draconian, Fry banned the Dramatics and Literary Societies and ordered masters to confine themselves to the common room whenever they had a free period. But Fry's crusade failed. His unpopularity among boys and masters alike led to his resignation.[3] Subsequent headmasters were no more successful. When in 1920 F.W. Sanderson (headmaster 1892–1922) requested that anyone who had been involved in passing *billets-doux* or notes stand up, half the school jumped to their feet.[4]

Contributions

DR HUGH FAULKNER. Medical Consultant and writer. At Oundle in the 1920s.

My only relevant memory of my time in Oundle was the preparation for confirmation carried out by the headmaster, Dr Kenneth Fisher, previously a housemaster at Eton . . . His talks in chapel to the confirmands were so obscure that I only realized years later that he was warning us against homosexuality. My family had always meant something very different when they had used the phrase 'deadly peril' and as a result I thought the headmaster was talking about constipation.

THE HON. CHRISTOPHER LAYTON. Economic Adviser to the Liberal Party, 1962–69. At Oundle in the 1940s.

I did not experience or come across much hero worship. As a quite good-looking younger boy I did however experience being on the receiving end of romantic love from an older boy. His gentle devotion was great and I found it acutely embarrassing. There were probably other cases, but fewer than were sniggered about.

Just about everyone masturbated to a greater or lesser extent and my guess is that most people, at some time or other, got into bed with someone or other, or put their hand into the next bed to caress or toss their neighbours off and enjoy being stroked themselves, or met in the woods on a Sunday afternoon to toss each other off . . . But I came across no buggery and in the house I was in all this went on very discretely. Some people had 'reputations', others less . . . It was in the attitude of the boys themselves to all these relationships that, I believe, some unpleasant aspects emerged, because of the unsavoury combination of hierarchical power, rules and rituals, and a monosexual way of life. There was, for example, a taboo on having friendships with anyone outside one's year because, it was suggested, such a friendship must mean an improper relationship. I found this potty at the time, having six older brothers and sisters, and being a bit of a brain who tended to make friends with older people. Actually I had two friends two years older and we used to stay with each other in the holidays and talk in the dorm at night about everything from quantum theory to *Jane Eyre*. Eventually this caused a scandal and at that point the housemaster realistically suggested we keep our friendship for the holidays.

The bottom line of all this was that there was a lot of repressed sexual energy about. Sometimes, when combined with the nasty habit of beating by prefects, this led to what were in my opinion unpleasant sado-masochistic happenings. One sturdy sixteen-year-old, X, enjoyed cheeking the head of one house, Y, and Y enjoyed hitting back. In this kind of flirtatious game of dare, Y beat X virtually every day of one term.

There could also be some uncomfortable ogling of smaller boys by bigger ones and some favouritism, but to my personal knowledge, actually getting into bed with people happened with consent. Dormitories were by age and unless the prefect in charge abused his position severely, anyone slipping into bed with someone else had to do it discreetly.

I don't think many of my contemporaries or circle were what you might now term gay. Most probably they ended up heterosexual or at any rate bisexual. Personally, from the age of about fifteen, I was much more interested in trying to get to bed with one of the maids. Other things were *faute de mieux*.

RICHARD SHEPLEY. *Farmer and forester. At Oundle in the 1960s.*

The greater number of homosexual 'relationships' were just spontaneous and gratuitous events. If A and B felt randy then off they went but this did not usually either 'make' or 'break' a friendship. The 'event' was rarely more than mutual masturbation. One assignment between two boys took place at 4 a.m. in the sewing room. I believe only one meeting took place but nonetheless, the phrase 'four o'clock in the sewing room' passed into the school vocabulary. Not strictly of a homosexual nature were the 'trying to break the record wanking races'. I believe it stood at fifteen seconds. These were of course conducted openly in the dormitory.

There was no bullying of those suspected of being interested in homosexual relationships. It was all accepted – every boy was very blasé about it. Those who weren't interested just ignored the matter. Those who were, were generally pretty brazen and public about it, both in conversation and display.

I must point out that I don't believe there was ever an occurrence of buggery. Such a thing would have been considered utterly disgusting and had it happened and become common knowledge, I believe the perpetrators would have been totally ostracized.

The housemaster gave some of the boys a good grilling – reminding all that such activities were illegal. The remarkable thing was that this happened almost a year after all this schoolboy experimentation had ceased. By this I mean that most of this behaviour had stopped around age sixteen and was non-existent by our final year. By then most of us were either trying to chat up girls or at least thinking about it.

Now I'm happily married with three children and for me the thought of any homosexual relationship is totally bizarre so hopefully I came out of the system unscathed.

RADLEY

Radley is one of the few schools where a limited form of fagging still survives. One of the most difficult chores for new boys is waking everyone up for the 7am breakfast.

In the nineteenth century, it was one of the first schools to begin regular sur-veillance of boys' dormitories. The headmaster, William Sewell, told the assembled school in 1849:

> Constantly we shall be visiting the dormitory, coming upon you suddenly – (until we feel you have strength enough to resist the temptation of being left alone) coming among you at all hours, myself, the fellows, the prefects, and if we should find it necessary even our confidential servants.[1]

Contributions

PETER GARDINER. *Headmaster of St Peter's School, York, 1967–79. At Radley in the 1940s.*

There was widespread homosexual hero worship in a community divided into house cells ('Socials') where our sole female company consisted of a fiercely boisterous matron, and occasionally some of the staff wives. My 'Social Tutor' was a bachelor.

'Homosexual' relationships were, as far as I know, all romantic and non-physical. I was once kissed by an older boy, an experience that puzzled and alarmed me, but I can remember no other physical contact at all, not even reports of any.

The prefects were very powerful in the running of the Social. They picked their private fags from boys in their second term onwards, and the main fagging duties were study-cleaning; cooking on gas-rings; making beds; and warming lavatory seats in the vast stand-alone pavilion known as the 'rears' – the cubicles were under cover but the approaches were open to the sky. There were no doors for the unprivileged, but the prefects had doors to theirs and so it was a luxury for the fags who could avail themselves of the privacy of the privileged loo. The fags were certainly picked for their looks . . . but they were invited, not coerced, and could decline the invitation and stay as public fags, on call to run errands at any time.

In my experience, both as fag and as prefect, conversation was hesitant, and seemly, and never developed into physical contact. Payment for fagging duties consisted of tips, the opportunity to use the gas-rings, generous portions of cake and, at the end of the year, the bequeathing of study furniture as the fag graduated to a study . . .

We were given no sex instruction or counselling. My prep school head had vaguely warned his leavers not to be pally with older boys (he didn't say why), but I certainly had no advice offered once I'd reached Radley . . . [although] hovering round our thinking was, of course, a vague aura of guilt but I'm not sure how this was induced . . .

I can illustrate the romantic hero worship from one experience that stands out with odd clarity in my memory. I was batting in the nets at the end of a summer's day and was about to emerge and de-pad when a good-looking boy in another Social, three years my junior, whose looks I had for some time admired, passed by returning from a game. He had a cricket ball in his hand. Presumably he knew of my admiration because with a smile he ran up and bowled a ball at me in the net. No words passed and the incident led to nothing. It was a curiously innocent thrill!

SIR ROWLAND WHITEHEAD. *At Radley in the 1940s.*

M in my house was known to fancy boys. One term a rather beautiful china-pale youth arrived – he was called Paul New. M was infatuated. We all knew it. The inevitable happened in chapel with the hymn, 'New every morning is the love – our waking and uprising prove.' The entire school collapsed in giggles.

NICHOLAS COLCHESTER. Deputy Editor of The Economist since 1989. At
Radley in the 1960s.

At Radley good-looking young boys were known (in 1960–64) as 'stigs': I
have no idea why. They were discussed by older boys, rather in the way that
pretty girls are in pubs, and I suspect that they were mainly a surrogate in an
all-boy school.

REPTON

Founded in 1557, the school is built in pink stone and stands amidst the hills
of south Derbyshire. Its most famous headmaster was the Revd Geoffrey Fisher
(later to become Archbishop of Canterbury). Soon after being appointed in
1914 Fisher was confronted with the 'problem' of homosexuality. Apparently
many boys were 'very badly astray' and '(even) some of the nicest (senior) boys
were deeply in this trouble'.[1]

Among Repton's most famous Old Boys are Harold Abrahams (of
Chariots of Fire) and Christopher Isherwood.

Contributions

SIR MAURICE FIENNES. Chairman of Davy-Ashmore Ltd., 1961–69. At Repton
in the 1920s.

I am a generation older than Ranulph [Sir Ranulph Fiennes – the explorer]
and went to Repton in 1920 and stayed there until 1925 . . . I cannot recollect
any incidents of a homosexual character during the time I was there . . . For
one thing, we were all kept much too busy. A programme was set for us from
7.30 a.m. until 9.30 p.m. on all days of the week except Sunday, when we were
busy up to and including lunch time. In the afternoon, one went for walks in
the country with friends. But I don't think any of these friendships were of
a homosexual character, except possibly one which, I know, lasted into later
life . . .

I think there was a pep talk from our housemaster during my first term, but
I don't think I really understood what he was talking about, which is perhaps
just as well.

I suppose there was an awareness of the sort of thing to which you refer. One was not encouraged to make friends with boys who lived in other houses in the school. If one did, eyebrows were raised, but it never seemed to get much further than that . . .

THE REVD PHILIP CROWE. Principal of Salisbury and Wells Theological College.

I was at Repton School from 1950 to 1955. It was a time when sexuality was not as public a matter as it is now. As a result, discussion about heterosexuality was not as open, which in turn had a significant effect on our understanding of homosexuality. It was a single-sex school, and homosexual talk and activity were widespread, but were not distinguished from heterosexual activity. The question of whether or not a person was gay didn't arise.

I have no recollection at all of any discussion about whether or not boys might be gay, no anecdotes, no crushes or 'affairs' which were explicitly identified as homosexual, simply because there was no possibility of anything else. If everyone is gay, no-one is gay!

It is, of course, quite possible that a boy who was genuinely homosexual might have a quite different perception, though even if he realized that he was doing it for real, while others were playing, that would not cause him any public problems.

From a Judge who was at Repton in the 1950s.

My English master, having read us the *Ballad of Reading Gaol*, was then asked what Oscar Wilde was doing inside. He answered that he was there for an offence (I assumed fraud) and that was all we got for a long time.

RUGBY

Founded in 1567, the school's most celebrated headmaster was Dr Thomas Arnold of *Tom Brown's Schooldays* fame.

Before Arnold's time the aim of public school education had been simply to educate. Discipline was subservient to this purpose. But Arnold felt that there should be much more emphasis on the formation of character, and this could only be achieved by extensive reform. Consequently he determined to rid schools of bullying and cruelty. He also strived to eliminate schoolboy homosexuality.

He was the first public school headmaster to launch a crusade against sexual experimentation between school boys. Previously, it had rarely attracted any special attention. Arnold wanted to change all that, and in an article he wrote in 1835 entitled *On the Discipline of Public Schools*, he voiced his concerns in thinly disguised metaphors:

> Public schools are made up of the very same persons whom we have known a few years earlier to be pure-minded and obedient children – whom we knew a few years later, to be at least decent and useful men. What special cloud hangs over this one part of our life's current, that the stream here will ever run dark and sullen, while on its earlier and its later course it is either all bright and lively or the impurity of its waters is lost to the distant view in the breadth and majesty of their volume?[1]

Subsequent headmasters were no less vigilant. John Percival (headmaster 1887–95) was reputed to have 'an unerring eye for the unwholesome boy'[2] and was so worried about the possibility of 'moral corruption' that he ordered all boys' football shorts to be retailored so as to reach below the knee. But the boys, finding it difficult to play football in the longer trousers, simply rolled their legs up. Furious and frustrated, Percival issued yet another decree, which declared that football shorts must be fitted with elastic to keep them firmly below the knee. But boys were not quick to comply; arguing, possibly with some justification, that the local tailors were overwhelmed with a backlog of work.[3]

The school's vigilance proved futile. Certainly the future poet Rupert Brooke ignored it, for it was at Rugby that he developed a passion for a younger boy who he named 'Antinous', sending him letters extolling his fervent and undying devotion.[4] Neither was Brooke by any means a sexual maverick. The writer A.N. Wilson recalled that homosexuality was the principal preoccupation of boys in his day:

> Romantic friendships were universal at Rugby . . . There was a certain amount of love, a certain amount of romantic friendship and . . . sex, sometimes casual and sometimes involving love affairs. The only difference from the outside world was that it was exclusively homosexual . . . It was not an orgy – It simply went on all the time as it does in ordinary life . . . In my house you would spend fifty per cent of the time talking about whom you had a crush on or who you thought had a crush on you.[5]

Contributions

LIEUTENANT-COMMANDER JOHN MILLER. At Rugby, 1916–22.

I am afraid you would find me very old-fashioned. I reached ninety years of age the other day and I must confess that your subject is in no way up my street.

I was at Rugby from 1916 to 1922, the last two years head of my house and the last year head of the school. In my day there were about 600 boys in the school but these were divided into a number of boarding houses mostly with about fifty boys in each. These houses were out of bounds to all boys except those who actually lived in them, so we really knew rather little about what was going on in the school as a whole.

Oddly enough, what I did find in my own case was that one of the masters – unsuitably a housemaster (not my own) – made an advance to me when we were out river bathing in the Avon near Princethorpe half way to Leamington. I was so shocked that I jumped into my clothes, grabbed my bicycle and rode back to Rugby alone as fast as I could. I think I can safely mention his name as he must be dead by now. The dear fellow's name was [. . .] and he was known to us boys as Roger Rum because of his peculiar proclivities. None of us ever split on him as we did not think we were entitled to wreck his career.

DR ALEC DICKSON. Founded Voluntary Service Overseas in 1958. At Rugby in the late 1920s/early 1930s.

So far as I can remember there were about 620 boys then. What a rich number to choose one's friends from, a stranger might comment. Not so. Divide 620 or so by twelve, approximately the number of houses: one did not make friends outside one's own house. Still, that leaves about fifty potential friends. Not so, again. One simply did not make friends outside the year in which one came, up or down, so to speak: it was 'not done'. So in fact one's circle of potential friends was very, very small. Of course one was aware of boys older and younger than oneself in one's own house, and aware of boys in other houses, for one mixed with them in classrooms and forms. But they did not offer a field for friendship.

One for whom I did develop deep admiration was dead before I came to the school! That was Rupert Brooke (1885–1915). I did not so much read his poems, I absorbed them: more to the point, they absorbed me. I sat for a year beneath the tablet with his lyrically beautiful profile and the accompanying sonnet, 'If I should die . . .'. All that he stood for, a Grecian model of male beauty, what Winston Churchill wrote of him, the whole concept of sacrifice that he personified – how cruel of fate that I was born too late to know him and revel in his friendship. I steeped myself in the romanticism of the First World War . . . Today I recognize that it is Wilfred Owen who has become the symbol of the awfulness and waste of the First World War. But . . . his [Brooke's] poetry captured me. I won the Rupert Brooke Prize in 1932 – with an essay, inevitably, on Rupert Brooke.

In 1931–1932, virtually my last year at Rugby, I developed a deep friend-ship for a boy of about my own age, X. He reciprocated, but the depth and intensity came from me. It can't have escaped the notice of those boys who knew us both that we cared for each other greatly. But nobody made snide remarks about us. Not even our fingers ever touched; we never embraced. However strange it may sound today in 1993, 'homosexual' did not enter our vocabularies at that time. I read the word for the first time when I got to Oxford. We were aware that love between two males was considered undesir-able, not to be encouraged, not to be discussed. It may seem incredibly inno-cent today, but that is how it was . . .

Those five years at Rugby were the unhappiest of my life. It was an unlov-ing place. None of the masters accorded us their friendship, far less their affec-tion . . .

SIR HAVELOCK HUDSON. *Chairman of Lloyds, 1975–77. At Rugby in the 1930s.*

Obviously you have never attended a single-sex boarding school or you would not have asked the questions in your letter. Everyone knows that these schools, such as the Rugby which I attended, are rife with homosexual activity, which has not precluded the vast majority of people, on leaving these schools, from having heterosexual affairs, and even marrying eventually.

THE RT. REVD JOHN BICKERSTETH. *Bishop of Bath and Wells, 1975–87. At Rugby in the 1930s.*

I had five very happy years at Rugby (1935–1940), the last year as head of house. I honestly do not believe there were active homosexual relationships on any scale. I remember discussing this with sixth-form boys from other schools where they seemed to be virtually the norm.

Our housemaster expelled one boy for dressing up in the matron's under-clothes. I recall that causing quite a stir among the sixths, but it never reached the rest of the house! . .

Certainly my housemaster had powerful views on homosexual matters, and would have pounced hard if he'd nosed out things he didn't approve of . . .

DR PETER ELMES. Consultant in lung diseases. At Rugby in the 1930s.

I was in School House from 1935 to 1939. There was plenty of hero worship (mainly centred on those good at games) and the occasional crush (usually between contemporaries) which lasted less than a term. But I don't remember anything you could call a romantic friendship, although outward shows of emotion were not the 'done thing' in those days . . .

Sex education . . . was carried out on a one-to-one basis with housemaster or tutor at about seventeen years except for one lecture (or was it two?) to the leavers by an 'expert' from London (a physician), mainly notable for telling you not to wear your old school tie when bent on extra-marital sexual behaviour.

PROFESSOR DONALD MICHIE. Senior Fellow, Turing Institute, Glasgow. At Rugby in the late 1930s/early 1940s.

I do not recall either the headmaster, or my housemaster, or any other member of Rugby teaching staff expressing any public attitude to homosexuality, or to any other facet of sex. Instead, a tall, thin man with glasses (described to us as 'a psychologist') visited the school every year to give a talk, plus private counselling if requested, on sex. His themes included masturbation, romantic friendships and physical intimacy between boys, especially between those of disparate ages. His material was superficially non-judgemental, and was regarded with polite ribaldry, more because of his earnestness of manner than because of his topic, which evidently gripped him more than his audience . . .

Sexual innuendo . . . was the small change of the constant invective, lam-poons and libels which spiced ordinary chit-chat. If the target of the moment was known or believed to be sexually active, then this would of course be worked into routine taunts; if not, then legends connecting alleged over-indul-gence in self-abuse would be linked to his nodding off in class, having a debauched and debilitated appearance, missing an easy conversion of a try on the rugger field, etc. etc.

I recall one or two private expressions of concern as to whether the coming reorientation to girls would go O.K.. But Rugby boys came mainly from prosperous Midlands merchants. Worrying about hypotheticals was not much part of the scene. Rugbeian attitudes were robust, perhaps to a fault.

COLONEL SIR GEOFFREY ERRINGTON. *At Rugby in the 1940s.*

There were of course certain people at school who were alleged to have crushes on others but I have no evidence of the truth of the rumours. As to the views of the headmaster and other staff, we were left in no doubt that it was a sack-able offence to be caught in a homosexual situation, even though it did not figure in the school rules nor was it alluded to verbally. The nearest indication we had of staff interest in such matters was when all the locks were removed from newly installed lavatory doors! Certain staff were thought to be homo-sexual and dark rumours used to fly around. However here again I have no evidence to offer.

SIR MARTIN BERTHOUD. *High Commissioner, Trinidad and Tobago, 1985–91. At Rugby in the 1940s.*

. . . There was masses of homosexuality in some of the houses while I was at Rugby, including mine . . . Very little buggery, though one or two people did get expelled for it.

In my house it (homosexuality) was certainly talked about and accepted, though almost always as a substitute for girls. I received a long *billet-doux* which embarrassed me intensely. I responded, negatively, by the same messenger.

SIR EWEN FERGUSSON. *Ambassador to France, 1987–92. At Rugby in the 1940s.*

I started a Scottish country dancing society. When housemaster's wives, daughters, matrons etc were unavailable, the younger boys acted as partners . . . I remember coming back to school after four months of heterosexual contact in France and being amazed at the reminder of how homosexual the ordinary tone of jokes/conversation was.

ST EDWARD'S

Founded in 1863, it moved to its present location two miles north of Oxford in 1873. The Old Boys are sometimes known as 'Teddies' and include the ITN newsreader Jon Snow and His Honour Judge Stephen Tumin, His Majesty's Chief Inspector of Prisons.

St Edward's was once regarded as one of the toughest and brawniest of all public schools. In his autobiography, *Of This Our Time*, the *Picture Post* Editor Tom Hopkinson recalled the freezing dormitories. Boys were allowed a maximum of only three blankets each and even in midwinter the windows had to remain open all night.[1]

During the First World War several boys were disciplined for homosexuality, but, contrary to standard procedure, none of them were expelled:

> 'There is no need for unsavoury details', Old Boy Patrick Lacey declared somewhat coyly. 'It is enough to remember that they led to the closing of two prefects' studies in the lobby of "Ceylon" and to six or seven "public", explosive and extremely authoritative episodes with the cane.'[2]

The school authorities appear to have believed that their offences were partly to be explained and hence mitigated by the overcrowded conditions and vacuum of authority brought about by the war. Many school prefects and members of staff had enrolled in the army and their authority had apparently not been equalled by the 'gallant band of substitutes' who took their place. It was thought that in the circumstances these 'cases' should be dealt with lightly. However, the boys themselves still considered the punishments unnec-essarily severe and were sympathetic to the victims. Patrick Lacey recalled how:

> In the congested changing-room . . . I was enormously impressed by a conversation between three or four senior boys which I could not help overhearing . . . Only a week before one of them had been 'summarily dealt with' in the presence of the whole school . . . and under the warden's personal supervision, for a moral offence of the first magnitude. The others in the conversation were criticizing and carping at the Warden in general terms, but this one boy reduced them to silence with a quiet, but extraordinarily sincere and effective word of praise and affection for him.[3]

Contributions

Anonymous Contribution. At St Edward's during the 1930s.

I am sorry that it has taken so long to answer your letter about homosexuality. The reason for the delay is that my wife knows nothing about my boyhood experiences of homosexuality. Please do not acknowledge this letter . . .

Homosexual relationships were a mixture of a game and some very deep and occasionally painful affairs. This was partly due to the fact that in those days life in a public school was like a closed order in a monastery and it was quite normal to go for a term without setting eyes on a girl. Although we discussed these affairs we did not mention any homosexual acts in which we may have indulged . . . I was only involved in one of these acts on two occasions and I think that they were comparatively rare in the school, though boys disappeared from time to time and we supposed that they had been caught and expelled . . . We were so carefully watched that if two boys managed to get away on their own they were probably breaking a rule somewhere.

AIR COMMODORE JAMES LEATHART. At St Edward's in the 1930s.

[Any] interest shown in the younger boys was referred to as 'tarting', but those who were known 'tartists' were in a small minority. Any senior boys caught doing what, I never really knew what at the time, were 'birched by the headmaster'. Birching was said to be much more painful than beating and its results could plainly be seen at the swimming pool. Those displaying these marks were generally despised by the majority.

Anonymous Contribution. At St Edward's during the 1950s.

Bathnight is my fondest memory. It was the only occasion when we were allowed to leave prep early. I hated prep. There was always some unfriendly senior in charge. One evening I was ordered to the prefect's room for eating an apple. As I explained my offence to a small circle of self-important prefects I didn't think it necessary to point out that it wasn't the most heinous of crimes. But my optimism about their interpretation of the law was ill-founded. 'Go away'. It was a ritualistic dismissal which always heralded a further summons minutes later to the bathroom. Why the bathroom? Well, it was one of the few places in our house that a cane-wielding prefect could get a long enough run up to deliver a painful sting.

I hated petty tyranny and as bathnight was the only moment in the weekly timetable which was unsupervised you can imagine how I looked forward to it. Only four of us had the privilege on any one night but myself and another boy called Jonathan [name changed] always made sure that on our bathnight we arrived there before the others. Neither were we slow to make use of those few moments of privacy. In fact Jonathan and I wanked each other so many times I can't remember what the first occasion was like.

At school I never thought of myself as gay. I don't think I even remember hearing the word 'homosexual'. Besides, none of the boys thought it particularly unusual either to have a crush on someone or to fool around a bit. I remember a friend of mine; he is now happily married with children. Then, however, he was always after the boys. 'Oh look there's Middleton [false name]', he would announce suddenly and we would follow Middleton discreetly round the whole school. He had such a beautiful profile but he was unattainable as he was in a different year and house.

My house had been built in the twenties and stood just a little back from the main quadrangle. But despite its relative modernity none of the toilets had any doors. It really was a humiliation not to be able to defecate in privacy and it was impossible to have a wank. That was a terrible inconvenience.

The house did however have one great asset. It had a day room on the first floor which was quite empty except for a few of us who would go up there to observe this or that boy crossing the quadrangle. In the summer this advantage was no longer valued. Then one could take up an even better observation post – a comfortable position on the quadrangle grass – where I would try or sometimes just pretend to read a book.

Whenever I grew bored of observing the boys on the quadrangle, I would walk down to the outside swimming pool where boys swam naked. I didn't stay in the pool for a moment longer than tact required as the water was always so cold; but I spent many a happy hour drying off in the sun and watching the more handsome youths parade their bodies along the water's edge.

It all seems so long ago but despite all the years that have passed since I'm still very nostalgic about my schooldays as you might guess from all my photographs. I'd kept them locked away for years and framed them just recently. The boy standing at the back there; that's Jonathan. I often wonder whether he turned out to be gay. I did, but I don't think that had anything to do with having gone to a boarding school.

SEDBERGH

This school does not need an introduction (except to mention that it was founded in 1525 and is situated on the edge of the Lake District) as the playwright John Arden has kindly supplied a vivid portrayal of Sedberghian life in his recollection below.

Contribution

JOHN ARDEN. Playwright. At Sedbergh in the 1940s.

Sedbergh was not one of those upper-crust public schools, nor a second-string establishment of the sort one might rudely describe as Home Counties twit-factories. The parents of most of the boys were professional class from the northern part of England and from Scotland; and there was a decidedly 'functional' attitude towards life – an ethos of responsible self-reliance based on the less excitable aspects of protestant ideology. The school's religious atmosphere was strong without being pietistic; and I would say that nearly all the boys subscribed to this – at least with part of their minds and for part of the time. It was balanced by a rather brisk no-nonsense sardonic cynicism, also maintained by most of the boys for some of the time. Contradictory characteristics, which I have found to be common throughout northern English and Scottish life. The contradiction was not resolved, I suspect it was not capable of resolution. But it did help to disperse that sort of adolescent guilt-obsession which religious schooling often seems to breed. The school's ethos was also largely bound up with a post-Wordsworthian cult of the fell-country. We were supposed to be inspired by the high bare hills surrounding the dale where Sedbergh lies, and to a considerable extent I believe we were. We had to run over them often enough.

All this, in relation to sex, particularly homosexual sex, meant that lustful and/or idealistic yearnings were always qualified by peer-group pressures towards a sense of the ridiculous, a desire to keep things in proportion, an understanding that what were known as 'moral fosses' (school slang for 'serious talks') by housemasters or headmasters were basically absurd as well as being probably worth listening to. Boys who were genuinely impressed by such discourses would also laugh at them afterwards and satirical imitations of them would crop up in end-of-term concerts. The masters were no less subject to these sanctions than the boys; in general, sanctimonious gush was totally avoided by them. Homosexuality was presented to us, by them, as being not so much perverted etc., as a self-indulgent waste of time.

Senior boys were (under strict limitations) allowed to beat younger ones with canes, very occasionally – or slippers – for the more minor infringements of school rules. In regard specifically to the caning, I know now that there was definitely a homosexual sadomasochism involved in the experience. I say, I know now: in fact, I knew it then. I never heard of anyone being in a position to indulge in it to a point of no return, but it was the subject of rather suspect humour; boys knew what to think of it, and knew that their own feelings were perhaps disreputable. Cruelty in the school was not ever-present as an underground current, as I believe it is at some schools, to judge from people's memoirs. In this area it was recognized and deprecated, but it continued to seep up because of the official sanction of this punishment-system.

If adult British attitudes toward homosexuality are all out-of-balance, as I think they are, the public-school canings have a lot to do with it: they teach or they used to teach the powerful a kind of lust which is indivisible from the coercion that accompanies it, and – in public life (as for example at a Tory Party Conference) – can be turned against homosexuality-as-an-expression-of-love in the name of robust moral values. Also, the canes used were the swagger-sticks carried by the cadet officers in the school corps; the associations were thus carried over into our (quite moderate, given the years – mid-1940s) cult of juvenile militarism.

The fagging system played its part in romantic attachments. The young boys acted as 'gentlemen's gentlemen' to the prefects, and very often there were warm feelings. I never heard of any carnal expression of them, as far as I remember they stayed at the level of romance. I myself, when seventeen or eighteen, and a prefect, had a definite crush on a younger boy aged about fourteen. I cannot remember whether he fagged for me; I think he did, for a time. I do remember that once, when I was chatting (I suppose flirtatiously) another prefect came past and said, 'I'd like a word with you about exams, if I can tear you away from your *lustknabe*?' (this was from his knowledge of German and not regular school slang.) I was very shocked. I had not realized my affections had been so noticeable, and I had never attempted physical contact with the boy; but I did realize, perhaps for the first time, that the imputation was essentially correct. I just hoped my younger friend would not understand that *lustknabe* meant 'pleasure-boy'; I didn't think he would, he would not have been in a form where they learned German, unlike myself and the other prefect. Which is, I daresay, why the other prefect used a German word; he was being mischievously discreet.

I never found myself taking part in sexual experiments, I was not in that sort of circle. I think some of my friends were; but they chose not to include me in their doings. Of course, we talked a lot about it; guessing at who was 'doing it', either homosexually in school or heterosexually at home or out in the town. I do not remember that this gossip made any distinction between homo and hetero, from a 'judgemental' point of view. We just felt that some boys were luckier or braver than we were. There were various rakes and 'sex-maniacs' (as sexually-experienced boys were often described) in the school whose alleged exploits were common currency. There was a lot of 'alleged' about it all.

In my last two years I discovered that a key to acceptance (if one could not shine at athletics) was to cultivate an artistic bohemianism. In order to do this I wore a long overcoat in all weathers. It wasn't exactly effeminate, it was just odd. It was a curious school, in one way; the arts were as 'respectable' as games. One could avoid a great deal of wretched physical exercise by joining an art class which met in the afternoon twice a week and went out of doors to do landscape painting. This was not (in general) sneered at; and no one suggested any sexual connotations.

Am I getting off the subject? Not really: for games, art and sex all seem to me to have hung together as different aspects of school life which one saw as a whole and from which one took what experiences one could. I was in love for a time with a boy of my own age in the art class; I don't think he realized my feelings, and I don't think they were reciprocated. But we were good enough friends, in any case, on a non-erotic level. As well as being an artist, he was a pretty good athlete. Then his younger brother played a female role in a school play in which I was also acting, and I fell in love with him. Again, it was not overtly requited and I did not press it.

I'd better say, I did not know any girls all the time I was at school; and at home (being an only child and shy) I never got to know any either. I was sufficiently aware of myself to feel that I was likely to have romantic attractions to boys as long as I was at a single sex school, and that after that the serious business of girls was going to come up, which I both longed for and dreaded!

There was an alarming event in my last year, when I was head prefect of my house. A friend of mine, a boy I'll call X, had left school and gone to work in business. He had told me, long before, that the headmaster of the prep school he'd been at had sexually abused him, and other little boys there. It was a prep school that [regularly] sent . . . boys to Sedbergh. Then two boys (not in the same house as myself) were caught 'shagging' (the school slang for mastur-bating) each other. Interrogation by the housemaster established that one of them – the instigator – had learned the habit at prep school. I was in corre-spondence with X at the time. I told him what had happened, and was horri-fied to get a letter from him giving a great list of others from that prep school whom he knew, most of whom were still at Sedbergh. He asked me to take some action, 'for the good name of Sedbergh', a dreadful sort of McCarthyite situation. I did not know what to do. There was quite enough inquisitorial horror going on in the school already without my adding extra names to it from an external informant. I never answered his letter, and I did nothing about it. The boys who were convicted on the basis of the existing investigation were . . . [I presume] severely caned . . .

The headmaster of the prep school was said to have been telephoned [and] . . . told 'All is known!' and given a week to sell his school and retire into private life or else the police would be informed. Everybody who was not personally involved in this great scandal was excited and entertained by it, except me – X's letter made me feel like a citizen of a totalitarian state. I think of it every time I read in the papers of people in [the former German Democratic Republic] who are now found to have been agents of the *Stasi*.

SHERBORNE

The origins of the school go back to the eighth century when it was part of the Benedictine Abbey of Sherborne. It is still (as of 1994) a boys-only school.

Traditionally much of a boy's school-life was confined to his house but the rigid segregations have gradually been eroded. Meals are now taken centrally and a boy may chose with whom he wishes to sit, although seniors wishing to mix with juniors might well be subjected to reproach from their peers.

Until recently it was not easy for a boy to make friends with boys in other houses. When the scientist and code-breaker Alan Turing fell for a boy called Christopher Morcom, Alan had to devise a means by which he could associate with Christopher. This proved almost impossible even though only a year separated their ages. One partial solution was a joint attendance at the gramophone society: 'There he could sit and steal glances at Christopher while the seventy-eights played out their disjointed versions of the great symphonies.'[1] Eventually, however, they began to write to each other in the holidays and as Turing's biographer explains, 'He did more than write to Christopher – he invited him to Guildford. Ross, as housemaster, would have been horrified by this audacious step.'[2]

The school's staff was paranoid about the possibility of the school acquiring a 'bad name'. Over ten years had passed since the publication of Alec Waugh's *Loom of Youth*. Though nominally fictional, its accounts of passionate friendships were clearly based on the author's experience of Sherborne and the book was still banned from the school. Predictably, however, the ban only encouraged boys to read it.[3]

Contribution

CAPTAIN JOHN MOORE. Editor, Jane's Fighting Ships, 1972–87. At Sherborne 1936–39.

On one occasion I dropped a heavy weight on to the toes of one of my closest friends. Most of his non-school time was spent with the horses and grooms at home so his agonized cry of 'Oh, you bugger' was not unexpected. Unfortunately it was overheard by X who immediately ordered a beating. I consulted the Oxford Dictionary where I found 'Bugger (noun): a term of friendship amongst sailors.' When I explained this to X and suggested that the term was appropriate as I was bound for the navy I nearly got beaten as well.

SHREWSBURY

The school is situated on a splendid site overlooking the river Severn and the old town of Shrewsbury. Originally, it was located in the city itself and the lack of room for expansion meant that it was not until the headmastership of Benjamin Kennedy (1836–66) that all boys were assigned single beds. By then it was considered such an urgent requirement that it was carried out despite the resulting drop in the number of boarders and income.[1]

James McConnell in *English Public Schools* comments, 'The Salopian of today . . . has a lot of personal freedom and is quite happy without girls in the school.'[2] Perhaps this is because the boys enjoy 'close links with several local girls' schools'.[3] However, the present situation is in sharp contrast with much of Shrewsbury's history during which there was little freedom – sexual or otherwise.

The restrictions on inter-house mixing used to be enforced rigorously. The Old Salopian David Walker, who was later imprisoned in the German fortress Colditz, referred to 1920s Shrewsbury as a 'regimented society' in which 'there was not much opportunity for assignation'. Yet despite these impediments to open flirtation he admitted that 'Romance was fairly rife at Shrewsbury. Big boys fell for appealing small boys, and the other way round.'[4] Brian Inglis (editor of the *Spectator*, 1959–62) had similar recollections: 'For a monitor to be 'crashed' on a 'doul' was fashionable. There was rarely any sexual consumma- tion but this did not prevent the affairs, while they lasted, being highly emotion- ally charged; pleasurably, though gooily romantic . . .'[5] A scandal rocked the school in 1932 when a wealthy housemaster, J.B. Oldham, confessed to an overly passionate night with a senior boy in London with the predictable result that the head received a furious letter from a parent demanding that justice be done. The solution arrived at, however, was something of a compromise, if only because Oldham held the leasehold of the house. After some difficult bargain- ing it was agreed that he should step down as housemaster, but that he be allowed to keep his post as school librarian. When the headmaster requested Sopwith, an assistant master, to take over Oldham's house because 'Oldham had had a breakdown', Sopwith protested that Oldham seemed perfectly normal, only to be told, 'I mean, he's going to have a breakdown.'[6]

Contributions

MICHAEL MORGAN. Ambassador to the Philippines (1981–85) remembers the late 1930s/early 1940s.

I was [already] 5' 7" when I went to Shrewsbury and never troubled by homo- sexuality myself and as far as I am aware there was no homosexuality in my house . . . but there was certainly a fairly general knowledge of what was involved.

There was during my time a fairly widely publicized incident, of which I cannot remember the details, but which caused the headmaster, H.H. Hardy, to preach a sermon about millstones hanging about our necks and I can remember the titters about a pretty young man who had been evacuated to Shrewsbury along with other pupils of Cheltenham School. But I suspect that he, in common with most of the other 'small boys' (the term for the pretty boys if I remember rightly), was fairly robust and not unduly susceptible to bullying.

Editorial Note:

Matthew 18 v6:

> Whoever causes one of these little ones who believe in me to sin, it would be better for him to have a great millstone fastened round his neck and to be drowned in the depth of the sea.[7]

JULIAN CRITCHLEY. Conservative MP for Aldershot since 1974. At Shrewsbury in the 1940s.

Nothing overt used to happen: too many cold baths, football and supervised activity. I.F. Wolfenden, however, would assemble school on Monday mornings in the Alington Hall (instead of in chapel). There would be a few hymns and then a pep talk about purity and dark threats of punitive action. Most of us had no idea what he was alluding to!

THE VEN. RICHARD MASON. Archdeacon of Tonbridge. At Shrewsbury in the 1940s.

My Salopian memories are now a little distant, but the aspects of school life you are covering were certainly real enough at the time. I think I may have been more innocent than many, but I certainly had 'crushes' and I can remember all the objects of my admiration, three in all. They were all in other houses and none of them could possibly have known about my 'infatuation'. This silent and distant worship was the limit of my romantic feeling at school.

I think I was aware that there were lots of other 'crushes' going on, but for the most part they weren't discussed and I wouldn't have dreamed of mentioning mine to anyone. I wasn't aware of any active homosexuality ... nor did it seem to be talked about excessively. Yet there were 'pretty' boys who were coveted by older ones and they tended to be known as 'tarts', with the letter 'T' formed by fingers to taunt them. Very often I suspect that these young boys were innocent enough but found it hard not to be flattered by the attentions of older 'men', not least because the barriers between 'years' were totally rigid and it was the custom (and in the circumstances rather a good and effective one) for there to be no communication across the great divide except in the most formal sense. Ordinary friendships consequently were confined to one's own year group.

Editorial Note:

It is interesting to note the changes of vocabulary during the next years. By the 1950s Old Salopian Dr Euan Clarkson recalls:

Attractive boys were known as 'T-boys'. Why, I have never been able to understand. I don't think that they were singled out to any great extent or bullied; rather they seemed to be favoured. Such was the nature of the strange environment which then prevailed that one might well be castigated far more by one's fellows for clandestinely kissing one of the kitchen maids than for boasting about homosexual prowess!

Anonymous Contributor. At Shrewsbury in the 1970s.

I am in my thirties. I was brought up outside a small town in Wales. I have one brother and two sisters. I went to a preparatory school in England when I was seven, and then to Shrewsbury school when I was thirteen.

When I went to prep school I was a spindly child, rather weak for my age, and very shy. During my first term, I was repeatedly sexually abused by an older boy; not much older, but for his age much better developed and stronger than me. Quite how an eight-year-old could have devised what he did to me, I do not know. I would rather not describe it further, if that is all right . . .

Although the boys could do hideous things to each other, as I well knew, there was nevertheless a sense that we were all together against the teachers. I had no such sense at Shrewsbury. I fairly soon appreciated that my contemporaries were the enemy.

I realized that I was gay when I was fourteen. My fantasies so far had been heterosexual, but had never featured any girl I had ever met, only some sort of idealized made-up woman cobbled together from books, etc.. I experimented one night with thinking about some of the older boys, and it was with a sense of relief, or release, that I recognized that I was gay.

Shrewsbury was considered a progressive school, and one of the manifestations of this, I assume, was the close links forged with local girls' schools. There were several school dances to which the girls were invited. I never went.

The culture at the place was homophobic (not that I had the word to hand at the time). I do not mean simply that the school rules were against it, though obviously they were, and there were occasional flurries of gossip about boys being found in bed together and expelled. What I mean is that the boys' culture was homophobic, intensely homophobic. The standard phrase was 'filthy queer'. No reference to homosexuality of any sort was voiced without this epithet.

As I have already said, I was extremely shy at prep school. This did not leave me. I was totally adrift at Shrewsbury. Almost everything about the interests and culture of my contemporaries was completely baffling. I simply did not understand why what they found important – the intense jostling for status as marked out by tiny details of achievement and dress, the obsessive interest in sport (both in the school and in the wider world), the overt and loudly voiced disparagement of anyone who was different or failed to fit in any way – was important. I sought refuge in anonymity (a 'non-entity' in the slang), simply hoping to get through each day without anyone, teachers or pupils, realizing that I was there at all. This was not a wholly successful strategy. The shabby, ill-repaired, ill-fitting and outdated garments that my mother foisted on me made me an obvious target. And of course, I was, although I never dared to show it, a 'filthy queer'.

I never told anyone that I was gay; I never made any attempt to make contact with anyone in the school who may have been gay; I did not know of anyone who may really have been gay. The bits of gossip I heard about various people were retailed to me with such an air of maliciousness that I assumed that it could not possibly be true, as animosity seemed to be the primary reason for the gossip. I passed through the place totally on my own, completely isolated and excluded from everything and everyone. I had no close friends, although I became pally enough with a few boys there. But we lost touch when I left, and I do not regret this; I have no intention of making any contact with anyone I knew there, and if I were to meet any one of them again, I would not know what to say to them, or indeed want to say anything at all.

I assumed for many years that my experience at Shrewsbury was typical; and that the notion that public schools were hotbeds of sexual activity was completely outmoded. I discovered a couple of years ago from a Wykehamist, two or three years younger than me, that in his day sexual activity was rife. Apparently they had a game called 'Chicken', which involved moving your hand further and further up someone's thigh, until the inevitable happened. Even the straights joined in with alacrity. It is utterly impossible for me to imagine this happening at Shrewsbury in my day. Even if it had, I do not know if I would have dared to join in.

The main point I am trying to make is the extreme sense of isolation and loneliness I felt, the utter desolation of my life there . . . I must make it clear that I have no complaints about Shrewsbury as a place of learning. It was excellent. I simply objected to the boys' culture of the place. Presumably all the petty absurdities and obsessions, the narrow-minded intolerance and horrible, relentless pressure to conform that my fellows displayed are simply manifesta-tions of the nature of closed communities, and not particularly their fault, as such. But I cannot help feeling now that (although I may have been let down by my parents) I was betrayed by my contemporaries and I find it difficult to forgive them even now.

STONYHURST

Originally founded in 1593 as a Jesuit School at St Omers in France, it fled the French Revolution to its present bleak location on the edge of the Longridge Fells in Lancashire in 1794.

Stonyhurst has long had a reputation for an austere moral climate. In his autobiography, *Memoirs and Adventures*, Sir Arthur Conan Doyle recalled that when he visited the school in 1871 masters constantly patrolled the dormitories and that even in the day boys were never left to their own devices. He claimed that, as a consequence, 'the immorality which is rife in public schools was at a minimum.'[1] By the 1920s the degree of vigilance had, if anything, increased. The biographer of Old Boy Charles Laughton explains:

> Watchful Jesuit officials were in charge of the boys every second – on or off the playground, in or out of the classroom – and worked in night shifts in the dormitories to suppress the slightest show of sexual feeling. They were grim plainclothes policemen, not permitted to smile while on duty, or to talk to their charges.[2]

Contribution

THE REVD JOHN COVENTRY. *Master, St Edmund's, Cambridge, 1976–85. At Stonyhurst in the late 1920s/early 1930s.*

I left school in 1932. My overriding impression then (and subsequently as a master in a boarding school) is that my contemporaries . . . having no feminine outlet, turned somewhat to the prettier boys. Those who did so included the rugger types, who demonstrated their heterosexuality in later life. So I don't think inter-boy relations should be taken so seriously . . .

The senior boys voted each year on the prettiest 'tart' among the new boys. I don't think I ever got a vote. But a nineteen-year-old master added to the staff at an early age got at least one.

STOWE

Stowe is surrounded by 750 acres of magnificent gardens laid out by Capability Brown and enriched with chestnut trees, rose beds and ready lakelets; but while the main mansion and its estate date back to the eighteenth century, the school itself is both relatively modern (founded in 1923) and by reputation progressive. Even in its early days there were no tail coats or stiff collars, but nevertheless it was according to Old Boy Sir Peregrine Worsthorne 'an entirely self-contained community'. Few women were ever seen on the school grounds and 'such feminine grace of charm as existed was supplied by pretty boys'.[1]

Neither did the school authorities demonstrate any latitude towards homo-sexuality. Roxburgh, the school's first headmaster, was keen to prevent it from becoming as prevalent as it had been during his own days as a pupil at Charterhouse. He insisted that the seats in chapel should not face inwards, an arrangement he considered perilous as it might have encouraged boys to engage in flirtatious glances. Similarly he prevented plans to raise the floor level for the choir. Comprised, as it was, mainly of juniors, he was worried that they might become the innocent targets of predatory glances.[2]

Later, when he heard that the most promising candidate for school head was himself consorting with juniors, Roxburgh warned him personally that even if the slightest shadow of suspicion was aroused again, it would bar him from any prospect of promotion. But Roxburgh realized he would be unable in most cases to suppress such passions. He even joked to one housemaster that the only solution to homosexuality would be to establish a school brothel.[3]

Old Stoic Peregrine Worsthorne remembered receiving both 'the patron-age of (the) older boys' and the attentions of at least one of his contemporaries who he claims seduced him one afternoon on the art room sofa. Years later they met again when by chance they were on the same television programme. 'He was defending permissiveness,' recalls Worsthorne, 'and I attacking it. After the show his very young new wife, who was accompanying him . . . gave me a contemptuous dressing-down as a typical example of buttoned-up, inhib-ited, bourgeois, kill-joy puritanism . . . "It might interest you to know, madam," I was able to reply, "that you and I have more in common than you care to recognize. We were both seduced in our teens by George Melly."'[4] Besides Worsthorne and Melly, other famous Old Stoics include David Niven, Lord Sainsbury and Richard Branson. Niven later recalled the jovial, almost perverse, pleasure with which boys and masters alike admired the marks of those who had been beaten. '"Pretty good shooting I'd call that . . . looks like a two-inch group." He [the housemaster] was his usual smiling, kindly self.'[5] When Niven returned to the dormitory he was again the centre of attention; 'In the darkness . . . the whispers started – "How many did you get?" . . . "Did you blub?" . . . "What sort of cane is it?" . . . "Promise to show us in the morning." All friendly whispers.'[6]

Contributions

MAJOR-GENERAL DAVID EGERTON. At Stowe in the late 1920s/early 1930s.

Your letter asking for help in your forthcoming book . . . set me wondering whether, in the case of Stowe, there was not a great deal more talk than practice . . . Quite obviously, there were crushes; some boys were obviously objects of desire, because of their looks, but I can only think of about two cases where there was actual buggery, mostly with consent. (There was a nastier case on an OTC [Officer Training Corps] field study when a boy was sacked for 'disgraceful conduct'.)

On the other hand, Stowe has a marvellous collection of follies and temples, which must have offered opportunities for clandestine affairs. They did happen, but I just do not know how much: I was rather naive myself. A friend of mine was a good deal more active, and I know he had two 'affairs' . . .

I remember worshipping a boy from afar; it got no further than lending him a cushion for some concert. I think I knew that anything further between two boys of different ages would lead to a lot of ragging, and would embarrass the younger. There would have been remarks that X was my 'bum boy' and I was very susceptible to that sort of ragging.

In those days we were even more worried about masturbation. We were all convinced that it would ruin our prowess at games!

JOHN DA SILVA. HM Diplomatic Service, retired. At Stowe in the 1930s.

I can recall only one boy at Stowe who I think was psychologically or, as people are now suggesting, genetically destined to be a homosexual, but there was in my time a certain amount of sexual groping between consenting juveniles who had no other outlet for their instincts except, as I used to do, gazing at the naked bosoms of the eighteenth century nymphs on the ceiling of the Painted Hall in which we ate.

PROFESSOR EDWIN BESTERMAN. Cardiologist. At Stowe in the late 1930s/early 1940s.

In reply to your queries about homosexuality at my school I recall that there was a lot of interest shown in the subject during my time there . . . A poll was conducted in my house (seventy-plus boys) on this and allied topics. Mutual masturbation was the commonest pastime and all except four of us admitted to this practice. No other physical relationship was admitted. 'Crushes' occasionally occurred between older boys and pretty younger ones; the latter always exploited this for favours of food, less arduous games and other innocent pleasures. However this was far rarer than encountered in girls' schools from what I have heard.

A TEACHER'S PERSPECTIVE

Anonymous Contribution

I'm gay. I've known it ever since September 1941 when aged seventeen I fell for an evacuee boy on the north beach at Tenby. My attraction to him was not overtly sexual but rather sentimental, perhaps even romantic. He was so friendly to me and I enjoyed his company so much for the hour or so we were together that when he cycled off I suddenly felt an emptiness inside me. It was then, I think, that I realized I was homosexual. The next year, 1942, I was called up, but I failed the medical because of bad asthma although at least I was fortunate enough to gain admission to Cambridge University to study mathematics and then to Bristol where I obtained a diploma in education.

My first teaching job was at a small school in the Lake District where I was a resident tutor for the thirty-eight boarders. Basically this meant that whenever the headmaster, who was also the school's housemaster, was busy, it was my job to look after the boarding boys.

I found a few of the boys very beautiful. I was certainly not captivated by the average spotty boy but there were occasional youths whose looks held an almost irresistible magnetism for me. I should stress, however, that I never touched any of them sexually and indeed I can't even remember hugging a boy.

Nevertheless I did get into trouble once. One of the prefects was very fond of hiking and for some reason one Whitsun holiday his parents had planned to travel abroad. I also had plans. I had decided to take time off in Keswick as it seemed an excellent location from which to explore the mountains and the homeless prefect kept asking me if he could come too. I eventually agreed under the condition that he wrote to his parents and obtained permission, which he did.

Unfortunately, after a long and tiring search of Keswick and its environs, the only vacant hotel bedroom we could find had just one double bed in it and so we took it and put the balustrade down the middle of the bed to act as a partition. I was completely naive and innocent as to the possible implications.

I felt nothing sexually for this boy though I confess I was happy enough to have him along as a holiday companion. Anyway, soon after we got back to school the headmaster sent for me and wanted to know what had happened. He waffled a little and then said, 'Don't you know that this sort of thing leads to gossip?' to which I replied that I had the parents' permission and had never considered that there was anything questionable about what we had done. I'm afraid after that the headmaster and I were daggers drawn.

In 1961 I joined the staff of a school situated near the edge of the Salisbury Plain. I was soon put in charge of a house and I enjoyed those five years greatly. The school received many boys who had failed to get into more famous schools, but the lads were a friendly lot and I think the quality of education was actually very good and later I was to come to regret leaving it for a more prestigious post at an HMC school.

I do, however, remember one difficult character. She was a colonel's widow and was the acting matron for one term. For some reason she took an instant dislike to me and one day made a very barbed comment: 'You imagine that you're the father of these boys. Why don't you marry and have children of your own?' She knew immediately she had hit her mark and marched off leaving me speechless.

There was another difficult incident back in my first year when I had not yet become a fully-fledged housemaster and held the second-in-command position of house tutor, a sort of housemaster apprenticeship I suppose. Anyway, I recall that one rather lonely boy developed a habit of coming up to my room for a chat. He wasn't the most charming or good-looking of boys, but I didn't like to discourage his visits as I thought it my duty to act *in loco parentis*. Then one day the head mentioned these visits to me. He was careful not to make the issue sound too important but it was very evident that he was more than a little anxious about the situation. I explained that I had never invited the boy and that the visits had been made entirely on his own initiative and the head seemed happy with my response. I don't know whether he then spoke to the boy, but in any event the visits tailed off.

But while there may have been the occasional unwelcome intrusion by the head into school life, it was only on going to my next school in the West Country that I became aware how oppressive and underhand school authorities could be. There was a pleasant and kindly school chaplain and it was rumoured in the staff room that he was the victim of the 'new broom' brought in by a change in the headmastership. Apparently the new head had asked the chaplain to let him know anything that the boys might reveal in confidence. The chaplain had refused but soon found himself under such pressure that he decided he had no option but to resign.

There were also other aspects of the school which I found somewhat unsavoury. Several members of staff, particularly the housemaster for whom I acted as a deputy, were always well informed about everything I was doing. I felt for the first time in twenty years of teaching that all my actions were being monitored. It was like living in a totalitarian state. I couldn't talk to a boy or take a walk across town without the housemaster knowing.

Neither did life appear much easier for the boys. The previous headmaster had introduced rules banning boys from talking to their seniors or even to their contemporaries if they lived in other houses. These regulations no longer existed on paper and were never mentioned in the staff room but they still exerted an unseen influence to such an extent that a housemaster would rarely give permission for two boys from different houses or of different ages to go out together, however legitimate the reasons advanced.

I don't think that any one headmaster can be blamed for the authoritarian ethos that pervaded the school. This seemed to have deep roots. It even appeared that large parts of the school had been designed to facilitate surveil-lance. My own study was a case in point. Built in the late nineteenth century, it had two large dormitories on either side; but in the dividing walls were two niches which until the recent past had evidently been windows enabling the housemaster to keep a wary eye on his boys. And as if this was not in itself a sufficient deterrent there were four prefects appointed to each dormitory, one to each corner, so that whatever a boy did he could not hide his actions from at least one of the prefects. I'm surprised the system was never introduced into prisons.

I never felt happy with the school. The only friendships I had in the staff room were very superficial. I think my activities in helping the scouts on several of their expeditions perhaps made me unpopular. I'm surprised they couldn't see that I had genuine reasons for being interested in such activities. I loved hiking and the outdoor life and many of the boys shared the same enthusiasms and as I had both my own transport and an ideally-located cottage in north Devon it would have been odd if I hadn't become involved. It's strange how the staff could be so suspicious.

UPPINGHAM

Uppingham can claim one of the nineteenth century's most celebrated head-masters, Edward Thring, founder of the Headmaster's Conference. His memory is lauded in the school's current promotional video but in his own time he had a reputation as an avid flogger. *Punch* commented, 'We don't know whether Mr Thring trains the boys' minds; but he makes them mind their trains.'[1] However, on rare occasions he did show affection:

> I had a little boy . . . in to speak to, who had been lying, and I spoke to him very seriously. When I had finished I held out my hand to him and he took it, and on my shaking hands and drawing him forward he fell on my neck weeping and kissed me, and I him.[2]

But Thring remained a firm disciplinarian, declaring in one of his sermons that 'This whole world is one great exercise ground for the practice of strength.'[3] It is even rumoured that following an outbreak of typhoid he warned that boys asking their parents to take them away would be considered 'cowards and deserters'.[4]

His immediate successor was equally severe. Dr Edward Selwyn (headmaster 1888–1907) was furious when he learned that some Sisters of Mercy had been waylaying his boys in the local town, even though it was in order to request charity. He immediately posted a notice in the school: 'All nuns are out of bounds, by order.'[5]

An infinitely more liberal Uppingham headmaster was Sir John Wolfenden who later chaired the inquiry that produced the 1957 report on prostitution and homosexuality.

Famous Old Uppinghamians include Ronald Firbank and Stephen Fry.

Contributions

JOHN GLEAVE. *Consultant Neurosurgeon Emeritus of Addenbrooke's Hospital. At Uppingham in the late 1930s/early 1940s.*

. . . I quite early acquired the idea that male comradeship was superior to heterosexual love as a result of receiving a good classical education and perhaps because in 1939 and 1940 we were in pretty desperate straights. The example of the Sacred Band at Chaeronea, never mind the general ethos of the Spartans, was very much on our minds . . .

I think on one occasion in my first year I was suspected of homosexual activity because I was found in an older boy's study after lights out. The fact that I was helping him with his prep did not save me from a beating.

Anonymous Contribution

I was at Uppingham in the 1950s. This was a school isolated on top of hills in the smallest county of England – Rutland. The previous headmaster – Wolfenden – was notorious for his liberal report on homosexuality but his successor, Martin Lloyd, returned the school to the strict Victorian virtues of Edward Thring, who, with Arnold of Rugby, had laid down the rules of the British public school system . . .

The only incident I can recall was when two senior boys were found together at the top of a church tower one Sunday afternoon. It was never disclosed what they were doing but our housemaster wept publicly that evening at house prayers and we were asked to pray for their forgiveness.

A WAR-TIME SCHOOL

Anonymous Contribution

Prior to school, my background was very ordinary. My father was an Anglican parson of a north London parish and although he normally deferred to my mother on most important family decisions, it was he who chose my school for me. Or perhaps it would be more accurate to say that he selected my older brother's school and I inevitably followed in my brother's footsteps.

I went to the junior branch of the school in 1937, aged nine. Its buildings were scattered close to some precipitous cliffs on the Channel coast and in the summer of 1940, just after the fall of France, its position became untenable. We had three nights of successive air-raid alarms and we were barely able to keep awake during class. Anyway, the Ministry of Defence came to our rescue by requisitioning a hotel in a mining village strung out along a remote valley several hundred miles away.

It was here that I lost my virginity to another boy in our makeshift dormitory. Until that moment, which came in the second year at senior school, I had had little or no sexual experience. I don't think that I even learned to masturbate until after leaving junior school. Neither had I ever had what I later learned was called a 'crush' on someone, though I do remember sitting in the back row of my father's church and admiring the legs of the boy scouts sitting in their shorts in the row in front. However, I can't remember exactly how I felt. Was it sexual desire? I don't know.

I think it was the evacuation which created the opportunity for sexual liai-sons. In the cramped confines of the hotel the house system which operated in the senior school was no longer viable and even the various age groups could no longer be so easily divided. At least, it now became possible to fraternize with boys of either a class above or below, who because of unavoidable over-crowding, often shared the same accommodation.

The hotel dormitory of my second year as a senior is a case in point. It had been the hotel lounge and wooden blackout shutters masked the windows. My neighbours comprised a sixth-former who was the dormitory captain and six other boys, both from my own year and the year above. After lights-out the windows were unshuttered and opened ajar to ventilate the room. This meant that no one could suddenly switch on the lights without contravening the blackout regulations and so we had, I suppose, an unfair advantage over the school authorities. Though, of course, it didn't pay to be persistently reckless.

One night the dormitory captain came in unexpectedly early. I and another boy were engrossed in a wanking contest and were so surprised that we both tumbled out of our beds. He was fortunately gentleman enough to recognize the inconsiderate timing of his entrance and was duly merciful. Another night, sometime before the captain was due to come up, a big boy from the year above sat on my bed in the dark and asked me very directly if he could climb in. Such candour might seem surprising but sex games, varying from size comparisons to mutual masturbation, had become common practice among most of the boys. Anyway, I was loath to refuse the request and after some initial explora-tion, he instructed me in the art of anal sex with myself as insertor and himself as recipient. With hindsight I am sure that he was very experienced, not just because of his confidence as instructor but because his anus was so loose. However, when he tried to penetrate me it proved too painful and we must have woken up the others in the dormitory, one or two of whom made comments later.

The next year we found ourselves in different dormitories but we deter-mined to continue our affair and used to meet at the outside bogs round the back of the hotel. Here there was one particularly useful cubicle which did not have any gap beneath its partition, and this became our regular rendezvous. At first, it was always he who was the initiator of these trysts but as time went past it was more often I who had to persuade him to accompany me.

Gradually I began to realize that I alone of my form mates remained pecu-liarly disinterested in their growing fascination with the opposite sex. Boys braved expulsion in their attempts to seduce the maids and returned from holidays bragging about girls they had conquered. All their friends sat enrap-tured, except me. I continued to remind my older partner that pleasure now was better than pleasure postponed, but in reality I was somewhat doubtful that the supposed allure of women would ever captivate me and whenever possible continued to frequent the little pleasure palace that stood so temptingly close to the hotel's back door.

Recently, when I was hiking in the area, I returned to the site and was at first disappointed to find no sign of any structure that might once have housed the outdoor toilets. Then I realized that the back of the building had been extended and on opening the door of the gent's washroom was pleasantly surprised to find the infamous bogs which, disregarding some minor decorative differences, were exactly the same as they had been all those years ago.

WELLINGTON

For many years Wellington led all other schools in providing the armed services with officers. Consequently it placed and still places a strong emphasis on character formation. Discipline remains strict with juniors still required to do chores for their house. The 1991 Harpers and Queen *Good Schools Guide* remarked, 'Sound traditional public school education for the pupil who likes structure and discipline. Not good for free spirits.'

Wellington used to enforce the rules restricting friendships between houses vigorously. Harold Nicolson explained:

> It was not thought proper that boys should become acquainted with other boys who were not in their own house or dormitory. The range of our acquaintance was thus limited to the thirty boys who happened to be housed under the same roof. Ten of these boys were too old, and ten too young, for intimacy. One's radius of friendship was thus reduced to ten companions ... Most (but not all) housemasters at Wellington would defend the system on the grounds that it restricts opportunities for vice. I can assure them that in my day, the only result was to confine that vice (which is inevitable) into a narrow space where it became foetid, secretive and squalid to the last degree.[1]

Homosexual affections flourished despite all attempts to suppress them. According to T.C. Worsley, who taught at the school in the 1930s, homoeroticism pervaded the school,[2] and the actor and Old Wellingtonian Robert Morley regretted that because of his 'wrong shape' he had been unable to attract the sort of friends and lovers of whom his school friends had boasted.[3]

Ironically it had been E.W. Benson, Wellington's first headmaster, who pioneered many of the procedures (subsequently adopted by many other public schools) designed to minimize the incidence of homosexuality. His notebooks were full of detailed accounts of the problems of maintaining order and segregation. 'The danger is in an evening,' he observed, '. . . also in the afternoon when boys are tired of playing.' Unfortunately nothing seemed to work,[4] and in desperation he even considered nailing a wire lattice over the top of the boys' bedroom cubicles to prevent night time assignations (see chapter one).

Contributions

GAVIN EWART. *Writer and poet. At Wellington 1929–33.*

I was in a house, and not a dormitory. Houses were where the richer, non-military boys lived. They were regarded as sissy or more refined, depending on your point of view. I always imagined that the dormitories were wickeder . . . [Not long] before I went to College, six boys had been expelled from the Murray for nameless homosexual acts.

Hero worship did exist for athletes, and many boys, I suppose, had close friends. There wasn't anything of this kind noticeable in my house. But I was very innocent and so were we all. There were two friends of mine (but slightly older) whom I now suspect of having sex together. I never thought of this at the time. There was one boy who used to lie on top of other boys in their rooms (each boy had a cubicle with a bed in it, a 'birdcage' bookcase, a table and a chair). He did this to me once or twice. I thought it was odd (we were both fully clothed) but no more. I later found out that this was a common practice of his. We just thought of him as a bit of a loony.

I wasn't aware of 'crushes', but I had a close friend, A, who was. He was always (at the age of sixteen plus) talking about the attractions of B in the Orange, or C, younger boys who seemed very conscious of being good-looking. I don't think A got very far with either. But it was genuinely believed that some of the senior prefects in their dormitories did. My hero was Martin Munro, a tall good looking athlete who was the best long-distance runner in the school. I admired him, mostly I think because my father had been a half-blue at Cambridge in the Hare and Hounds and had cups and medals to prove it.

I also knew a boy called D, in one of the dormitories, who was always telling me of his exploits. He was in the shooting VIII, and said that masturbation before a match steadied his nerves. I think he did have sex with people. For me, he had the fascination of the disreputable. I wasn't moved in this way; my interest was in girls, and probably I was too afraid of the 'homosexual component'. At the age of seventeen plus, I remember, I did imagine for a short time that I was in love with A and I wrote him a letter to this effect in the holidays (we both lived in London). He rebuffed me (by letter) and that was the end of that; though he was always a friend of mine.

MICHAEL MEYER. *Author and translator. At Wellington in the 1930s.*

In my time the official attitude, as expressed by our headmaster F.B. Malin who left in 1937, was that 'sex does not exist'. Although I had crushes on several boys I never had sex with any of them (yes, with one, I now remember after fifty years). As far as I recall, I had tremendous guilt feelings about it, as of course about masturbation, which we were taught was practically the ultimate sin. There was a horrid book we were encouraged to read called *I Commit to Your Intelligence*, by I forget whom, which detailed the dreadful things that might happen to us if we masturbated. I thought . . . that I was the only boy in the school who committed this wickedness, and it left me with guilt feelings which persisted for years.

I don't know how many boys actually had sex together. It was something one felt one couldn't talk about. I wrote a novel about it, *The End of the Corridor*, which appeared in 1951, and was rather well received, though not at Wellington where it was banned, which ensured a steady underground circulation there. Over forty years later the current headmaster asked me if I would present a signed copy to the College library!

SURGEON VICE-ADMIRAL SIR JOHN RAWLINS. *At Wellington in the 1930s.*

My three brothers and I were in a house, the Wellesley, which was a quarter of a mile from College on the edge of Crowthorne village, and we had as little to do with our contemporaries in the other houses and dormitories as was humanly possible. We all hated Wellington, as did many others, mainly because we had a wonderful home life in the country in a Hampshire village, and our attitude to College was comparable to that of an inmate to an open prison . . .

When I was in my third term a house prefect had a crush on me for a brief period, which I found embarrassing: but it was not a problem and it didn't last long. I developed a similar interest in a fourteen-year-old during my last term but I very much doubt if he was aware of it. I suppose there must have been other such romances in house and certainly in College but they were no concern of mine and I couldn't hazard a guess at their prevalence . . .

There were young boys who were at one time or another alleged to be the flavour of the month and there were senior boys who had dark reputations as seducers, but how much truth there was in the allegations I have no idea. I suspect a good deal of it was wishful thinking. It wasn't my scene and I wasn't interested. In general, however, my guess is that around 95% of boys at public schools have had some sort of homosexual experience, mainly trivial . . .

As to the attitude of the boys [to homosexuality], many of us who were introduced to the facts of life by boys a year or so older than ourselves . . . were initially horrified. [However] as we grew older we accepted it as a facet of life at school. After all there wasn't much in the way of an alternative outlet for our burgeoning sexuality and the term 'homosexuality', in this context, although technically correct, is misleading. It was not based upon a desire for sexual expression with members of the same sex but was a substitute for the highly desirable but (largely) unobtainable sexual expression with members of the opposite sex, and I do not know of anyone whom I knew personally at Wellington who became an overt homosexual in adult life . . .

My tutor did subject us all to what you term a pep talk during our second term, for which we were all prepared in advance by our friends so that it was very difficult to keep a straight face. The burden of his short lecture was, 'I don't mind a fellow having a game with himself now and then but never let another fellow fiddle with your privates!' That was all.

In the Wellesley we were required to take a cold bath every morning, an unhygienic practice which, together with the shared hot baths after games, left most of us with various forms of epidermophytosis (athlete's foot), which stayed with some of us for the rest of our lives and was duly passed on to our families. It was the job of one of the fags to fill the bath and a junior house prefect was supposed to see that none missed out. We were not given any reason: we supposed it was a sort of toughening-up ritual which was inseparable from public school life, as were other absurdities, like wearing our house caps on the backs of our heads when in Crowthorne. Perhaps it was genuinely intended to curb our sexual desires and fantasies and promote 'healthy' thoughts: if so it was a singular failure.

PROFESSOR COLIN PENNYCUICK. Professor of Ornithology, University of Miami, 1983–92.

In my time (1947–51) the smoke was suffocating but there was very little fire. Younger boys who had 'crushes' on older ones were usually tolerated like over-affectionate dogs, shooed away if their attachment became embar-rassing. An older boy might be rumoured to have a 'patch' on a younger one, who was then described as his 'little man'. Younger boys suspected of exploit-ing their charms for ulterior motives were derided as 'tarts'. These largely imaginary goings-on were the subject of ceaseless ribald jokes and lewd innu-endo.

Actual buggery was something else. I believe it was very rare. I only knew of one case, and that was a scandal that rocked the school. A very senior boy, who had perhaps forgotten that the law still applied to him, buggered his room fag, who complained to his tutor. The tutor immediately hauled the culprit before the Master, and had him summarily deposed from his position of authority, and expelled. Nobody was in any doubt about the attitude of the school. Such behaviour was absolutely not tolerated. To us boys, it was a shocking aberration. The dirty jokes were suddenly no longer funny. If people had been doing it all the time we would have known, and our reaction would have been different to what it was.

LORD FALKLAND. Deputy Whip, Liberal Democrats, House of Lords, from 1989. At Wellington in the late 1940s/early 1950s.

. . . The occasional case of boys being expelled created an enormous scandal. There was one just after I arrived and to my immense relief a great brute of a prefect who had made a point of making my first days very unpleasant indeed was quickly removed. The victim of his attentions was a likeable red-faced boy of quick wit who was thereafter nicknamed, strangely, 'Tartoy' . . .

My first housemaster was a retired officer who had an enormous sleepy-looking bulldog. He did take upon himself some rudimentary sex education which involved pointing and poking at the unfortunate dog's genitals, but nothing further was ventured. As for the attitude of the boys to homosexuality I doubt whether there was anything as advanced as attitude as such. I think we thought of that as part of the adult world and a wary eye was kept on the teach-ing staff.

WINCHESTER

Founded in 1382, its original statutes stipulated that women were not to be employed as servants or allowed into the school grounds, except one washer-woman who was to be admitted only so far as the outer gate where a male servant would meet her to hand in or hand out the linen.[1]

George Ridding, appointed headmaster in 1867, is acclaimed as one of the great Victorian 'reformers'. He was particularly anxious to improve the 'moral tone' of the school and decreed that juniors were no longer to worship along-side the seniors in school chapel. Instead they were to be confined to their own chapel created in 1874 by the transformation of the chantry.[2] But he remained uneasy about the layout of pews in senior chapel which made it possible for boys' feet on the front rows to touch during prayers and after some hesitation, in deference to the antiquity of the seating, which was centuries old, he ordered the seats to be ripped out and replaced by 'smart yellow pews'.[3]

The fagging system however proved itself to be relatively immune to Ridding's reforms and remained unchanged well into the twentieth century. Under it not all juniors suffered equally. Richard Crossman, who later became an MP and cabinet minister, was fortunate in being allocated a kindly fagmaster, Anthony Asquith, son of one of Britain's longest-serving prime ministers. Asquith soon developed a crush on Crossman. When one day Crossman tumbled down the stairs, spilling a can of water, he feared he would be severely punished, possibly caned. Instead, Asquith rushed out of his room to see if his beloved was all right.[4]

Another future MP, Alan Herbert, was also the focus of considerable atten-tion. He explained: 'I was considered attractive and classed as a 'tart': but my innocence was, rather incredulously, respected . . .'; and added as a verdict on his monastic existence at Winchester, 'It will be, I fancy, a shocking confes-sion that my wife was the first woman I kissed.'[5]

Contributions

DR EDGAR ANSTEY. *Author of several books on interviewing and psychological tests. At Winchester in the 1930s.*

. . . There was a lot of hero worship. I myself particularly admired a boy three years older than myself who became head boy, captain of football and cricket, and won the school prize for maths (as I did three years later). He took no particular interest in me. This man now lives close to me in Cornwall and we are friends, but not particularly close ones. At school my particular friends shared common interests in work, games, literature and politics. I was vaguely aware that some boys had 'crushes' on other boys, but these seemed innocent enough . . .

One personal anecdote might amuse you. When I was about fifteen, the housemaster summoned me to his study and asked me a question which puzzled me. I thought he asked, 'Are you interested in sects?' and that we would go on to discuss various heretical branches of the Christian faith. Then I realized he had said 'sex', and the conversation took its normal course. I assured him that I was acquainted with the facts of life, though I had as yet no practical experience. He left it at that.

GENERAL SIR HUGH BEACH. *Has contributed chapters to several books on nuclear proliferation and disarmament. At Winchester in the late 1930s/early 1940s.*

As I recall the existence of romantic friendships among boys . . . was taken for granted by all concerned. I never heard the Head Man utter on the subject. My housemaster . . . himself a confirmed bachelor, was obviously disapproving and one boy was expelled for obsessive mutual masturbation with other boys. I guess that we virtually all did this to a greater or lesser degree. I masturbated with six other boys, all in my house and roughly contemporary, but seldom more than once with any boy: in dormitory, house reading room, changing room, darkroom and once in a cornfield. The one in bed, by moonlight, was the best. Two older boys expressed a romantic interest in me but it came to nothing.

While at Winchester I took no interest in females whatsoever – there were none. After leaving school I took no interest in any male, romantically or sexually. I married at age twenty-eight, still a virgin, and remained faithful to my wife (we had four children) for the ensuing thirty-seven years. She is now dead and I have had one other sexual partner. You could say, I suppose, that homosexuality at Winchester did me no harm.

PROFESSOR FREEMAN DYSON. *Professor of Natural Sciences. At Winchester in the late 1930s/early 1940s.*

The culture of the place was strongly homosexual, but on a lofty and literary rather than physical level. Probably more Platonic than Plato himself. I remember one of my friends came down to his desk each morning to find a sonnet written to him personally by an older boy who happened to be the College poet. My friend enjoyed the poems but remained, so far as I am aware, unresponsive. This little romance was not regarded as unusual or shameful. After all, if Shakespeare could write sonnets to the boy he loved, why should our College poet not do the same?

Another part of our daily lives that you may find worth recording is the ceremony of making the toast. Every day we ate tea at six o'clock in the ancient College Hall which was heated by a big open coal stove in the middle. Only the prefects had the privilege of standing with long toasting-forks around the stove and making the toast. The younger boys had to sit on wooden benches away from the stove and wait to be served. The official reason for this rule was that there was not enough room around the stove for everyone to make his own toast. But everyone knew that this was not the real reason. The real reason was that the serving of the toast was a mating-game. The reward for the prefect was the smile on the face of the loved one when he took the toast from the fork. There was intense competition among the prefects to make a perfect piece of toast for a younger boy who happened to be particularly beautiful. The toast was a completely open, and still harmless, declaration of love. And nobody had to go hungry. After the scramble to bring toast to the beautiful boys was over the ugly ducklings were fed too, and only after all the younger boys were fed did the prefects make toast for themselves. I remember taking great delight in this ceremony, both as a receiver and as a giver of toast. The ceremony had some of the symbolism of the Christian Eucharist, combined with the rough-and-tumble of schoolboys enjoying themselves. Looking back fifty years later, I think this daily ritual of the toast epitomizes better than anything else the strangely innocent homosexuality of the Winchester schoolboy society in which I lived.

REAR-ADMIRAL JOHN MYRES. At Winchester in the early 1950s.

Whilst I was at the school, there . . . took place at Winchester Assizes the prosecution of Lord Montagu of Beaulieu for alleged indecency . . . Some sixth form men were allowed to attend some of the sittings – I was a junior as I recall. Whether this caused others to think about the subject with more understanding I do not know.

DR RAYMOND CRAWFURD. In general practice since 1971. At Winchester in the 1950s.

The college porter came to me one day in some embarrassment to say he had found something I ought to see. He took me to a classroom where a fresh graffito showed a heart with an arrow through it. At one end were my initials and at the other were the initials C.C.F. [Combined Cadet Force]. The porter had clearly feared the worst, but the explanation was rather different. College, normally a very unmilitary house, had briefly become moderately competent on the parade ground and had a sporting chance of winning the forthcoming drill competition. As the Senior NCO in College at the time, I thought it might be a good idea to have a briefing for the house and called a meeting in one of the classrooms for the purpose. It was not a popular move, and all I achieved for my pains was this neat and pithy insult!

Anonymous Contribution. At Winchester in the late 1950s/early 1960s.

Gunner's Hole was the name given somewhat euphemistically to the Winchester College swimming pool. In fact this was a fairly filthy stretch of the river, surrounded by a high wooden fence, impenetrable to the outside world. Each end of the 'pool' was cordoned off by a heavy metal grill to prevent large pollutants (like dead animals) floating into the swimming area. The water was uncleansed in any way – it was pea-soup green. This had some advantages, as we shall see.

It was the rule that all swimming was to be in the nude, for boys and masters. This rule was compromised a little after my time when swimming trunks became optional. Members of the school sheltered round the perimeter of the pool in house order, with a section devoted exclusively to men in College (scholars lived separately from humbler mortals, known as commoners).

My house had its changing area next door to the College men. It was in Gunner's Hole that I first set eyes on Jonathan (not his real name). He was dazzlingly beautiful with soapsud curls. He walked with a slight waddle, like a duck. I was far too shy and inhibited to make contact with him but the gods smiled on our friendship because he sent a message to me via an intermediary, and I realized that my feelings for him were reciprocated.

We managed to meet. The intensity of my attraction for him was impaired by a strong sense of guilt. I went through a profoundly religious phase at Winchester which went a long way to preventing me from deriving full enjoyment from my love for Jonathan. But not entirely.

The water in Gunner's Hole was so dirty as to provide camouflage. It was my favourite pastime to wait for Jonathan to plunge into the pool, dive in after him and feel him under the water without fear of detection. He came to stay with me during the holidays. We used to go off together for the day on *absit* days. But we faced the fundamental problem that we were in different houses. A solution was found. The classrooms were built round a courtyard. Up against the end of these buildings was a lavatory. It had no roof but was private in all other respects. We discovered that it was left unlocked after hours. It was here by prior arrangement that we used to have contact of the most intimate kind.

At the end of one summer, I decided to leave Winchester early. Apart from Jonathan, it was a fairly miserable place for me.

I only saw Jonathan once after I left. I saw him in the Crush bar at Covent Garden Opera House but he didn't recognize me. He became a distinguished fellow of an Oxford College. He died of Aids a few years ago.

WREKIN COLLEGE

Founded in 1880, the most unusual feature of the original school was that the classrooms had glass walls so that at a glance the headmaster at his dais could see if any boy in the school was misbehaving.[1]

Unfortunately the Orwellian architecture did not prevent one headmaster from being dismissed by the governors in July 1923 for allowing too much 'immorality'. The mother of one boy had complained that her son was being subjected to wicked and shameful language and J. Hammerton, the headmaster, had foolishly attempted to console her with 'But think what a good influence your son must have on his fellows'. To which she had tersely replied, 'Mr Hammerton, I did not send my boy here to be a missionary.'[2] Matters deteriorated further when the son of an influential parent was sacked for immorality. The parent seems to have convinced the governors that his boy had been unfairly singled out, but instead of simply reinstating the boy, the governors decided the most expedient action was to summon Mr Hammerton to the Charing Cross Hotel at London to inform him that he would have to go.

The school's historian, B.C.W. Johnson, commented, 'The indignation, the turmoil, the gossip and speculation which this high-handed action caused are easier to imagine than to describe.'[3]

Contribution

GEOFFREY HOLROYDE. *Director, Coventry Cathedral Chapter House Choir. At Wrekin in the 1940s.*

My school was a hotbed of homosexual activity. Such would have been fiercely denied by the staff . . . The whole subject was taboo, and [many boys] talked about 'homos' (the term queer came later) as though they were lepers, whilst engaging in the activity.

The masters used to talk about 'self abuse' at house meetings and in chapel, and we were all made to feel very very guilty about masturbation – a state of mind which haunted me till I was nearly forty years old. Indeed, it did much to destroy my self-confidence, by persuading me that because I enjoyed and wanted sex with other males, I was odd, and because I masturbated I was effeminate and likely to go mad! It was not until my third year as an undergraduate that I regained my self-esteem, and you will see from *Who's Who* that my subsequent career did not suffer. I got married when I was thirty-one and soon had four children.

I messed around with many other boys, mainly of my own age, from the beginning, in bed, behind sheds, on walks in the woods etc., but most of this was exploration of possibilities, not affection. Much of it went on. It was considered courageous to wank off a boy sitting next to you in class or chapel or dining hall without the master noticing you had done it.

When I was sixteen I had a terrible crush on a beautiful newly-arrived thirteen-year-old. We spent hours together reading poetry and talking about God. I fantasized about him when masturbating. We did not have sex together at school, but did so several years later in our twenties. He is not gay. Crushes were common and talked about a lot. Boys sought opportunities to be with their crushes – in public to attract attention and proclaim victory – but I suspect not much sex took place across the age gap . . .

I had sex often with a boy of my own age, and in our last year at school we fell in love and had really nice, lingering sex in bed and elsewhere. I visited him during the term after I had left and had sex with him in the darkroom. That alas was the last time. The taboo prevented us from admitting even to each other that we were in love, so it all finished. I often think of him now, but don't know where he is.

During my last year I was a prefect and supervised a dormitory of fourteen-year-olds. One of them had a crush on me, which I enjoyed, and he used to get into my bed often. We did not have sex (alas) as I was aware of my authority and responsibility. After we had both left (he left at sixteen) when I was twenty,

I visited his home and tried to seduce him, but by then he was really into girls and didn't want it.

A YORKSHIRE SCHOOL

An anonymous contributor recalls his experience at a Yorkshire school in the early sixties.

It was the family doctor who recommended that I should go to a boarding school. I lived in a tiny house in Watford with my mother and father, my elder brother and two sisters. There were constant arguments and, not wishing to be involved, I would spend a lot of time sitting quietly by myself. My parents thought that was odd and that there must be something wrong with me. They consulted the doctor and yielded to his novel prescription. Five years to absorb the fresh air and vigour of a school which he knew of, located in one of the remoter parts of Yorkshire. It would do me the world of good.

So one September day my Dad deposited me at King's Cross station into the care of Mr Chaucer (name changed), the portly deputy head, who was also shepherding several other boys of disparate ages. They were such an uncouth lot, swearing loudly and comparing size and sharpness of penknives. I watched them nervously and clutched my pet rabbit, Pinnochio. My Dad had insisted I be allowed to take him with me despite the vain protests of Mr Chaucer. Now I began to wish I had left him at home. Poor Pinnochio. He did not survive the spartan conditions of boarding school for more than a few days.

But his death was not my only torment in those first days of school. I was always hungry as I refused to eat the school meals. On Sundays I almost starved. Cold porridge for breakfast and pilchard pie for lunch! The other torment was the constant cold. The radiators were never on and the windows in the dormitories were kept wide open. I remember waking up one morning to find my top blanket (we each had a total of two) covered in snow.

I also had to find a way of surviving in a dormitory of boys most of whom were older, bigger and more aggressive than I was. (The school population numbering only forty-eight and spanning the ages eleven to seventeen, didn't permit the luxury of age-segregated bedrooms.) One of these older boys appointed himself Inspector General and lined all the juniors up naked. All except me. I refused and was teased mercilessly for being shy. This infuriated me and I reported the older boy to my form master and he got into terrible trouble. Six of the best, I think. I was not very popular with any of the seniors for a while afterwards.

When I first arrived a strange system operated whereby the position of the beds in the dormitories was changed every three weeks. I think the intention was to prevent relationships from developing, but actually it had the opposite effect. Most boys were far more forward than the staff imagined and the bed shuffling merely led to more frequent changes of partner, although I was one of the few boys who usually remained aloof from the cruder games and competitions that engrossed the others.

I admit I was more prudish at certain times than others. On Saturday after-noons I would often seek an attractive boy to go for a walk with. These outings were encouraged by the staff. It was a very isolated school, miles from any-where, and I think they felt that if we got up to mischief no one would be likely to notice.

I suppose as a blond eleven-year-old I was quite attractive and one Saturday afternoon, when I was lingering near the fire place in the Great Hall, my house captain accosted me and coolly asked if I would like to stroll with him down to the river. (The school still retained the house system from former days when it had had a much larger number of pupils.) I had been at the school long enough, though it was probably only my second term, to know what this older boy desired. I was flattered by his attention as in those early days at school I was something of a loner and the house captain was a popular sporting type and very handsome. However I don't wish to divulge in any detail what happened that spring day except that his charm and experience quickly won me over.

But it was not a one-afternoon affair. I remember particularly how when I was consigned to sickbay for several weeks he came to visit me every day and I soon came too depend on his friendship enormously. Unfortunately, at the end of a blissful summer term, he left. I was devastated. I only ever saw him once again. He returned the next Old Boys day as a married man and as I wan-dered over to where he and his wife were standing, he gave me an anxious glance. I think he was worried in case his wife might guess the nature of our friendship.

It was not long before I was in a relationship with the roles reversed. This time I was house captain and keeping a certain David (name changed), a gor-geous junior, under my wing. Apparently he had been in some sort of trouble at his previous school so my form master had asked me to keep an eye on him and I'm afraid my interest went somewhat further than intended when I seduced him one afternoon in the school's infamous hollow tree. It was the somewhat indelicate debut to what was to become the first and most intense love affair of my life.

I wanted to be with David all the time but we were both wary of being seen together during the day and we used to arrange night-time assignations in the vast castle cellars, which were known by the boys as the 'Crypt'. Once we had a narrow escape when I was caught returning to my dormitory. Fortunately David had taken a different route back and I tried to look innocent and confused and said I had just gone to get a drink of water.

Our relationship thrived but was running out of time as it was now my final year. I will always remember the last day we were together. The sixteenth of July 1964. It was the most unhappy day of my life. David lived in Barking in East London and we travelled down together on the train, but we couldn't talk intimately as we normally did as our compartment was crowded with other passengers. The result was an awkward and sad silence. When the train finally pulled into King's Cross my father was waiting impatiently at the top of the platform and as I looked back I waved to David. He smiled sadly. It was the last time I ever saw him. I suppose I could have tried to contact him, but I was frightened that another meeting wouldn't live up to the magic of my memories. Yet the loss of his friendship was so painful that for twenty years I refused to use King's Cross station.

Those years, trapped in a nine-to-five job in London, were unbearably dull. It was supposed to be the swinging sixties but I had to wait two years for my first sexual encounter and that was with an older man who had been following me round the Tate Gallery.

It was a long time before I was able to rediscover any great joy in life and not until I was almost forty did I tell anyone about my schoolday passions. For years I hated the happy memories, the frustrating contrast of past and present. One day I could take it no more and I burnt all my diaries, meticulous records of every day of school life. In retrospect I regret that but at least I still have David's football sweater which he used to wear in goal.

CONCLUSION

The architecture and organization of today's boarding school has been shaped by over one hundred years of homophobia. Superficially one might imagine that the post-*Tom Brown* evolution of the boarding school was conditioned by the gradual ascendancy of liberal reformers over uncompromising traditionalists. Unfortunately, however, the great 'reforming' headmasters also had an illiberal agenda which has now been conveniently forgotten; the desire to efficiently manage the sexuality of adolescent boys and the 'problem' of homosexuality.

At times, particularly in the late Victorian period, this goal was clearly articulated in journals, letters and school sermons. At other times it remained an unspoken undercurrent affecting the direction of school reforms. Either way the resulting changes in school organization continued relentlessly.

Only in the last thirty years has there been any manifest dismantling of the less subtle products of this trend towards ever tighter sexual control. Cold showers, sewn-up pockets and doorless toilets had always been crude and futile methods, but now they were also depicted as barbarous relics of the Dark Ages, although ironically all were inventions of the late nineteenth century.

In their place schools introduced less obvious but more ingenious mechanisms for managing and directing a 'healthy', 'heterosexual' adolescence. These included a trend towards coeducation (dressed up in the rhetoric of gender egalitarianism) and the debachelorization of housemasterships (evidenced in the 'all our housemasters are married' protestations of several school prospectuses).

Some of the old taboos, though rarely articulated, continue. It is obvious, but apparently now an unremarkable fact, that older and younger boys rarely mix socially. They sleep in age-segregated dormitories, they work in classes categorized by age (rather than ability), they eat at detached tables and they chat in separate common rooms and the whole process is carried on in such a spontaneous, unquestioned way that it is easy to imagine that this has always been the natural order of things. Victorian headmasters, if alive today, would be astounded by the effortless efficiency of it all.

So I hope this book has helped to forge a new interpretation on this revolution in boarding school organization, one which emphasizes the extent to which institutional homophobia (often unjustly ridiculed as a meaningless cliché) can have direct repercussions on so many disparate aspects of our lives. For if such superficially unrelated features of public school life as the layout of the pews in chapel, the content of the curriculum, the taboos on inter-class and inter-house friendships, and the architecture of classrooms, corridors, toilets and dormitories can be shown to be shaped, at least in part, by negative attitudes to homosexuality then one has to acknowledge that the fear of homosexuality is indeed pervasive. It is proof that homophobia does not manifest itself merely in the taunts of the gutter press and the threats of queer-bashing thugs, and that its insidious impact is not confined 'merely' to the lesbian and gay population, but affects the life experience of everyone.

Studies of various institutions – the army, the church, the city and the law – have already demonstrated that homophobia has profound and far-reaching consequences. What is so interesting about the boarding school, however, is that the homophobic elements are so well concealed by what appears to be an unplanned assemblage of architecture and tradition, an innocuous and charming accident of history. I hope this book has helped to end this deception.

That a homophobic culture was so influential in shaping the organization of boarding schools begs the question to what extent the changes to that system reinforced the homophobia of the wider culture. If boarding schools were striving to imbue their pupils with a sense of guilt and shame, what momentous consequences might this have had when those boys became the governing élite of the country? And if those same schools were sending out men to administer the Empire and if these men in turn were replaced by local élites, often educated either in English boarding schools or the local equivalents modelled on the English system, the repercussions must obviously have been considerable on a world-wide scale. The influence of sex-negative attitudes learned at an early age is likely to have been a major factor in determining the beliefs and values of the ruling class in many English-speaking and Commonwealth countries.

Finally, one cannot escape the question, 'Do single-sex boarding schools make pupils homosexual? Most gay men I interviewed did not attribute their sexual orientation to school and the few straight men who bravely admitted to homosexual experimentation at school often stressed that it was just a phase or that it was a substitute heterosexuality – hence the emphasis on 'pretty' juniors and the comical and unserious aspects of romance. There is no evidence to refute their stories, but one senses that sometimes a certain anxiety lurks behind such protestations.

It is probably true that in most cases sexual preferences are established at a very early age prior to school, but it is also likely that the spectrum of human sexuality is far wider than the labels 'gay' and 'straight' imply. Many people, however, find such ambiguities confusing and threatening. For a straight man, to admit to a serious affair at school would lead him to question his own sexuality; and for a gay man, to suggest that school might have had some influence on the evolution of his own desires would imply that his sexuality too was not entirely fixed.

It is difficult to gauge the extent to which the shame and opprobrium attached to physical homosexuality at school has subsequently influenced the recollections of most pupils who now think of themselves as heterosexual. It is easy for Old Boys to deny the prevalence of homosexuality at their alma mater (only their school colleagues might contradict them) and it is equally tempting to remember only the humorous and frivolous. The memories of the latter type might often be more truthful, but nevertheless I suspect that sometimes behind the laughs and innuendos there lurks that same fear of self-discovery which dawns on the main character in *Another Country*: 'All this acting it up – making a joke of it even to myself – it was only a way of trying to pretend it wasn't true. But it is.'[1]

GLOSSARY

'An "institutional lingo" develops through which inmates describe the events that
are critical to their particular world.'
Erving Goffman, *Asylums*

Bad name: A reputation for homosexuality. A favourite term of Old Boys, often
with the inference that another house, certainly not their own, was a virtual
Sodom and Gomorrah.

Bijou: (Charterhouse term): A boy on whom another had a crush (qv).

Bounder: (in use up to the 1930s): A disreputable boy, especially a senior boy
who associated with juniors. In the words of Thomas Hughes, 'big fellows
of the wrong sort, boys whose friendships and tastes had a downward tendency'.

Bounds: The geographical limitation to a boy's leisure time activities which
might or might not be more lenient at some times (for example, weekends)
than at others. Anywhere *out of bounds* was an area strictly forbidden to
pupils. These areas, such as the railway arches at Eton, were often those
where surveillance was almost impossible and which thus offered a relatively safe refuge for the amorous.

Bum-boy: A pretty boy, particularly a pretty junior.

Bum-freezer: A short jacket or blazer, normally worn by junior boys, of
insufficient length to cover the bum. Formally known as an Eton
jacket, although Eton finally abolished it in 1967 and allowed juniors to
wear tails.

Cavalier: An uncircumcised boy.

Cherub (Fettes term): Any boy who was more than averagely keen on sex with
other boys.

Chum (Commonly in use up to the 1930s): A school friend with whom one
was on sufficiently intimate terms to use his Christian name. Hence a proliferation of books around the turn of the century with such titles as Florence
Combe's (1896) *A Chum Worth Having*, Forsyth Grant's (1899) *Chums at
Last* and John Finnemore's (1910) *Teddy Lester's Chums*.

Civilize: A somewhat ambiguous verb used frequently by headmasters and staff when arguing the benefits of coeducation, as in, 'We hope the admission of girls will civilize our boys'; a phrase which casts the girls in the role of missionaries. Usually it is a mere euphemism for 'heterosexualize'.

Cock-up: A punishment practised by some boys at Charterhouse and inflicted for poor sportsmanship; all that is known is that a cricket stump was used on the victim. The problem was that when fags were employed to field they would 'stand about in a listless way, often with their backs to the batsman'.[1] Presumably that's why their elders felt they deserved a painful surprise.

Compart: An enclosure used in some school dormitories which either partly or fully enclosed a boy's bed.

Confirmation chat: A sexual pep talk preceeding a boy's confirmation.

Corps (full name – Officer Training Corps): An organization of school boys, supervised by masters and prefects (q.v.) with the purpose of teaching military skills and reinforcing codes of discipline.

Crate (Framlingham term): The junior partner in any relationship.

Crush: Either an infatuation (as in, D had a crush on E) or the boy who was the focus of such desires (E being D's crush).

Cushy (Malvern term): pretty.

Debagging: The forceful removal of a boy's trousers by another boy or boys.

Ding List (Lancing term): A list of the best looking boys in the school drawn up once a term by sixth-formers.

Doul (Shrewsbury term): A pretty junior.

Eton jacket: See 'bum-freezer'.

Extra tuition: Help with school work given by a master to a boy or boys outside his regular hours or a euphemism for an affair between a master and a boy or boys.

Fag: A junior boy who had to undertake regular chores for a senior boy or prefect. These might vary from routine cooking and cleaning to more unusual tasks such as delivering secret notes or warming lavatory seats.

Flog off (verb): To masturbate.

Four o'clock in the Sewing Room (Oundle term): Any pre-arranged night-time rendezvous.

Frig (verb): A nineteenth-century term for masturbate.

Hags: A term commonly used in public schools to describe female domestic staff.

Haggish (Downside term): Any behaviour considered effeminate (see 'hags').

Head of House: A boy appointed from among the senior boys to help the housemaster (q.v.) maintain order and discipline within his house (q.v.).

Headmaster's Conference: A formal association of 244 public schools (q.v.) whose headmasters meet annually. Established in 1869 by Edward Thring, headmaster of Uppingham, the purpose of the conference is to discuss the financial, educational and other problematic issues facing member schools. Eligibility is based on a school's independent status and academic record.

Housemaster: A member of staff responsible for the boys in his house (q.v.). In the nineteenth and early twentieth centuries housemasters often owned their houses and the headmaster had very little control over how a housemaster ran his house but, gradually, as the headmaster's powers increased, house-masters were chosen, increasingly from among the senior members of the teaching staff.

House spirit: A quality measured by a boy's loyalty to his house (q.v.), his contribution in team games against other houses and his reluctance to make close friendships with boys outside his own house.

Landing boy: A prefect (q.v.) who would stand as sentinel outside a dormitory or dormitories and report any noise to the housemaster.

Library: That room in a house (q.v.), often devoid of any books, which was both a sort of social club for prefects and the site of a self-appointed court which judged any offences committed 'in house' and enforced the penalties deemed appropriate.

Little man (Wellington term): The junior partner in a relationship.

Lustknabe (Sedbergh term – limited usage): A boy, especially a junior, on whom another had a crush (q.v.). As the term was not in general use it could be employed discreetly by students of German.

Monitor: Another word for prefect (q.v.).

M'Tutor: The name by which a housemaster (q.v.) was known at Eton.

Nervous breakdown: The normal explanation given to schoolboys and parents to cover up the sacking of a master for sexual misconduct.

Oppidans: Fee-paying Etonians, as opposed to those studying on scholarships.

Outward Bound: A movement which started in the 1930s at Gordonstoun in which boys participated in arduous expeditions, often involving rock climbing, map navigation, long route-marches and canoeing. The idea was that such activities would toughen the mind and help boys fight off sexual temptation, but in reality camping out at night offered the perfect opportu-nity for sexual experimentation.

Pash: Another term for crush (q.v.).

Patch (Wellington term): A crush (q.v.).

Pillow fight: A mock fight between boys in a dormitory, or between boys of different dormitories, in which the protagonists pummel each other with pillows.

Prefect: A senior boy who is given limited powers in order to help staff super-vise the school.

Prep school (full name, preparatory school): A private school attended by boys and/or girls aged seven to twelve. When first established its manifest purpose was to prepare children for public school (q.v.), but its real purpose may have been to protect young children from becoming the sexual targets of their teenage elders.

Prowlers: Prefects (q.v.) who patrolled corridors outside dormitories and reported any noise they heard to the housemaster (q.v.).

Public school: Any of a select number of private fee-paying independent schools for pupils aged thirteen to eighteen (sometimes eleven to eighteen) and fully entitled to call themselves a public school only if associated to the Headmaster's Conference (q.v.). Public schools can be either single-sex or coeducational and can be either a predominantly boarding or day-school establishment. Since the 1960s the tendency has been increasingly towards coeducation and day schooling.

Roundhead: A circumcised boy.

Rears (Radley term): The communal lavatory area.

Sneaking: The act of a boy informing a member of staff about another boy or other boys who have broken school rules.

Socius (Winchester term): Either of a pair of school friends who were per-mitted by their housemaster (q.v.) to walk together from their house (q.v.) to the classrooms. Each boy had to have one, but only one, socius.

Stigg (Radley term): A good-looking younger boy.

Storm (Late nineteenth-century Japanese term): During their first year new boys' dormitories in Japanese boarding schools would be attacked by a gang of seniors. This much feared rite of passage, known as 'the storm', often included homosexual rape.[2]

Swagger stick: A cane carried by cadet officers in the schools corps (q.v.) which could be used for beating juniors.

Swell (no longer used): A senior boy, especially a popular senior and/or one prominent in school sports.

Tart: Any young boy who was open to advances from his seniors, especially any pretty boy thought to be 'available'. At Shrewsbury older boys taunted younger ones by forming the letter 'T' with their fingers.

T-Boy (Shrewsbury term): Any junior boy considered pretty or a tart (q.v.).

Toss off (verb): masturbate.

Tuck shop: A shop located in or near the school which sells food, especially sweets and cakes.

Usual reasons: A slanderous term used to indicate that a master had been sacked for having had an affair with a boy/boys.

Whizz Kids (Harrow term): Boys, especially juniors, who were considered attractive because of their girlish looks.

APPENDIX

Figures on Recent Changes in Gender Ratios at Public Schools

TABLE A: BOY/GIRL RATIOS IN HMC SCHOOLS (1993)

Percentage Boys	40–50	50–60	60–70	70–80	80–90	90–95	95–100
Number of Schools	17	33	34	15	30	27	80

NOTE: HMC schools comprise all those independent boys and coeducational schools which are affiliated to the Headmaster's Conference.

SOURCE: *Independent Schools Information Service Annual Census 1992.*

TABLE B: NUMBERS OF BOYS AND GIRLS AT HMC SCHOOLS 1974–1993

Year	Number of schools	Boys boarding	Girls boarding	Total	Girls as % of total
1974	207	46,208	1,195	47,403	2.3
1979	208	44,849	2,752	47,601	5.8
1984	221	41,901	4,478	46,382	9.7
1992	233	33,249	7,983	41,232	19.4
1993	236	31,748	7,999	39,747	20.1

SOURCE: *Independent Schools Information Service Annual Census,* 1974–1993 editions.

TABLE C: FULL-TIME STAFF AT HMC SCHOOLS 1984–1993

	Full-time Men	Full-time Women	Total full-time	Women as % of total
1984	9,316	929	10,245	9.1
1993	10,918	2,907	13,825	21.0

SOURCE: *Independent Schools Information Service Annual Censuses,* 1984 and 1993.

NOTES AND REFERENCES

Chapter One

1. Quoted in Monica Furlong, *Genuine Fake: A Biography of Alan Watts*, Unwin Paperbacks, London, 1986, p. 31.
2. Even the sociologist Ian Weinberg claimed that 'they try to avert their gaze from the phenomenon altogether.' Ian Weinberg, *The English Public Schools*, Atherton Press, New York, 1967, p. 108.
3. Evelyn Waugh, *Decline and Fall*, Penguin Books, Harmondsworth, 1976, p. 188.

Demarcation

1. Borstals eagerly copied the power structure, building up their own system of house-masters, matrons and prefects in which sometimes each cell-landing officially became a 'house'. See Roger Hood, *Borstal Re-Assessed*, pp. 108–109.
2. Wilfred R. Bion, *The Long Weekend 1897–1919: Portrait of a Life*, Free Association Books, London, 1986, p. 77.
3. Ian Stephens, *Unmade Journey*, Stacey International, London, 1977, p. 42.
4. S.P.B. Mais, *A Public School in War Time*, John Murray, London, 1916, p. 145.
5. T.C. Worsley, *Flannelled Fool: A Slice of Life in the Thirties*, Hogarth Press, London, 1985.
6. Brian Inglis, *Downstart: The Autobiography of Brian Inglis*, Chatto and Windus, London, 1990, p. 39.
7. Osbert Lancaster, *With an Eye to the Future*, John Murray, London, 1967, p. 44.
8. Catherine Dupré, *John Galsworthy: A Biography*, Collins, London, 1976, pp. 23–24.
9. Andrew Boyle, *Montagu Norman: A Biography*, Cassell, London, 1967, p. 19 and p. 256.
10. Roger Wilkes, *Blood Relations: Jeremy Bamber and the White House farm Murders*, Robinson, London, 1994, p. 330.
11. Frances Donaldson, *Edward VIII*, Futura Publications, London, 1978, pp. 28–29.

12. Michael Davidson, *The World, the Flesh and Myself*, Gay Men's Press, London, 1985, pp. 52–53.

13. Arthur Marshall, *Life's Rich Pageant*, Hamish Hamilton, London, 1984, p. 64.

14. Anthony Kenny, *A Path from Rome: An Autobiography*, Sidgwick and Jackson, London, 1985, p. 24.

15. John Rodgers, *The Old Public Schools of England*, B.T. Batsford, London, 1938, p. 39.

16. Ibid., p. 38.

17. Ibid., p. 39.

18. Dai San Koto Gakko Dosokai, 'Kohon Jinryoshie', unpublished manuscript quoted in Donald Roden, *Schooldays in Imperial Japan*, University of California Press, Los Angeles and London, 1980, p. 37.

19. 'Boy's Accommodation in 1758' in *Etoniana 1950*, reprinted in P.S.H. Lawrence (ed.), *The Encouragement of Learning*, Michael Russell, Salisbury, 1990, p. 110.

20. Louis Crompton, *Byron and Greek Love*, Faber and Faber, London, 1985, p. 79.

21. Ann Monsarrat, *An Uneasy Victorian: Thackeray the Man 1811–1863*, Cassell, London, 1980, p. 17.

22. Felix Clay, *Modern School Buildings*, Batsford, London, 1902, pp. 240–241.

23. T.W. Bamford, *Rise of the Public Schools*, Thomas Nelson, London, 1967, p. 64.

24. A.H. Trelawny-Ross, *Their Prime of Life: A Public School Study*, The Wykeham Press, Winchester, 1956, p. 19.

25. 'Boarding Houses and a Prep School in Common Lane, 1861–69' in *Etoniana 1954*, reprinted in P.S.H. Lawrence (ed.), *The Encouragement of Learning*.

26. Wilfrid Blunt, *Married to a Single Life*, Michael Russell, Wilton, 1983.

27. C.C. Somervell, *A History of Tonbridge School*, Faber and Faber, London, 1947, p. 115.

28. Tom Hopkinson, *Of this Our Time: A Journalist's Story 1905–50*, Hutchinson, London, pp. 53–54.

29. 'How is the Life in Dormitory Organized?' (22 September 1893) quoted in Derek Sederman, *A History of Abbotsholme School 1889–1989*, Abbotsholme School, Uttoxeter, 1989, p. 29.

30. Trelawny-Ross, p. 80.

31. Roy Fuller, *The Ruined Boys*, Hogarth Press, London, 1987, pp. 224–225.

32. M.C. Morgan, *Cheltenham College*, Richard Sadler, Chalfont St Giles, 1968, p. 101.

33. A.K. Boyd, *The History of Radley College 1847–1947*, Basil Blackwell, Oxford, 1948, p. 209.

34. Christopher Lee, *Tall, Dark and Gruesome: An Autobiography*, W.H. Allen, London, 1977, p. 52.

35. Quentin Crisp, *The Naked Civil Servant*, Fontana, London, 1981, p. 18.

36. David Newsome, *Godliness and Good Learning: Four Studies on a Victorian ideal*, Cassell, London, 1961, p. 45.

37. Edward Lyttelton, *The Causes and Prevention of Immorality in Schools*, Social Purity Alliance, 1887, p. 17.

38. Ibid.

39. Ascott R. Hope, 'Cave' in *Journal of Education*, May 1885, p. 195.

40. Quoted in Lord Birkenhead, *Rudyard Kipling*, Weidenfeld and Nicolson, London, 1978, p. 41.

41. Philip Mason, *A Shaft of Sunlight: Memories of a Varied Life*, André Deutsch, London, 1978, p. 25.

42. See for example F.D. Roosevelt's experience at Groton School for Boys, modelled after the English public school. Here all boys were instructed not to go for a walk in pairs. See Ted Morgan, *F.D.R. A Biography*, Grafton Books, London, 1987, p. 57.

43. Boyd, p. 60.

44. Stephens, p. 42.

Denunciation

1. Julian Amery, *Approach March: A Venture in Autobiography*, Hutchinson, London, 1973, p. 48.

2. Nicholas Elliott, *Never Judge A Man by his Umbrella*, Michael Russell, Salisbury, 1991, p. 28.

3. Diana B. Webster, *Hawkes Eye: The Early Life of Christopher Hawkes*, Alan Sutton, New Hampshire, USA, 1991, p. 61.

4. Thomas Hinde, *Sir Henry and Sons: A Memoir*, Macmillan, London, 1980, p. 108.

5. Elliott, p. 28.

6. E.F. Benson, *David Blaize*, Thames & Hudson, London, 1989, pp. 115–116.

7. The Revd A.A. David, *Life and the Public Schools*, Alexander Maclehouse, London, 1932, pp. 159–160.

8. H. Montgomery Hyde, *Walter Monkton*, Sinclair-Stevenson, London, 1991, p. 5.

9. Edward James, *Swans Reflecting Elephants: My Early Years*, Weidenfeld and Nicolson, London, 1982, p. 36.

10. Robin Maugham, *Escape from the Shadows*, Hodder and Stoughton, London, 1972, p. 32.

11. Quentin Crewe, *The Autobiography of an Optimist*, Hutchinson, London, 1991.

12. Revd David, pp. 159–160.

13. See for example Wilfrid Blunt, *Married to a Single Life*.

14. Lord Drogheda, *Double Harness: Memories by Lord Drogheda*, Wiedenfeld and Nicolson, London, 1978, p. 14.

15. Hinde, p. 146.

16. Lyttelton, p. 20.

17. Ibid.

18. Edward Thring quoted in J.R. de S. Honey, *Tom Brown's Universe*, Millington Books Ltd., London, 1977, p. 171.

19. George Parkin, *Edward Thring: Life, Diary and Letters*, Macmillan, London, 1900, p. 275.

20. Ibid., p. 276.

21. Peter Ustinov, *Dear Me*, Heinemann, London, 1977, p. 58.

22. G.W.S. Howson, *Sermons by a Lay Headmaster Preached at Gresham's School 1900–1918*, Longmans, Green and Co., London, 1920, pp. 61–62.

23. F.W. Farrar, *St Winifred's or The World of School*, Ward Lock, London, pp. 230–231.

24. Robert Skidelsky, *English Progressive Schools*, Penguin Books, Harmondsworth, 1969, p. 110.

25. From the 1952 Shrewsbury School play quoted in Philip Cowburn (ed.), *A Salopian Anthology*, Macmillan, London, 1964, p. 262.

26. Anthony Powell, *To Keep the Ball Rolling. The Memoirs of Anthony Powell: Volume One: Infants of the Spring*, William Heinemann, London, 1976.

27. Beverley Nichols, *The Unforgiving Minute: Some Confessions from childhood to the Outbreak of the Second World War*, W.H. Allen, London, 1978, pp. 4–5.

28. Elfrida Vipont, *Ackworth School*, Lutterworth Press, London, 1959, pp. 145–146.

Diversions and Defeminization

1. T.E. Page et al., *The Public Schools From Within*, Sampson Low, Marston and Company, London, 1906, p. 183.

2. Clement Dukes quoted in J.R. de S. Honey, *Tom Brown's Universe*, p. 173.

3. J.G. Cotton Minchin, *Our Public Schools*, 1901, p. 230.

4. The Revd J.M. Wilson, 'Morality in Public Schools and its Relation to Religion' in *Journal of Education*, November 1881, p. 255.

5. Colonel Meadows Taylor, *Story of My Life*, Pluto Press, London, 1989, p. 6.

6. J.A. Mangan, *Athleticism in the Victorian and Edwardian Public School*, Cambridge University Press, Cambridge, 1981, p. 17.

7. Lytton Strachey, *Eminent Victorians*.

8. Mangan, p. 18.

9. James Sabben-Clare, *Winchester*, Paul Cave Publications, Southampton, 1981, p. 40.

10. J. d'E Firth, *Winchester College*, Winchester Publications, 1936, p. 115.

11. Vipont, pp. 57–58.

12. Rodgers, p. 17.

13. Thomas Steele, *Musings of an Old Schoolmaster*, The Sylvan Press, London, 1932, pp. 20–22.

14. T.C. Worsley, pp. 68–69.

15. Lee, p. 58.

16. Boyd.

17. John Barber, *The Story of Oakham School*, Sycamore Press, Wymondham, 1983, p. 84.

18. Michael Holroyd, *Lytton Strachey: Volume One: The Unknown Years 1880–1910*, Heinemann, London p. 58 and p. 62.

19. Lyttelton, p. 27.

20. Quoted in Skidelsky, p. 109.

21. G.F. Campbell in Various Authors, *Memories of Old Fettesians 1870–1920*, T. and A. Constable, Edinburgh, p. 28.

22. Boyd, p. 40.

23. Nicholas Fairbairn, *A Life's too Short*, Quartet Books, London, 1987, p. 46.

24. Hugh Boustead, *The Wind of Morning*, Chatto and Windus, London, 1972, p. 12.

25. Ronald Tree, *When the Moon was High: Memoirs of Peace and War 1897–1942*, Macmillan, London, 1975, p. 24.

26. David Spinney, *Claysmore: A School History*, Dovecote Press, Standbridge, 1987, p. 31.

27. Trelawny-Ross, p. 245.

28. Dennis Sloan, *The Twenty-Third Little Varmint*, Dennis Sloan in Association with the Self Publishing Association Ltd., 1988, pp. 60–61.

29. Mark Cocker, *Richard Meinertzhagen: Soldier, Scientist and Spy*, Secker and Warburg, London, 1989, p. 16.

30. Adrian Bell, *My Own Master*, Faber and Faber, London, 1961, p. 67.

31. Stephen Roskill, *Hankey: Man of Secrets Volume One 1877–1918*, Collins, London, 1970, p. 30.

32. Arnold Brown, p. 44.

33. Hugh Heckstall-Smith, *Doubtful Schoolmaster*, Peter Davies, London, 1962, pp. 135–136.

34. R.D. Hill, *A History of St Edward's School*, St Edward's School Society, 1962, p. 115.

35. Boyd, p. 89.

Debarment

1. Chandan Mitra, *Constant Glory: La Martiniere Saga 1836–1986*, Oxford University Press, Calcutta, 1987, p. 27.

2. Dillibe Onyeama, *Nigger at Eton*, Leslie Frewin, London, 1972, p. 165.

3. Imogen Thomas, *Haileybury 1806–1987*, The Haileybury Society, Haileybury, 1987, p. 65.

4. Noel Annan, *Roxburgh of Stowe*, Longmans, London, 1965, p. 174.

5. Onyeama, pp. 170–171.

Detection

1. Bion, p. 45.

2. Newsome, *Godliness and Good Learning*, pp. 41–42.

3. John Chandos, *Boys Together: English Public Schools 1800–1864*, Hutchinson, London, 1984.

4. Lord Home, *The Way the Wind Blows*, Collins, London, 1984, pp. 26–27.

5. Patrick Lichfield, *Not the Whole Truth: An Autobiography*, Constable, London, 1986, p. 23.

6. M.C. Morgan, p. 46.

7. Richard Ollard, *An English Education: A Perspective of Eton*, Collins, London, 1982, p. 128.

8. Arthur P. Stanley, *The Life and Correspondence of Thomas Arnold*, John Murray, London, 1882, p. 150.

9. Extract from a letter to Wilfrid Blunt. See Wilfrid Blunt, *Slow on the Feather: Further Autobiography*, Michael Russell, Salisbury, 1986, p. 127.

10. Quoted in Revd David, p. 147.

11. Davidson, p. 53.

12. Kenneth Grubb, *Crypts of Power*, Hodder and Stoughton, London, 1971.

13. J. d'E Firth, p. 171.

14. Reg Ferm, *Ice Cold Charity*, The Book Guild Ltd., Sussex, 1990.

15. Boyd, *The History of Radley College 1847–1947*, p. 119.

16. Ferm, p. 25.

17. *Oxford English Dictionary*. See also Iona and Peter Opie, *The Lore and Language of School Children*, Oxford University Press, Oxford, p. 373. They date the origin of the term to Eton in 1750 and argue that its usage 'only rarely extends to boys who do not possess any Latin.'

18. W.F. Farrar, *Eric or Little by Little: A Tale of Roslyn School*, Adam and Charles Black, London, 1905, p. 97.

19. See for example Victor Alexander's speech in 'Report of Meeting at O.Y.S.A. and M.O.S.A. held at Clifford Street, York, on Monday 21st May 1956' in *Bootham: The Magazine of Bootham School*, Vol. XXVI – No. 4, November 1956.

20. Annan.

21. Quoted in Jonathan Gathorne-Hardy, *The Public School Phenomenon*, Penguin Books, Harmondsworth, 1979.

22. Peter F. Carter-Ruck, *Memoirs of a Libel Lawyer*, Weidenfeld and Nicolson, London, 1990, pp. 4–5.

23. Jeffrey Amherst, *Wandering Abroad: The Autobiography of Jeffrey Amherst*, Secker and Warburg, London, 1976, p. 21.

24. Ferm, p. 25.

25. Stephens, p. 44.

26. Robert Henriques, *From a Biography of Myself: A Posthumous Selection of the Autobiographical Writings of Robert Henriques*, Secker and Warburg, London, 1969, p. 17.

27. Peter Medawar, *Memoir of a Thinking Radish*, Oxford University Press, Oxford, 1986, p. 38.

28. Felix Clay, p. 241.

29. Lord Rothschild, *Meditations of a Broomstick*, Collins, London, 1977, p. 14.

30. Lyttelton, p. 39.

31. Lord Rothschild, p. 14.

32. George Orwell, 'Such, Such were the Joys,' in *The Penguin Essays of George Orwell*, Penguin Books, Harmondsworth, 1984, p. 441.

33. H.E. Wortham, *Victorian Eton and Cambridge: Being the Life and Times of Oscar Browning*, Arthur Baker, London, 1956, pp. 97–98.

34. David Newsome, *A History of Wellington College 1859–1959*, John Murray, London, 1959, p. 242.

35. Boyd, p. 58.

36. Clay, p. 241.

37. Skidelsky, p. 111.

38. Sederman, p. 27.

39. Quoted in R.J. Mackensie, *Almond of Loretto*, Archibald Constable and Company, London, 1905, p. 206.

40. Tim Card, *Eton Renewed: A History from 1860 to the Present Day*, John Murray, London, 1994, p. 109.

41. The Duke of Windsor, *A King's Story*, Cassell and Company, London, 1953.

42. See for example Philip Mason, *A Shaft of Sunlight: Memories of a Varied Life*, André Deutsch, London, 1978, pp. 24–25.

43. James MacVeigh, *Gaskin*, Jonathan Cape, London, 1982, p. 25.

44. Amherst, p. 21.

45. Hugh Cecil, 'My Father at Eton,' in H. Cranborne (ed), *David Cecil*, Dovecote Press, Stanbridge, 1990, pp. 20–21.

Deterrence

1. Christopher Hollis, *Eton: A History*, Hollis and Carter, London, 1960, p. 142. The term 'undesirable' may have meant merely his unorthodox behaviour in associating with boys above himself in social status.

2. Chandos, pp. 301–302.

3. Newsome, *Godliness and Good Learning*, p. 45.

4. Simon Gray, *Little Portia*, Faber and Faber, London, 1986, p. 105.

5. Laurence Irving, *The Precarious Crust*, Chatto and Windus, London, 1971, pp. 222–223.

6. Card, p. 109.

7. George R. Parkin, *Edward Thring: Life, Diary and Letters*, Macmillan, London, 1900, p. 280.

8. Andrew Gibson-Watt, *An Undistinguished Life*, The Book Guild Ltd., Sussex, 1990, p. 40–41.

9. Edward Blishen, *Sorry Dad – An Autobiography*, Hamish Hamilton, London, 1978, p. 116.

10. George Orwell, 'Such, Such were the Joys,' in *The Penguin Essays of George Orwell.*

11. Gathorne-Hardy.

12. Crisp, pp. 18–19.

13. Cyril Norwood, *The English Tradition of Education*, John Murray, London, 1929, pp. 74–75.

14. Mackensie, p. 205.

15. Arnold Brown, p. 225.

Chapter Two

Friendships Between Masters and Boys

1. Evelyn Waugh, *A Little Learning*, Penguin Books, Harmondsworth, 1983, p. 84.

2. H. Hamilton Fyfe in Various Authors, *Fifty Years of Fettes*, p. 86.

3. Frank Fletcher, *After Many Days: A Schoolmaster's Memories*, Robert Hale and Company, London, 1937, p. 96.

4. Richard Holmes, *Shelley: The Pursuit*, Penguin Books, Harmondsworth, 1987, pp. 25–26.

5. Edward Carpenter, *Selected Writings Volume One: Sex*, Gay Men's Press, London, 1984, p. 206.

6. Quoted in Boyd, p. 193.

7. Hollis, p. 218.

8. Boyd, p. 194.

9. Blunt, p. 78.

10. Ibid., p. 77.

11. Lord Drogheda, p. 14.

12. Nigel Hamilton, *JFK. Volume One: Reckless Youth*, Arrow Books, 1993.

13. Quoted in James Lees Milne, *The Enigmatic Edwardian: The Life of Reginald Second Viscount Esher*, Sidgwick and Jackson, London, 1986, p. 8.

14. Ibid., p. 10.

15. Ibid., p. 8.

16. Robert Rhodes James, *Rosebery: A Biography of Archibald Philip, Fifth Earl of Rosebery*, Weidenfield and Nicolson, London, 1963, p. 27.

17. Kenneth Rose, *Superior Person: A Portrait of Curzon and his Circle in Late Victorian England*, Weidenfeld and Nicolson, London, 1969, p. 30.

18. Ibid., p. 31.

19. Ibid., p. 31.

20. Ibid., pp. 31–32.

21. Ibid., p. 32.

22. Letter from Curzon to Browning, 15 February 1876, *Oscar Browning Collection*, Modern Archives, King's College, Cambridge.

23. Oscar Browning, *Memories of Sixty Years*, John Lane, London, 1910, p. 75.

24. Lord Chandos, *The Memoirs of Lord Chandos*, The Bodley Head, London, 1962, p. 9.

25. Blunt, p. 132.

26. Michael Cox, *M.R. James: An Informal Portrait*, Oxford University Press, Oxford, 1983, p. 24.

27. Worsley, pp. 68–69.

28. Gerald Priestland, *Something Understood: An Autobiography*, André Deutsch, London, 1986, pp. 49–50.

29. Duff Hart-Davis, *Peter Fleming: A Biography*, Jonathan Cape, London, 1974, p. 34.

30. Blunt, *Married to a Single Life*, pp. 203–204.

31. Ibid., p. 225.

32. Rose, p. 32.

33. Letter from Curzon to Browning, 6 February 1877, *Oscar Browning Collection*.

34. Letter from Curzon to Browning, *Oscar Browning Collection*.

35. Rose, p. 33.

36. Ibid.

37. Faith Compton Mackenzie, *William Cory: A Biography*, Constable, London, 1950, p. 28.

38. Ibid., p. 25.

39. Ibid., p. 43.

40. Quoted in Edward Graham, *The Harrow Life of Henry Montagu Butler*, Longmans, London, 1920.

41. Earl of Gowrie interviewed by Danny Danziger, *Eton Voices: Interviews by Danny Danziger*, Penguin Group, London, 1988, p. 112.

42. Trelawny-Ross, p. 303.

43. Ted Morgan, *FDR: a biography*, Grafton Books, London, 1987, p. 57.

Dreams and Desires

1. Blunt, p. 85.

2. Rhodes-James, p. 26.

3. Ibid., p. 28.

4. Dudley Barker, *The Man of Principle: A View of John Galsworthy*, Heinemann, London, 1963, p. 31.

5. Francis Warre Cornish (ed.), *Extracts from the Letters and Journals of William Cory*, p. 283.

6. Worsley, pp. 112–113.

7. Ibid., p. 113.

8. Quoted in David Newsome, *On the Edge of Paradise: A.C. Benson: The Diarist*, John Murray, London, 1980, p. 83.

9. Martha Vicinus, 'Distance and Desire: English Boarding School Friendships 1870–1920', in M.B. Duberman *et al.*, *Hidden from History: Reclaiming the Gay and Lesbian Past*, Penguin Books, London, 1991, p. 223.

10. Compton Mackenzie, p. 27.

11. Cox, pp. 23–25.

12. John Addington Symonds, *The Memoirs of John Addington Symonds*, Hutchinson, London, 1984, p. 112.

13. Ibid., pp. 112–113.

14. Quoted in Rhodes James, pp. 27–28.

15. John Rae, *Letters from School*, Collins, London, 1987.

16. Compton Mackenzie, p. 25.

17. Rose, p. 30.

18. Letter from Curzon to Browning, 28 September 1878, *Oscar Browning Collection*.

19. Inglis, p. 38.

20. Woodrow Wyatt, *Confessions of an Optimist*, Collins, London, 1985, p. 52.

21. Blunt, p. 85.

22. S.P.B. Mais, *A Public School in War Time*, John Murray, London, 1916, pp. 52–53.

23. Edward Thomas, *The Childhood of Edward Thomas*, Faber and Faber, London, 1983, p. 66.

24. Quoted in Newsome, *On the Edge of Paradise*, p. 83.

The Teacher as Hero

1. Edward Carpenter, 'My Days and Dreams', in Edward Carpenter, *Selected Writings: Volume One: Sex*, p. 83.

2. Robert Calder, *Willie: The Life of W. Somerset Maugham*, William Heinemann Ltd., London, 1989, p. 27.

3. Crisp, pp. 20–21.

4. Hallam Tennyson, *The Haunted Mind*, André Deutsch, London, 1984, p. 47.

5. Bernhard Zeller, *Herman Hesse: An Illustrated Biography*, Peter Owen, London, 1972, pp. 21–22.

6. Michael Holroyd, *Augustus John: Volume One: The Years of Innocence*, Heinemann, London, 1974, pp. 25–26.

Chapter Three

Le Coup de Foudre

1. Quoted in Hollis, 1960.

2. Davidson, p. 52.

3. John Betjeman, *Summoned by Bells*, John Murray, London, 1974, p. 72.

4. Frank Norman, *Banana Boy*, Secker and Warburg, London, 1969, pp. 54–55.

5. Betjeman, p. 72.

6. Derek Malcolm interviewed in Danziger, *Eton Voices*, p. 200.

7. Amherst, pp. 27–28.

8. Ferm, p. 49.

9. Horace Vachell, *The Hill: A Romance of Friendship*, John Murray, London, 1917, p. 136.

10. Quoted in Francis Wheen, *Tom Driberg: His Life and Indiscretions*, Chatto and Windus, London, 1990, p. 32.

11. Davidson, p. 53.

The Enslavement Paradox

1. Ted Morgan, *Literary Outlaw: The Life and Times of William S. Burroughs*, The Bodley Head, London, 1991, p. 51.

2. Cyril Connolly, *Enemies of Promise*, André Deutsch, London, 1973, p. 202.

3. Blunt.

4. H.E. Wortham, *Victorian Eton and Cambridge: Being the Life and Times of Oscar Browning*, p. 32.

5. Quoted in Peter Parker, *The Old Lie: The Great War and the Public School Ethos*, Constable, London, 1987, p. 110.

6. Dudley Barker, *G.K. Chesterton: A Biography*, Constable, London, 1973, pp. 34–37.

7. Benson, p. 183.

8. George Hayim, *Thou Shalt Not Uncover Thy Mother's Nakedness*, Quartet Books, London, 1988, p. 49.

The Incongruity Paradox

1. Ludovic Kennedy, *On My Way to the Club*, Collins, London, 1989, p. 41.

2. Christopher Elliot-Binns, *Too much Tenderness: An Autobiography of Childhood and Youth*, Routledge and Kegan Paul, London, 1983.

3. Quoted in Rose, p. 34.

4. Ibid.

5. John Cowper Powys, *Autobiography*, Pan Books, London, 1982, p. 115.

6. Arthur Marshall, *Life's Rich Pageant*, Hamish Hamilton, London, 1984, p. 70.

7. Anthony Hopkins, *Beating Time*, Michael Joseph, London, 1982, p. 50.

8. Maugham, p. 33.

9. Ibid., p. 34 and p. 38.

10. Lord Drogheda, p. 15.

11. Davidson, p. 53.

12. Quoted in David Newsome, *On the Edge of Paradise*, p. 30.

The Reluctant Hero Paradox

1. Benson.

2. J.E. Morpurgo in *The Christ's Hospital Book (1953)*, Hamish Hamilton, London, pp. 311–312.

3. Ibid., p. 312.

4. Quoted in Hollis, p. 293.

5. John Lehmann, *In the Purely Pagan Sense*, 1976.

6. Osbert Lancaster, *With an Eye to the Future*, John Murray, London, 1967, p. 54.

7. Christopher Hibbert (ed.), *Captain Gronow: His Reminiscences of Regency and Victorian Life 1810–1860*, Kyle Cathie, London, 1991, pp. 16–17.

Götterdämmerung

1. Brian Masters, *The Life of E.F. Benson*, Chatto and Windus, London, 1991, p. 72.

2. Connolly, p. 190.

3. Paul Wright, *A Brittle Glory: An Autobiography*, Weidenfeld and Nicolson, London, 1986, p. 13.

4. Wyatt, p. 19.

5. *Gay News*, No. 121, 16 June–29 June 1977, p. 19.

Chapter Four

1. Letter from Peter Tatchell, July 1994.
2. Letter received by the author in September 1994.
3. Paul Monette, *Becoming a Man*, Harcourt Brace Jovanovich, New York, 1992, p. 69. Monette was at Andover, an American boarding school, but the cult of games there mirrored that at English schools.
4. Quoted in Royston Lambert, *The Hothouse Society*, Weidenfeld and Nicolson, London, 1960.
5. HMC schools comprise all those independent boys' and coeducational schools which are affiliated to the Headmaster's Conference (see glossary).
6. Dean Welldon, *Thirteen Essays in Education by members of the XIII*, 1891.
7. Geoffrey Walford, *Life in Public Schools*, Methuen and Company, London, 1986, p. 146.
8. Lambert, p. 357.
9. John Buchanan quoted in John Rae, *The Public School Revolution: Britain's Independent Schools 1964–1979*, Faber and Faber, London, 1981, p. 142.
10. John Rae, *The Public School Revolution*, p. 131.
11. Quoted in Brian Gardner, *The Public Schools*, Hamish Hamilton, London, 1973, p. 166.
12. Letter received 27 July 1994.
13. Lambert, p. 271.
14. Letter received from Ian Small, headmaster of Bootham, in August 1994.
15. Thomas, p. 60.
16. Letter received by the author in July 1994.
17. Quoted in Kim Hayes, *Practising Virtues*, University of California Press, Los Angeles, 1994.
18. Letter received from J.H. Arkell, headmaster of Gresham's, on 20 August 1994.
19. Letter from Peter Tatchell, July 1994.

Part Two

Bradfield

1. John Blackie, *Bradfield 1850–1975*, St Andrew's College, Bradfield, 1976, p. 40.
2. Ibid., p. 64.
3. Ibid., p. 104.
4. David Owen, *Personally Speaking to Kenneth Harris*, Weidenfeld and Nicolson, London, 1987, p. 7.

5. The *Daily Telegraph*, 31 March 1979, p. 18.
6. Blackie, p. 110.

Bryanston

1. Gathorne-Hardy, *The Public School Phenomenon*, p. 287.

Charterhouse

1. John Pollock, *John Wesley*, Hodder and Stoughton, London, 1989.
2. F.A.M. Webster, *Our Great Public Schools*, Ward Lock, London, 1937, p. 58.
3. Quoted in Gathorne-Hardy, p. 68.
4. A.H. Tod, *Charterhouse*, George Bell and Sons, London, 1900, p. 85.
5. Ann Monsarrat, *An Uneasy Victorian: Thackeray the Man, 1811–1863*, p. 25.
6. Lancaster, pp. 47–48.
7. Gerald Priestland, *Something Understood: An Autobiography*, André Deutsch, London, 1986, p. 54.
8. Quoted in Martin Seymour-Smith, *Robert Graves: His Life and Works*, Hutchinson, London, 1982.

Cheltenham

1. Gathorne-Hardy, p. 280.
2. Morgan, pp. 193–194.
3. Michael Gilbert, *Prep School: An Anthology*, John Murray, London, 1991, pp. 17–18.

Christ's Hospital

1. *The Christ's Hospital Book (1953)*, p. 365.
2. This early aspiration is still evident in the number of scholars who are admitted each year from families whose gross annual income is less than £10,000.
3. *The Christ's Hospital Book (1953)*, p. 195.
4. Ibid., p. 338.
5. J.E. Morpurgo, *The Autobiography of Leigh Hunt*, The Crescent Press, London, 1948, p. 83.
6. Chandos, p. 236.
7. Ibid., p. 236–237.

Churcher's College

1. J.H. Smith, *Churcher's College*, Manchester University Press, Manchester, 1936, p. 65 and p. 69.

Clifton

1. N.G.L. Hammond (ed.), *Centenary Essays on Clifton College*, J.W. Arrowsmith, Bristol, 1962, p. 6.
2. Michael Redgrave, *In My Mind's Eye: An Autobiography*, Weidenfeld and Nicolson, London, 1983, p. 34.
3. Ibid., p. 35–36.
4. Ibid., p. 36.

Downside

1. Dom Hubert Van Zeller, *Downside By and Large*, Sheed and Ward, London, 1954.
2. Ibid., p. 244.

Eastbourne College

1. Wyatt, pp. 50–51.

Eton

1. Hollis, *Eton: A History*, 1960.
2. Christopher Hollis, *The Seven Ages, Their Exits and Their Entrances*, William Heinemann, London, 1974, p. 37.
3. Rose, *Superior Person*, p. 33.
4. Derek Malcolm interviewed in Danziger, p. 199.
5. Ranulph Fiennes, *Living Dangerously: The Autobiography of Ranulph Fiennes*, Macmillan Books, London, 1987, pp. 15–16.
6. Ibid. Eton jackets for juniors were finally abolished in 1967 from which time all boys have been allowed to wear tails. (See Card, p. 257).

Fettes

1. J.S. Muirhead in *Fifty Years of Fettes*, p. 189.
2. Quoted in Paul Delany, *The Neo-Pagans: Friendship and Love in the Rupert Brooke circle*, Macmillan, London, 1987, p. 11.
3. Quoted in Jim Perrin, *Menlove: The Life of John Menlove Edwards*, Victor Gollancz Ltd., London, 1985, pp. 42–44.

Gresham's

1. Gathorne-Hardy, p. 296.
2. W.H. Auden in Graham Greene, *The Old School: Essays by Divers Hands*, Oxford University Press, Oxford, 1984, p. 8.

3. J.H. Simpson, *Schoolmaster's Harvest: Some Findings of Fifty Years 1894–1944*, Faber and Faber, London, 1954, p. 101.
4. Quoted in Robert Cecil, *A Divided Life: A Biography of Donald Maclean*, Hodder and Stoughton, London, 1988, p. 41.
5. Ibid., p.42.

Haileybury

1. Blunt.
2. Thomas, p. 192.
3. J.R. de S. Honey, p. 181.
4. Ibid., p. 182.
5. Thomas, p. 78.
6. Ibid., p. 49.
7. James McConnell, *English Public Schools*, The Herbert Press, London, 1985, p. 166.

Harrow

1. Hollis, *The Seven Ages* p. 27 and p. 37.
2. Lord Rothschild, p. 13.
3. Hayim, p. 49.
4. Michael Darlow and Gillian Hodson, *Terence Rattigan: The Man and His Work*, Quartet Books, London, 1979, p. 40.

King's School, Canterbury

1. Quoted in Furlong, p. 31.
2. Calder, p. 27.
3. Quoted in Thomas Hinde, *Imps of Promise: A History of King's School*, James and James, London, 1990, p. 93.
4. Ibid., p. 94.

Lancing College

1. Davidson, p. 51.
2. Basil Handford, *Lancing College*, Phillimore and Company, Chichester, 1986, p. 63.

Marlborough

1. McConnell, p. 128.
2. Medawar, p. 38.

3. Ibid., pp. 30–31.
4. Beverley Nichols, *The Unforgiving Minute: Some Confessions from Childhood to the Outbreak of the Second World War*, W.H. Allen, London, 1978, p. 4.

Oundle

1. McConnell, p. 70.
2. Peter Scott, *The Eye of the Wind*, Hodder and Stoughton, London, 1968, p. 50.
3. Raymond Flower, *Oundle and the English Public School*, Stacey International, London, 1989, pp. 86–88.
4. Gathorne-Hardy, p. 163.

Radley

1. Chandos, p. 343.

Repton

1. Edward Carpenter, *Archbishop Fisher – His Life and Times*, The Canterbury Press, Norwich, 1991, p. 19.

Rugby

1. T.W. Bamford, *Thomas Arnold*, The Cresset Press, London, 1960, pp. 108–109.
2. Peter Ustinov, *Dear Me*, Hutchinson, London, 1977, p. 58.
3. J.B. Hope Simpson, *Rugby Since Arnold: A History of Rugby School from 1842*, St Martin's Press, New York, 1967, p. 117.
4. Parker, pp. 110–111.
5. Tim Devlin and Hywel Williams, *Old School Ties*, Sinclair-Stevenson, London, 1992, p. 153.

St Edward's

1. Hopkinson, pp. 47–48.
2. P. Lacey quoted in R.D. Hill, *A History of St Edward's School*, St Edward's School, 1962, p. 183.
3. Ibid., pp. 183–184.

Sherborne

1. Andrew Hodges, *Alan Turing: The Enigma of Intelligence*, Unwin Hyman, London, p. 36.
2. Ibid., p. 39.

3. John Le Mesurier, *A Jobbing Actor*, Elm Tree Books, London, 1984, p. 15.

Shrewsbury

1. Colin Leach, *A School at Shrewsbury*, James and James, London, 1990, p. 52.
2. McConnell, p. 48.
3. Klaus Boehm and Jenny Lees-Spalding, *The Equitable Schools Book (1993): The Independent Guide to Independent Secondary Schools*, Bloomsbury, London, 1993, p. 685.
4. David Walker, *Lean, Wind Lean – A Few Times Remembered*, Collins, London, p. 25.
5. Inglis, p. 49.
6. Ibid., pp. 44–45. Also Leach, pp. 83–84.
7. Division of Christian Education of the National Council of the Churches of Christ (USA), *The Bible: Revised Standard Version*.

Stonyhurst

1. Gathorne-Hardy, p. 91.
2. Charles Higham, *Charles Laughton: An Intimate Biography*, W.H. Allen, London, 1976, p. 4.

Stowe

1. Peregrine Worsthorne, 'Boys made Man' in Paul Johnson et al, *The World of the Public School*, Weidenfeld and Nicolson, London, 1977, p. 90.
2. Annan, p. 137.
3. Ibid., p. 138.
4. Peregrine Worsthorne, 'Boys made Man' in Paul Johnson et al, pp. 90–91.
5. David Niven, *The Moon's a Balloon: reminiscences by David Niven*, Hamish Hamilton, London, 1971, pp. 39–40.
6. Ibid.

Uppingham

1. Donald Leinster-Mackay, *The Educational World of Edward Thring*, The Falmer Press, London, 1987, p. 14.
2. Ibid., p. 15.
3. Ibid., p. 53.
4. Ibid., p. 54.
5. John Graham, *Forty Years of Uppingham: Memories and Sketches*, Macmillan, London, 1932, pp. 39–40.

Wellington

1. Harold Nicholson, 'Pity the Pedagogue' in Greene, pp. 99–100.
2. Worsley, p. 75.
3. Robert Morley, *Around the World in Eighty-One Years*, Hodder and Stoughton, London, 1990, p. 22.
4. David Newsome, *Godliness and Good Learning*, pp. 44–45.

Winchester

1. J. d'E Firth, *Winchester College*, Winchester Publications, Winchester, p. 53.
2. Ibid., p. 168.
3. Ibid., p. 161.
4. Tam Dalyell, *Dick Crossman: A Portrait*, Weidenfeld and Nicolson, London, 1989, p. 16.
5. Sir Alan Herbert, *A.P.H. His Life and Times*, Heinemann, London, 1970, pp. 19–20.

Wrekin College

1. B.C.W. Johnson, *Wrekin College*, Wilding and Son Ltd., Shrewsbury, 1965, pp. 14–15.
2. Ibid., pp. 53–54.
3. Ibid., p. 54.

Conclusion

1. Julian Mitchell, *Another Country*, Amber Lane Press, Oxford, 1982, p. 89.

Glossary

1. H.A. Tod, *Charterhouse*, p. 85.
2. Donald Roden, *Schooldays in Imperial Japan*, University of California Press, Los Angeles, 1980.

SELECT BIBLIOGRAPHY

School Histories

BAMFORD, T.W., *Rise of the Public Schools*, Thomas Nelson, London 1967

BARBER, JOHN, *The Story of Oakham School*, Sycamore Press, Wymondham 1983

BLACKIE, JOHN, *Bradfield 1850–1975*, Bradfield 1976

BOYD, A.K., *The History of Radley College 1847–1947*, Basil Blackwell, Oxford 1948

BROWN, ADAM A., *Unfolding Character: The Impact of Gordonstoun*, Routledge and Kegan Paul, London 1962

CARD, TIM, *Eton Renewed: A History from 1860 to the Present Day*, John Murray, London 1994

CHANDOS, JOHN, *Boys Together: English Public Schools 1800–1864*, Hutchinson, London, 1984

COWBURN, PHILIP (ed.), *A Salopian Anthology*, Macmillan, London 1964

DANZIGER, DANNY, *Eton Voices: Interviews by Danny Danziger*, Penguin 1988

DAVID, REVD A.A.., *Life and the Public Schools*, Alexander Maclehouse, London 1932

FIRTH, J. D'E, *Winchester College*, Winchester Publications, Winchester 1949

GATHORNE-HARDY, JONATHAN, *The Public School Phenomenon*, Penguin Books, Harmondsworth 1979

GRAHAM, JOHN P., *Forty Years of Uppingham: Memories and Sketches*, Macmillan, London 1932

HAMMOND, N.G.L. (ed.), *Centenary Essays on Clifton College*, J.W. Arrowsmith, Bristol 1962

HILL, R.D., *A History of St Edward's School*, St Edward's School Society 1962

HINDE, THOMAS, *Imps of Promise: A History of King's School*, James and James, London 1990

HOLLIS, CHRISTOPHER, *Eton: A History*, Hollis and Carter, London 1960

HONEY, J.R. DE S., *Tom Brown's Universe*, Millington Books, London 1977

HOPE SIMPSON, J.B., *Rugby since Arnold: A History of Rugby School from 1842*, St Martin's Press, New York 1967

JOHNSON, B.C.W., *Wrekin College*, Wilding and Son, Shrewsbury 1965

LAWRENCE, P.S.H., (ed.) *The Encouragement of Learning*, Michael Russell, Salisbury 1980

LEACH, COLIN, *A School at Shrewsbury*, James and James, London 1990

MAIS, S.P.B., *A Public School in War Time*, John Murray, London 1916

MANGAN, J.A., *Athleticism in the Victorian and Edwardian Public School*, Cambridge University Press, Cambridge 1981

MITRA, CHANDAN, *Constant Glory: La Martinière Saga 1836–1986*, Oxford University Press, Oxford 1987

MORGAN, M.C., *Cheltenham College*, Richard Sadler, 1968

NEWSOME, DAVID, *A History of Wellington College*, John Murray, London 1959

——, *Godliness and Good Learning*, Cassell, London 1961

——, *On the Edge of Paradise: A.C. Benson: The Diarist*, John Murray, London 1980

OLLARD, RICHARD, *An English Education: A Perspective of Eton*, Collins, London 1982

PARKER, PETER, *The Old Lie: The Great War and the Public School Ethos*, Constable, London 1987

RAE, JOHN, *The Public School Revolution: Britain's Independent Schools 1964–1979*, Faber and Faber, London 1981

RODEN, DONALD, *Schooldays in Imperial Japan*, University of California Press, Los Angeles and London 1980

RODGERS, JOHN, *The Old Public Schools of England*, Batsford, London 1938

SABBEN-CLARE, JAMES, *Winchester*, Paul Cave, Southampton 1981

SEDERMAN, D., *A History of Abbotsholme School*, Abbotsholme School, Uttoxeter 1989

SKIDELSKY, ROBERT, *English Progressive Schools*, Penguin Books, Harmondsworth 1969

SMITH, J.H., *Churcher's College*, Manchester University Press, Manchester 1936

SOMERVELL, D.C., *A History of Tonbridge School*, Faber and Faber, London 1947

SPINNEY, DAVID, *Clayesmore: A School History*, Dovecote Press, Standbridge 1987

THOMAS, IMOGEN, *Haileybury 1806–1987*, The Haileybury Society, Haileybury 1987

TOD, A.H., *Charterhouse*, George Bell, London 1900

TRELAWNY-ROSS, A.H., *Their Prime of Life*, The Wykeham Press, Winchester 1956

VIPONT, ELFRIDA, *Ackworth School*, Lutterwoth Press, London 1959

ZELLER, DOM HUBERT VAN, *Downside By and Large*, Sheed and Ward, London 1954

Autobiographies and Biographies

ANNAN, NOEL, *Roxburgh of Stowe*, Longmans, London 1965

BAMFORD, T.W., *Thomas Arnold*, The Cresset Press, London 1960

BLUNT, WILFRID, *Married to a Single Life*, Michael Russell, Salisbury 1983

——, *Slow on the Feather: Further Autobiography*, Michael Russell, Salisbury 1986

BROWNING, OSCAR, *Memories of Sixty Years*, John Lane, London 1910

CONNOLLY, CYRIL, *Enemies of Promise*, André Deutsch, London 1973

CORNISH, FRANCIS W. (ed.), *Extracts from the Letters and Journals of William Cory*, Oxford 1897

CRISP, QUENTIN, *The Naked Civil Servant*, Fontana, London 1981

DAVIDSON, MICHAEL, *The World, the Flesh and Myself*, GMP Publishers, London 1985

FERM, REG, *Ice Cold Charity*, The Book Guild, Sussex 1990

GRAHAM, EDWARD, *The Harrow Life of Henry Montagu Butler*, Longmans, London 1920

MACKENSIE, R.J., *Almond of Loretto*, Archibald Constable and Company 1905

MACKENZIE, F.C., *William Cory: A Biography*, Constable and Company, London 1950

MAUGHAM, ROBIN, *Escape from the Shadows*, Hodder and Stoughton, London 1972

ONYEAMA, DILLIBE, *Nigger at Eton*, Leslie Frewin, London 1972

PARKIN, GEORGE, *Edward Thring: Life, Diary and Letters*, Macmillan 1900

ROSE, KENNETH, *Superior Person: A Portrait of Curzon and his Circle in Late Victorian England*, Weidenfeld and Nicolson, London 1967

SIMPSON, J.H., *Schoolmaster's Harvest*, Faber and Faber, London 1954

STANLEY, ARTHUR P., *The Life and Correspondence of Thomas Arnold*, John Murray, London 1882

STEELE, THOMAS, *Musings of an Old Schoolmaster*, The Sylvan Press, London 1932

SYMONDS, J.A., *The Memoirs of John Addington Symonds*, Hutchinson, London 1984

WAUGH, EVELYN, *A Little Learning*, Penguin Books, Harmondsworth 1983

WORSLEY, T.C., *Flannelled Fool: A Slice of Life in the Thirties*, Hogarth Press, London 1985

WORTHAM, H.E., *Victorian Eton and Cambridge: Being the Life and Times of Oscar Browning*, Arthur Baker, London 1956

Fiction

BENSON, E.F., *David Blaize*, Thames and Hudson, London 1989

FARRAR, F.W., *Eric or Little by Little*, Adam and Charles Black, London 1905

——, *St Winifred's or the World of School*, Ward Lock, London

FULLER, ROY, *The Ruined Boys*, Hogarth Press, London 1987

GRAY, SIMON, *Little Portia*, Faber and Faber, London 1986

VACHELL, HORACE, *The Hill: A Romance of Friendship*, John Murray, London 1917

WAUGH, ALEC, *The Loom of Youth*, Grant Richards, 1917

WAUGH, EVELYN, *Decline and Fall*, Penguin Books, Harmondsworth 1976

Other

AUDEN, W.H., *The Old School: Essays by Divers Hands*, Oxford University Press, Oxford 1984

CARPENTER, EDWARD, *Selected Writings Volume One: Sex*, Gay Men's Press, London 1984

CLAY, FELIX, *Modern School Buildings*, Batsford, London 1902

CROMPTON, LOUIS, *Byron and Greek Love: Homophobia in Nineteenth Century England*, Faber and Faber, London 1985

DELANY, *The Neo-Pagans: Friendship and Love in the Rupert Brooke Circle*, Macmillan, London 1987

DELVIN T. and WILLIAMS, H., *Old School Ties*, Sinclair-Stevenson, London 1992

GARDNER, BRIAN, *The Public Schools*, Hamish Hamilton, London 1973

GILBERT, MICHAEL, *Prep School: An Anthology*, John Murray, London 1991

GOFFMAN, ERVING, *Asylums*, Penguin Books, Harmondsworth 1968

HAYES, KIM, *Practising Virtues: Moral Traditions at Quaker and Military Boarding Schools*, University of California Press, Los Angeles 1994

HOOD, ROGER, *Borstal Re-Assessed*, Heinemann, London 1965

HOSWON, G.W.S., *Sermons by a Lay Headmaster Preached at Gresham's School 1900–1918*, Longmans, London 1920

LAMBERT, ROYSTON, *The Hothouse Society*, Weidenfeld and Nicolson, London 1960

LYTTELTON, EDWARD, *The Causes and Prevention of Immorality in Schools*, Social Purity Alliance 1887

NORWOOD, CYRIL, *The English Tradition of Education*, John Murray, London 1929

PAGE, T.E. et al, *The Public Schools from Within*, Sampson Low, London 1906

RAE, JOHN, *Letters from School*, Collins, London 1987

VICINUS, MARTHA, 'Distance and Desire: English Boarding School Friendships 1870–1920', in M.B. Duberman et al, *Hidden from History: Reclaiming the Gay and Lesbian Past*, Penguin Books, London 1991

WALFORD, GEOFFREY, *Life in Public Schools*, Methuen, London 1986

WEBSTER, F.A.M., *Our Great Public Schools*, Ward Lock, London 1937

WEINBERG, IAN, *The English Public Schools*, Atherton Press, New York 1967

INDEX